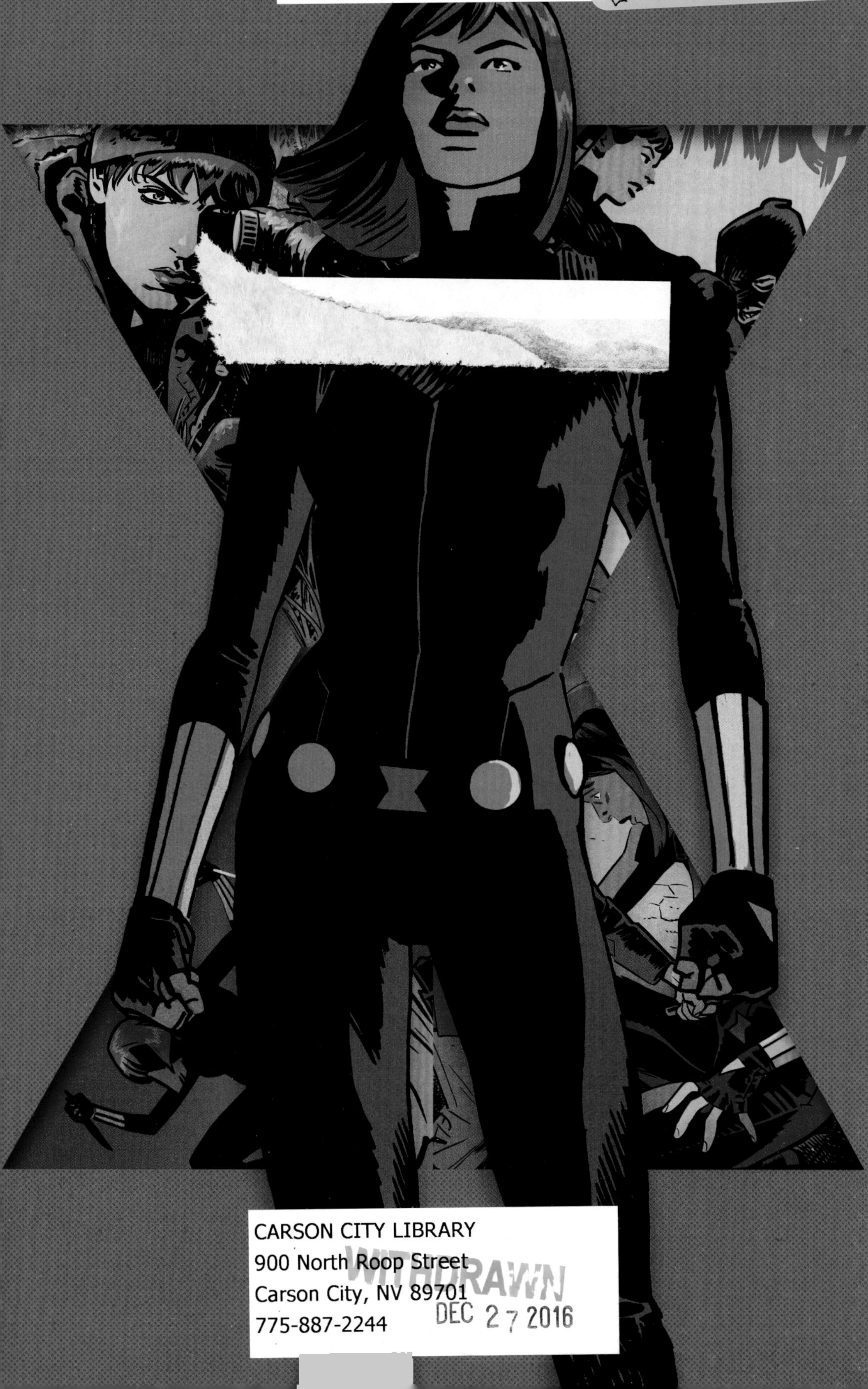

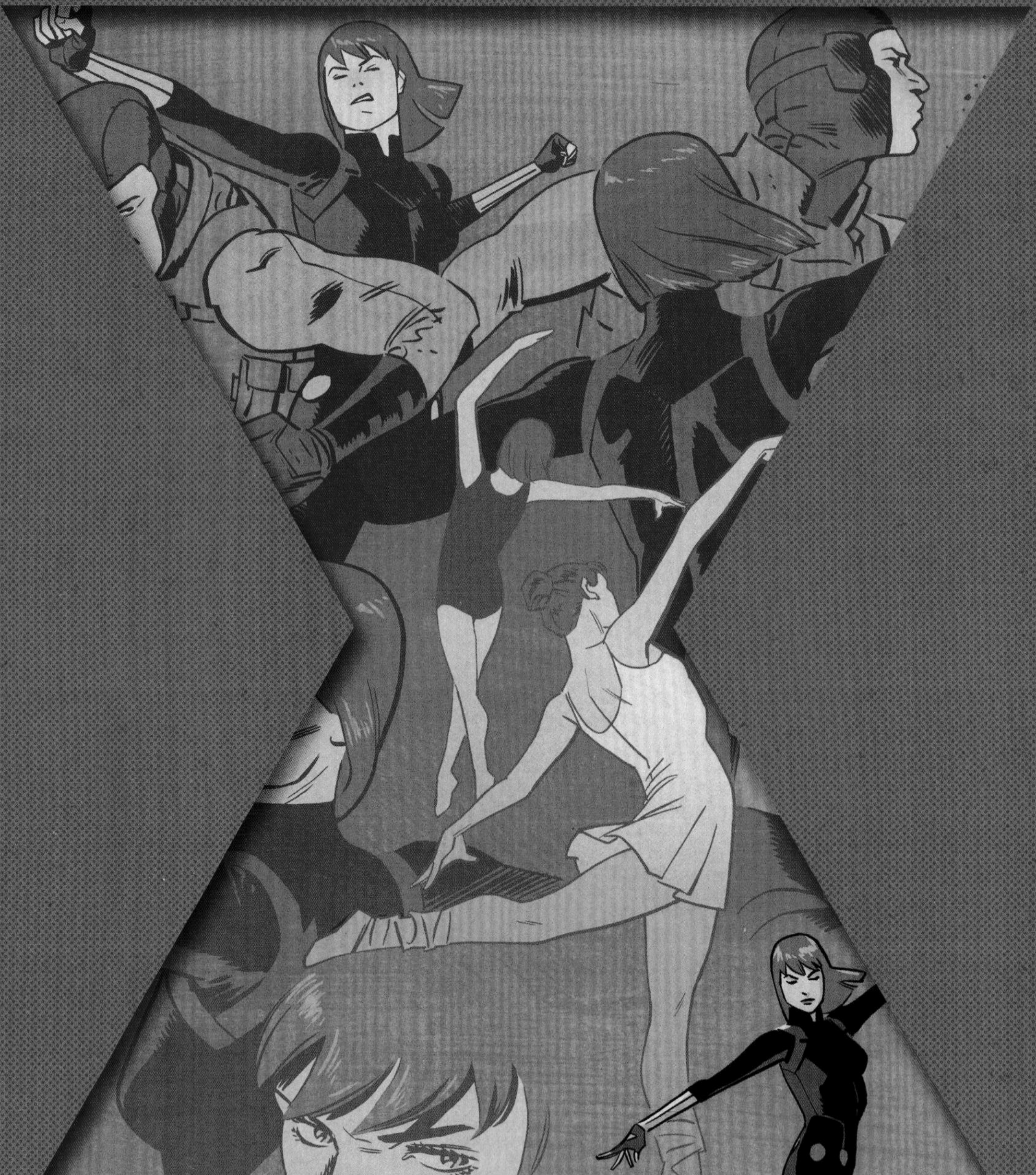

BLACK WIDOW

S.H.I.E.L.D.'S MOST WANTED

MARK WAID & CHRIS SAMNEE
WRITERS

CHRIS SAMNEE
ARTIST

MATTHEW WILSON
COLOR ARTIST

VC's JOE CARAMAGNA
LETTERER

CHRIS SAMNEE & MATTHEW WILSON
COVER ART

KATHLEEN WISNESKI
ASSISTANT EDITOR

JAKE THOMAS
EDITOR

COLLECTION EDITOR **JENNIFER GRÜNWALD**
ASSOCIATE MANAGING EDITOR **KATERI WOODY**
ASSOCIATE EDITOR **SARAH BRUNSTAD**
EDITOR, SPECIAL PROJECTS **MARK D. BEAZLEY**

VP PRODUCTION & SPECIAL PROJECTS **JEFF YOUNGQUIST**
SVP PRINT, SALES & MARKETING **DAVID GABRIEL**
BOOK DESIGNER **ADAM DEL RE**

EDITOR IN CHIEF **AXEL ALONSO**
CHIEF CREATIVE OFFICER **JOE QUESADA**
PUBLISHER **DAN BUCKLEY**
EXECUTIVE PRODUCER **ALAN FINE**

BLACK WIDOW VOL. 1: S.H.I.E.L.D.'S MOST WANTED. Contains material originally published in magazine form as BLACK WIDOW #1-6. First printing 2016. ISBN# 978-0-7851-9975-5. Published by MARVEL WORLDWIDE, INC., a subsidiary of MARVEL ENTERTAINMENT, LLC. OFFICE OF PUBLICATION: 135 West 50th Street, New York, NY 10020.

Printed in Canada. ALAN FINE, President, Marvel Entertainment; DAN BUCKLEY, President, TV, Publishing & Brand Management; JOE QUESADA, Chief Creative Officer; TOM BREVOORT, SVP of Publishing; DAVID BOGART, SVP of Business Affairs & Operations, Publishing & Partnership; C.B. CEBULSKI, VP of Brand Management & Development, Asia; DAVID GABRIEL, SVP of Sales & Marketing, Publishing; JEFF YOUNGQUIST, VP of Production & Special Projects; DAN CARR, Executive Director of Publishing Technology; ALEX MORALES, Director of Publishing Operations; SUSAN CRESPI, Production Manager; STAN LEE, Chairman Emeritus. For information regarding advertising in Marvel Comics or on Marvel.com, please contact Vit DeBellis, Integrated Sales Manager, at vdebellis@marvel.com. For Marvel subscription inquiries, please call 888-511-5480. **Manufactured between 9/2/2016 and 10/10/2016 by SOLISCO PRINTERS, SCOTT, QC, CANADA.**

10 9 8 7 6 5 4 3 2 1

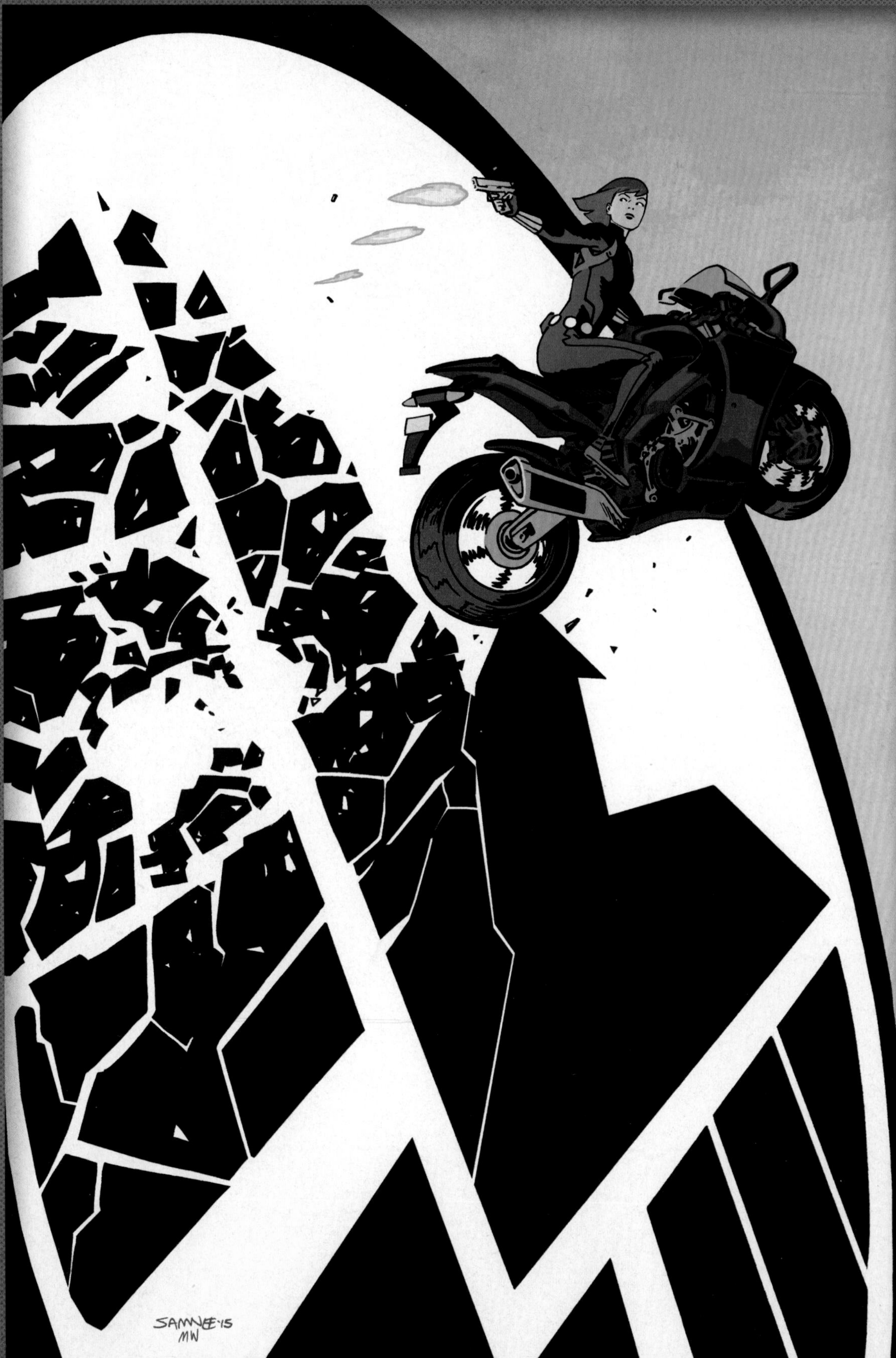
SAMNEE '15
MW

1

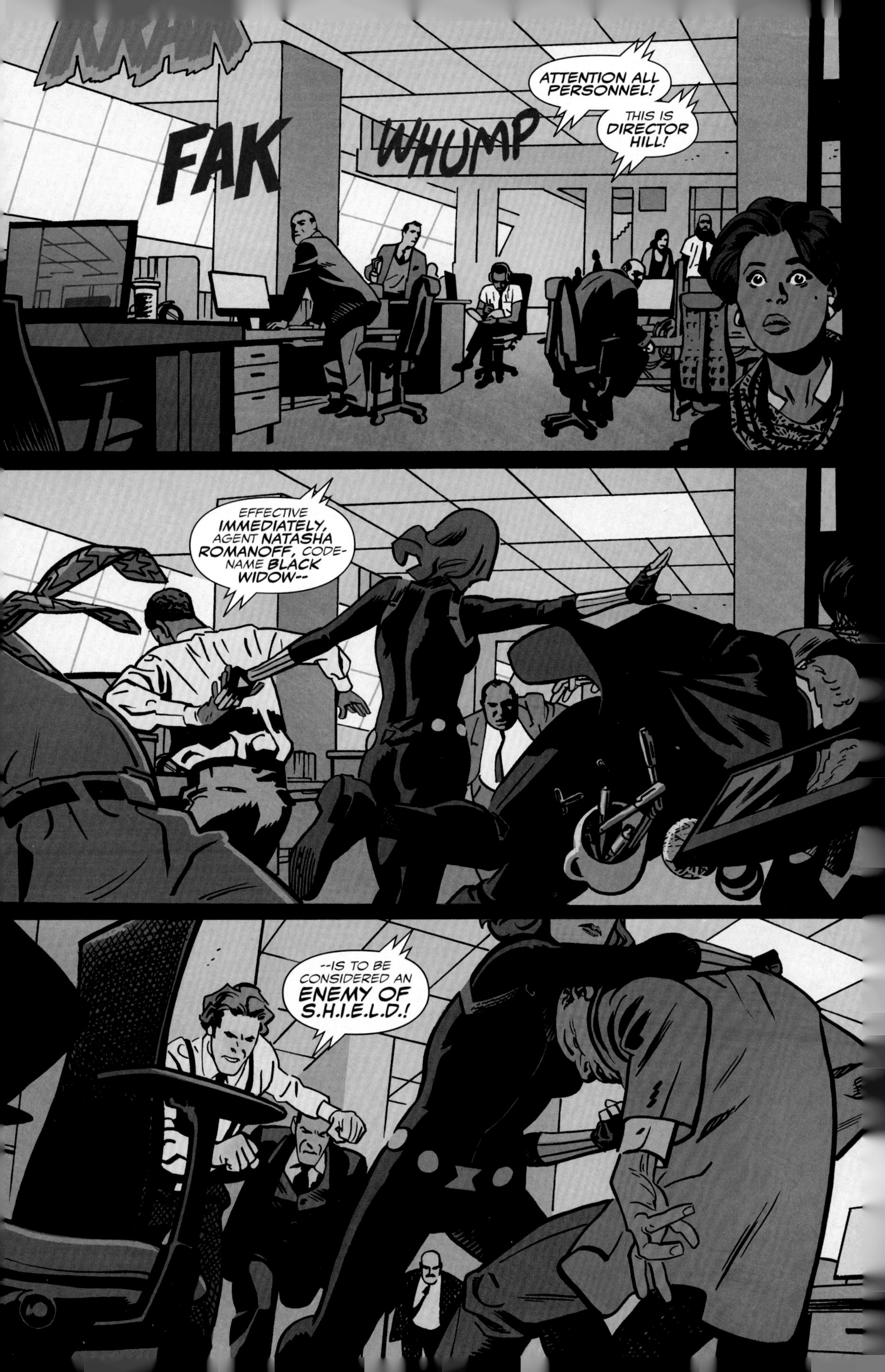
FAK
WHUMP
ATTENTION ALL PERSONNEL!
THIS IS DIRECTOR HILL!
EFFECTIVE IMMEDIATELY, AGENT NATASHA ROMANOFF, CODE-NAME BLACK WIDOW--
--IS TO BE CONSIDERED AN ENEMY OF S.H.I.E.L.D.!

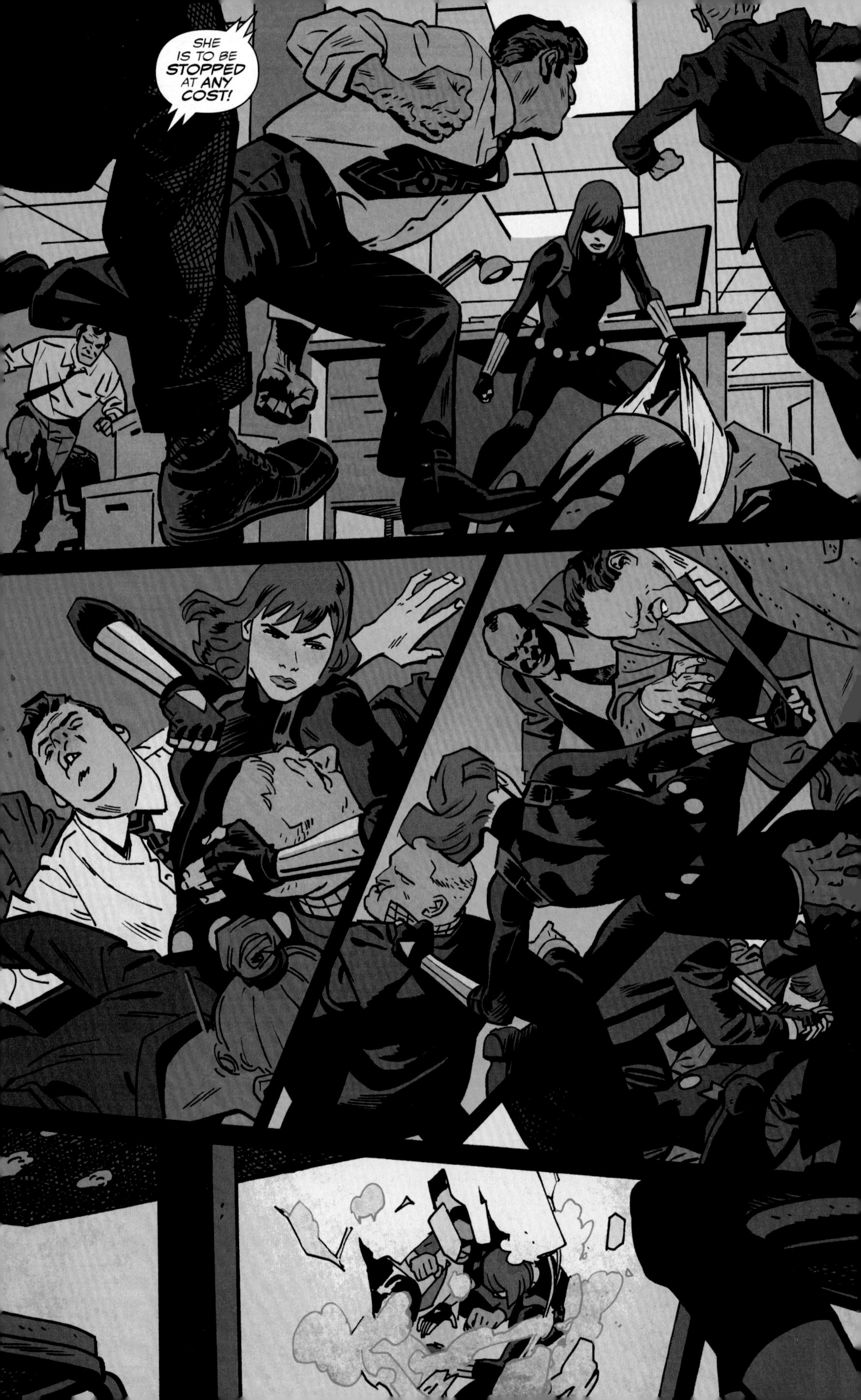
SHE IS TO BE STOPPED AT ANY COST!

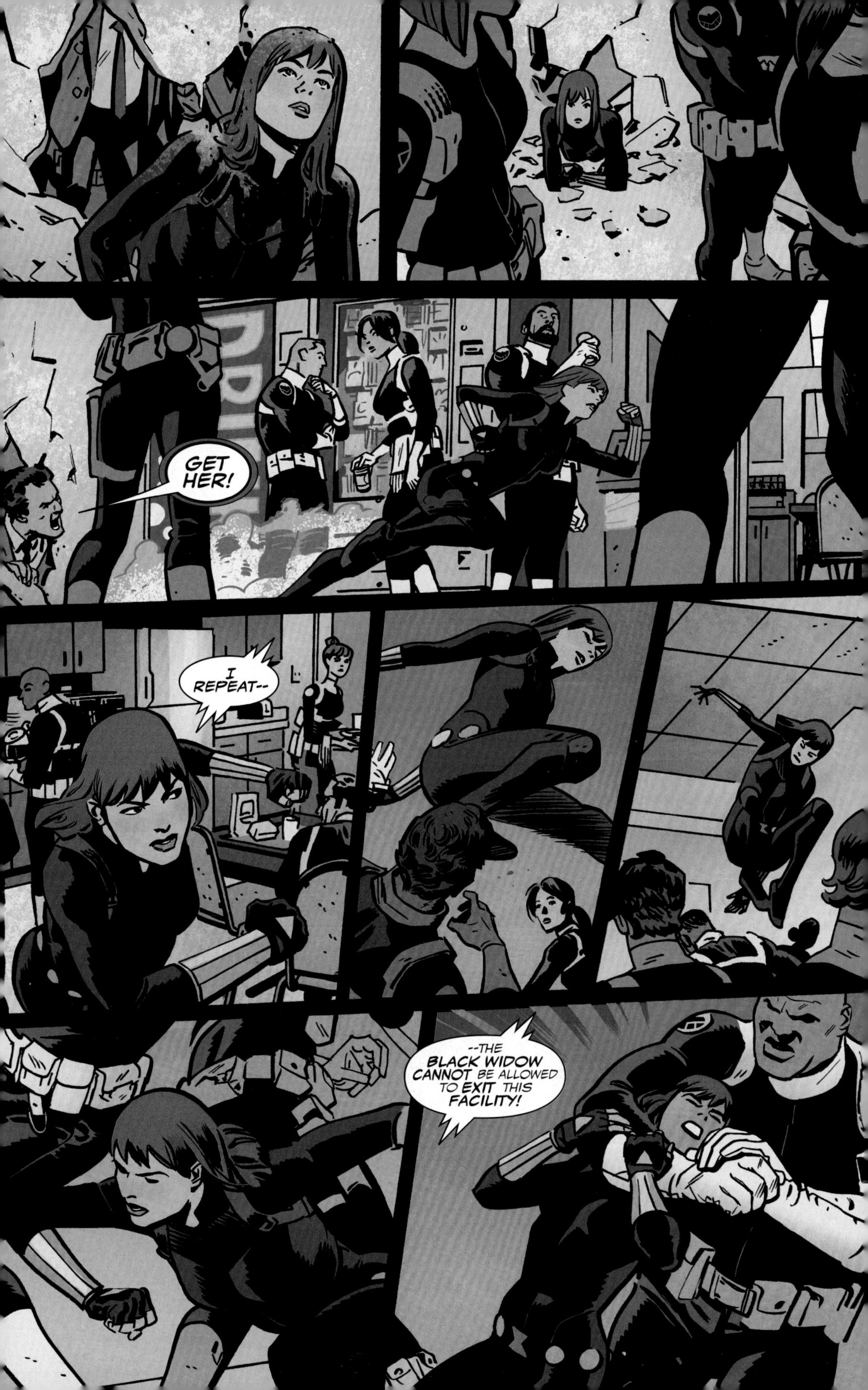
GET HER!
I REPEAT--
--THE BLACK WIDOW CANNOT BE ALLOWED TO EXIT THIS FACILITY!

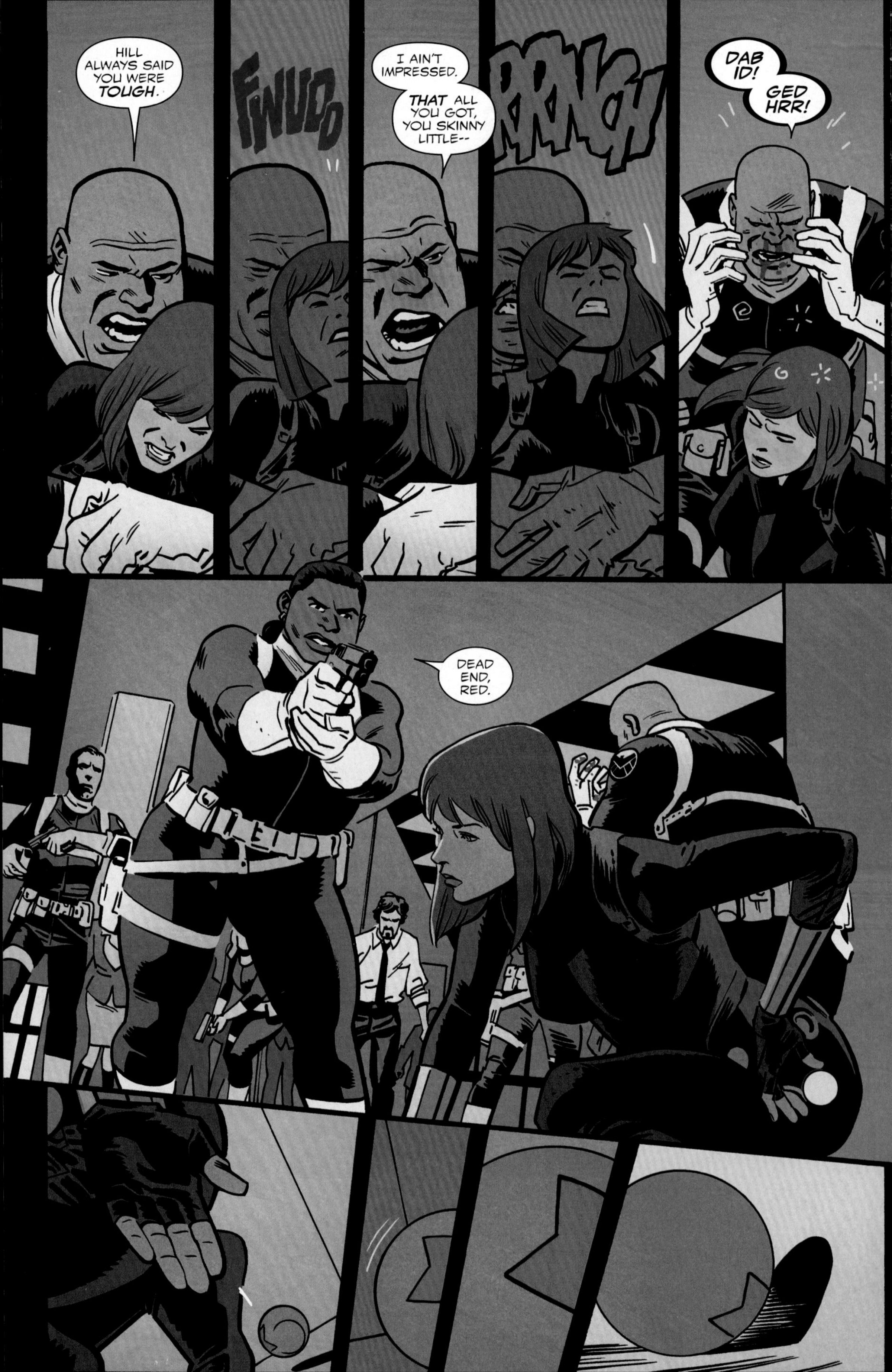
HILL ALWAYS SAID YOU WERE TOUGH.
FWUDD
I AIN'T IMPRESSED.
THAT ALL YOU GOT, YOU SKINNY LITTLE--
PRANCH
DAB ID!
GED HRR!
DEAD END, RED.

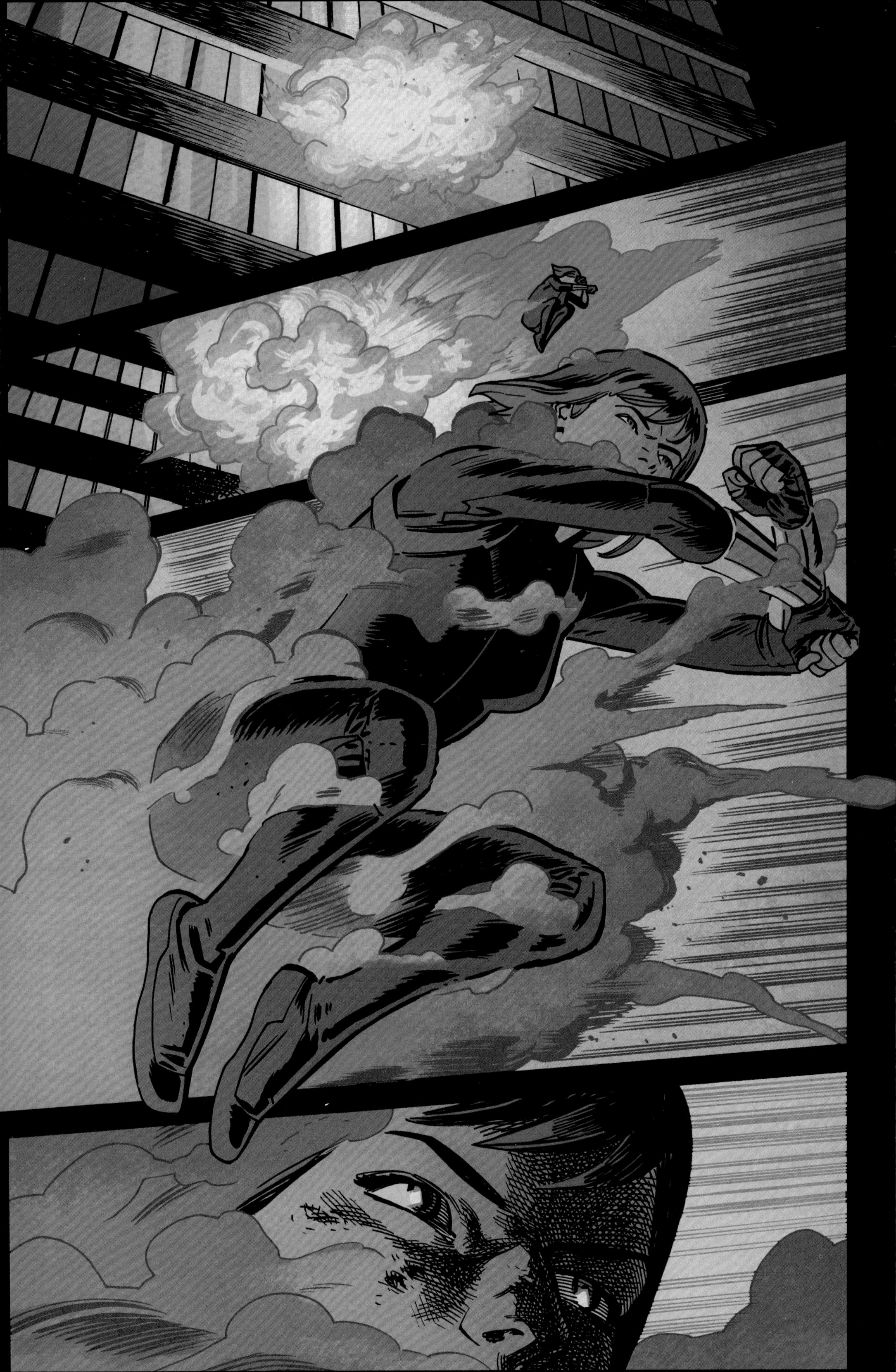

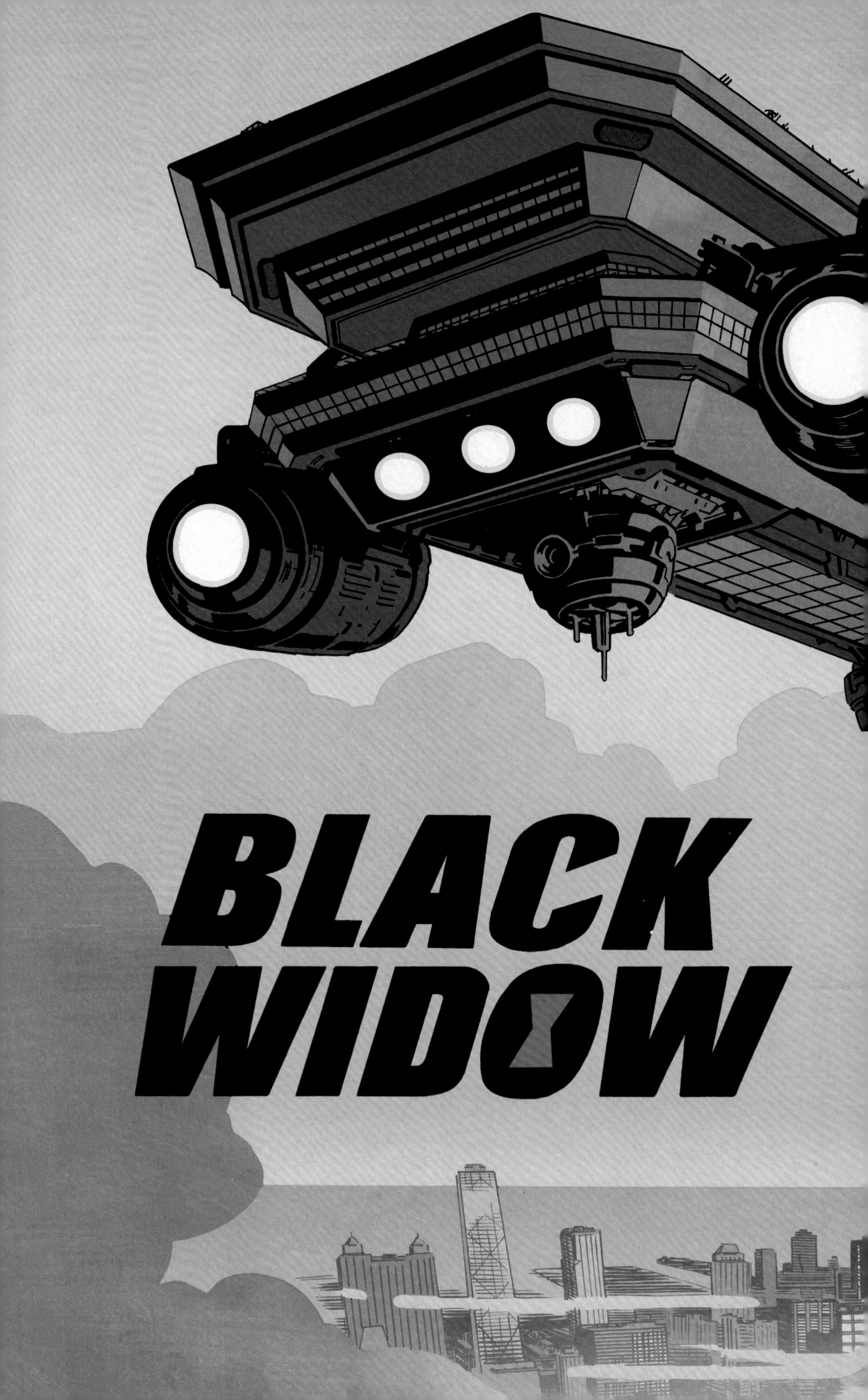
BLACK
WIDOW

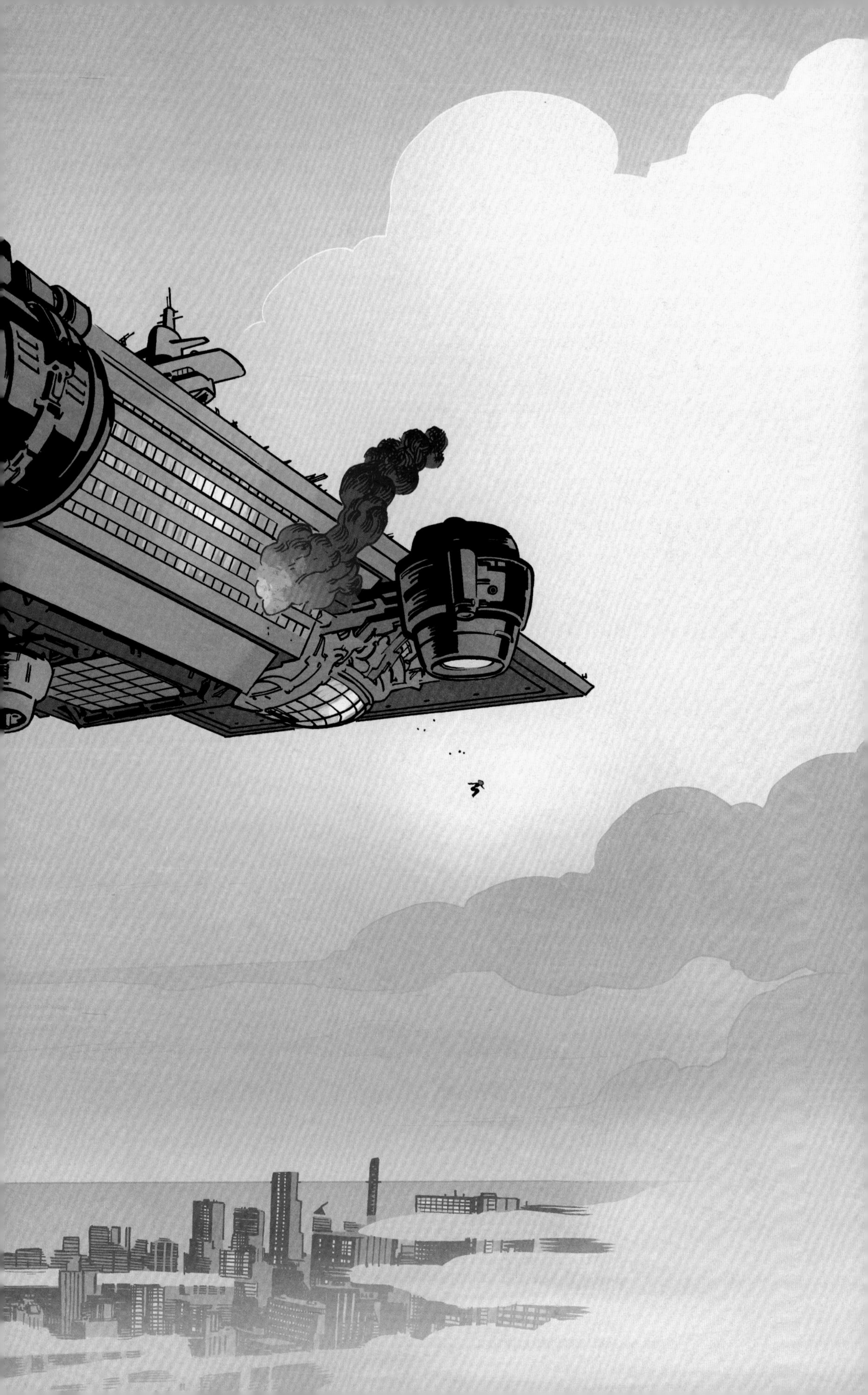

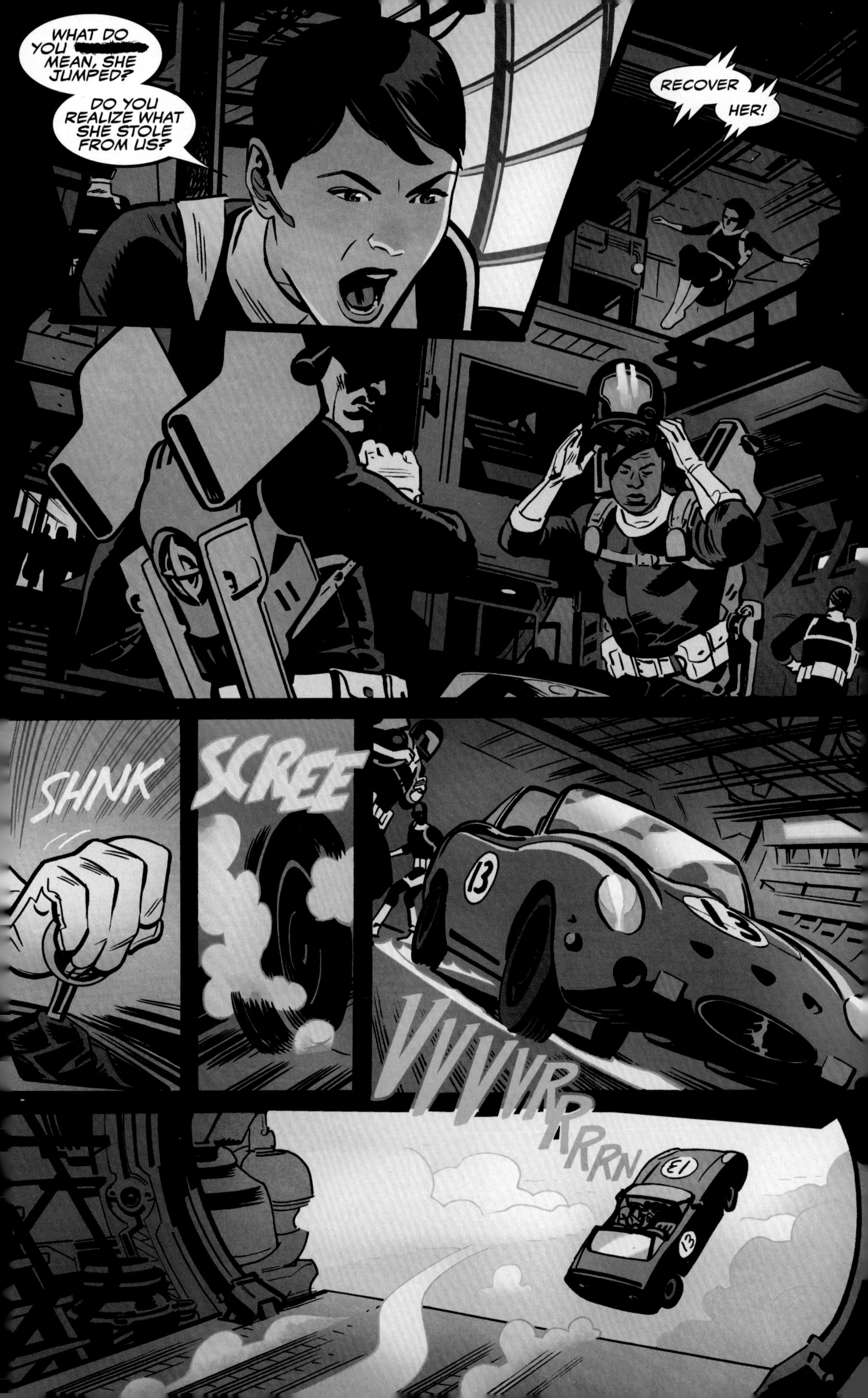
WHAT DO YOU [redacted] MEAN, SHE JUMPED?
DO YOU REALIZE WHAT SHE STOLE FROM US?
RECOVER HER!
SHNK
SCREE
13
VVVVRRRRRN

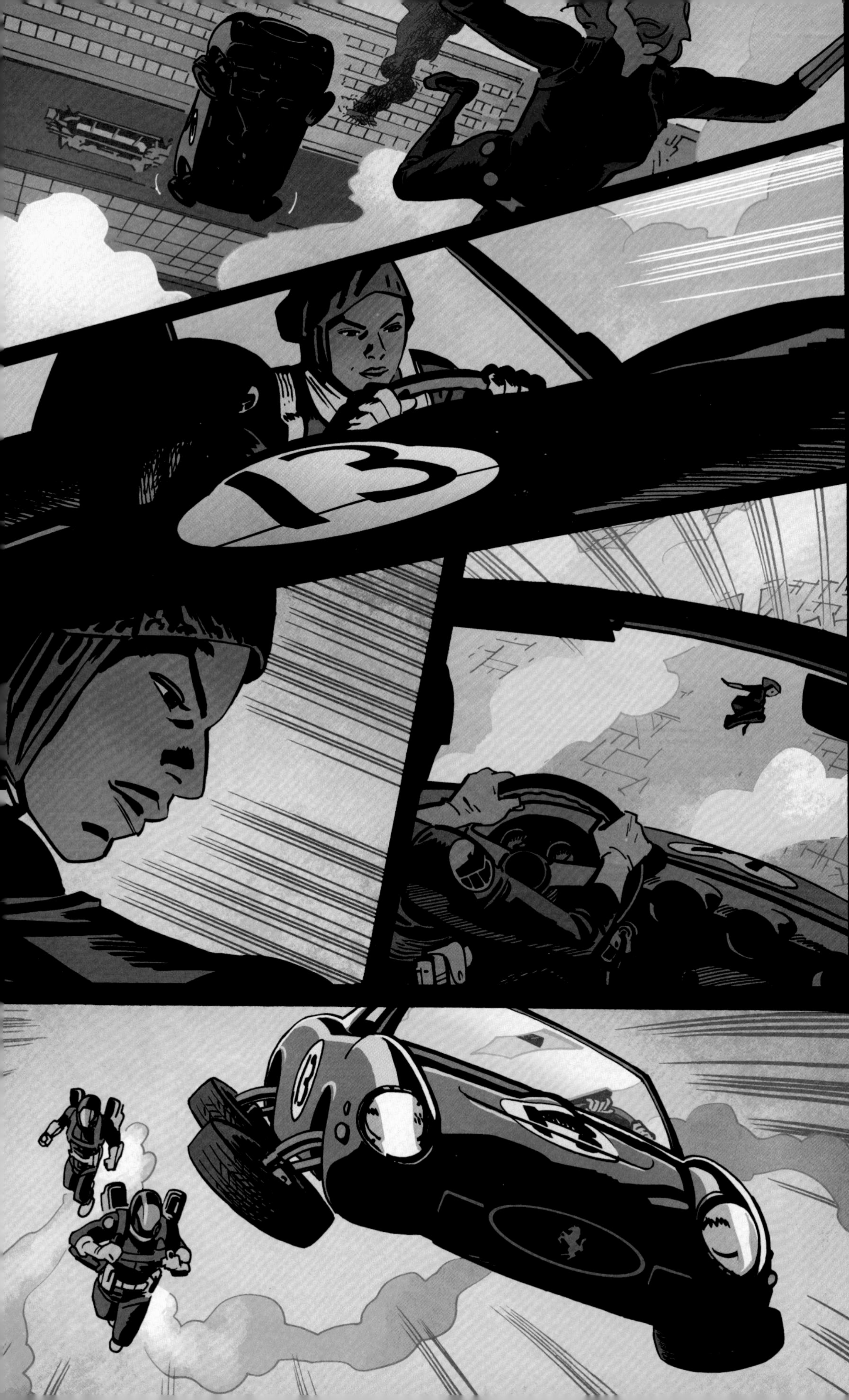
13

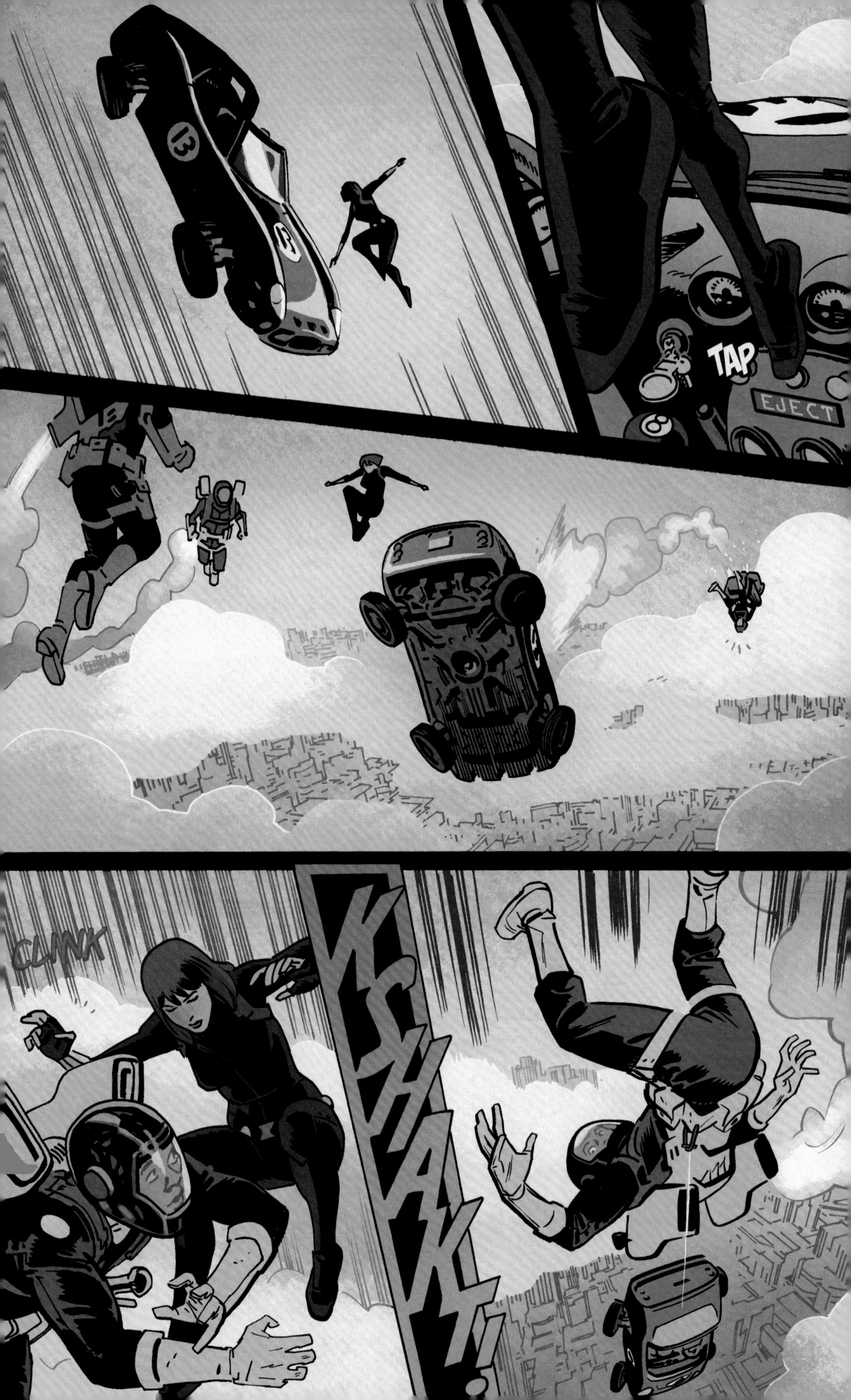
TAP
EJECT
CLINK
KSHAKT!

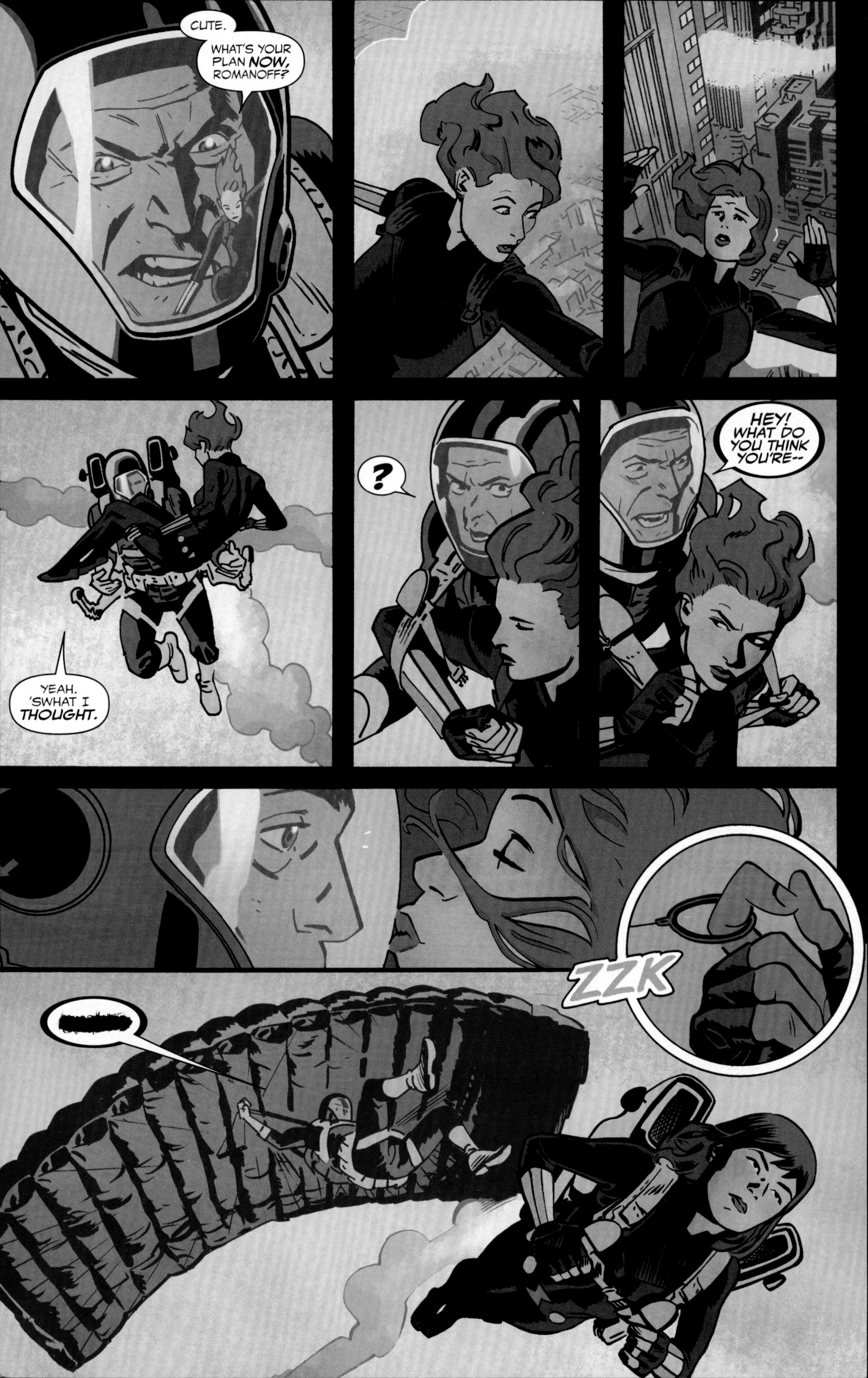
CUTE.
WHAT'S YOUR PLAN NOW, ROMANOFF?
YEAH. 'SWHAT I THOUGHT.
?
HEY! WHAT DO YOU THINK YOU'RE--
ZZK

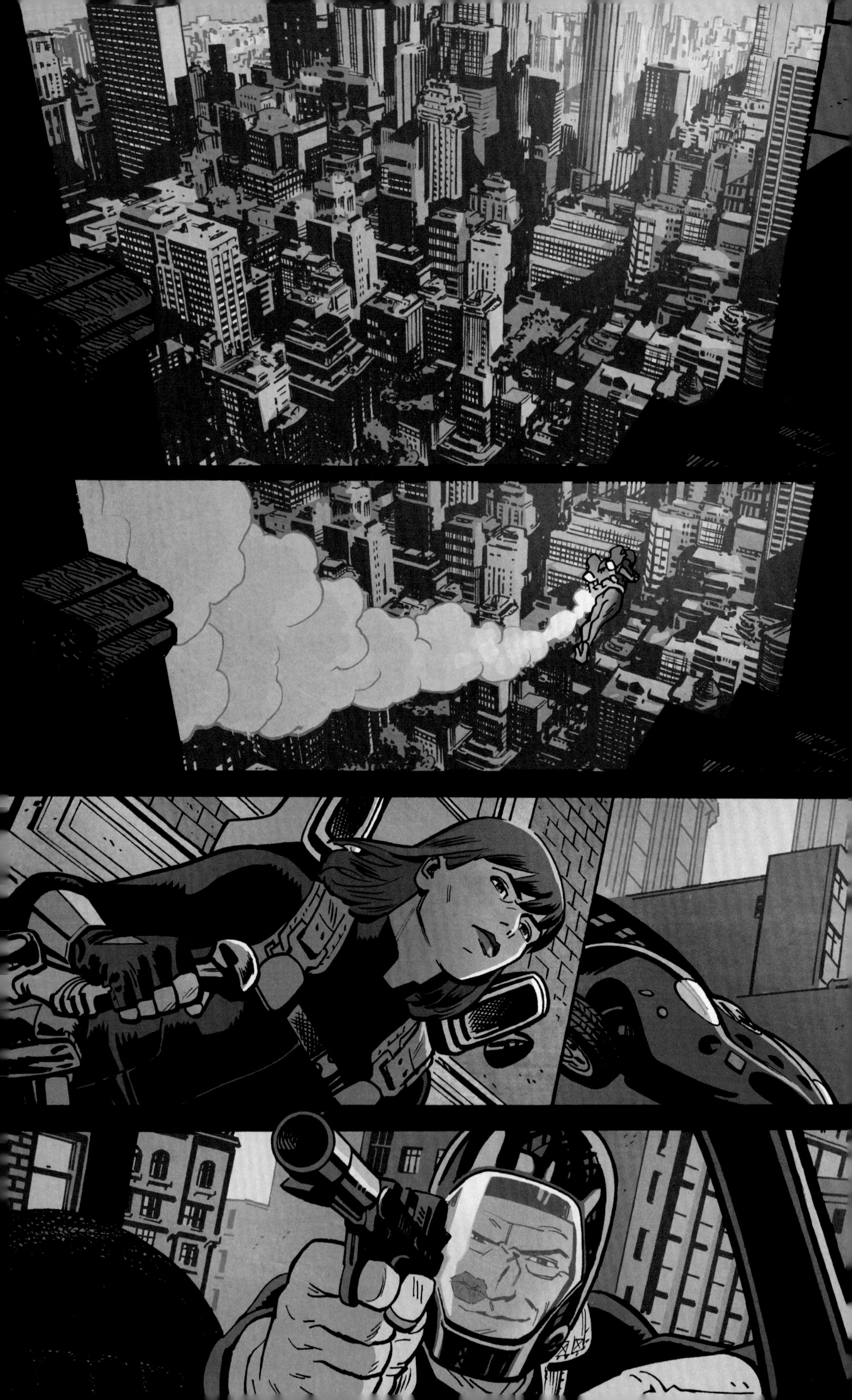

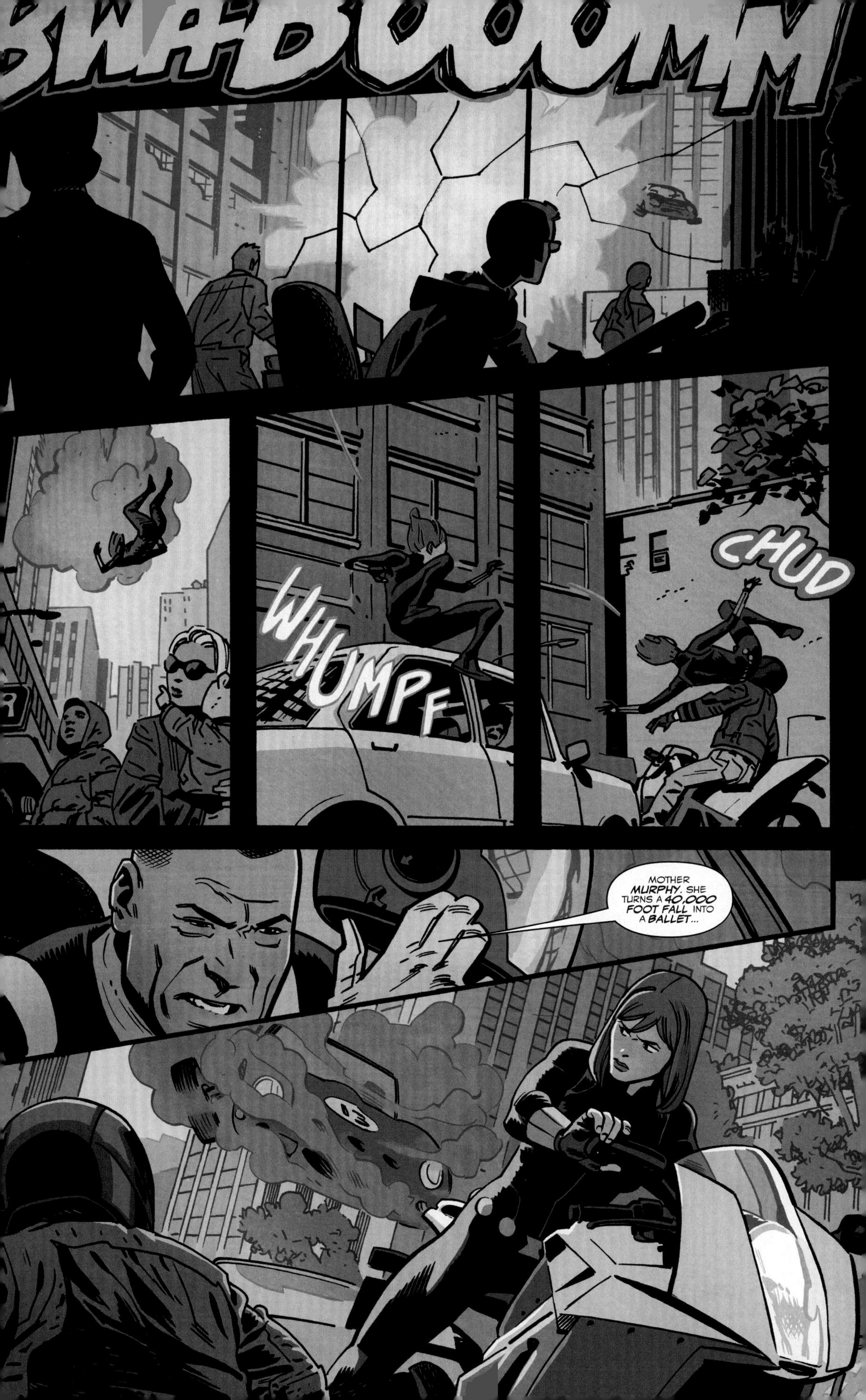
BWADOOOM
WHUMPF
CHUD
MOTHER MURPHY. SHE TURNS A 40,000 FOOT FALL INTO A BALLET...

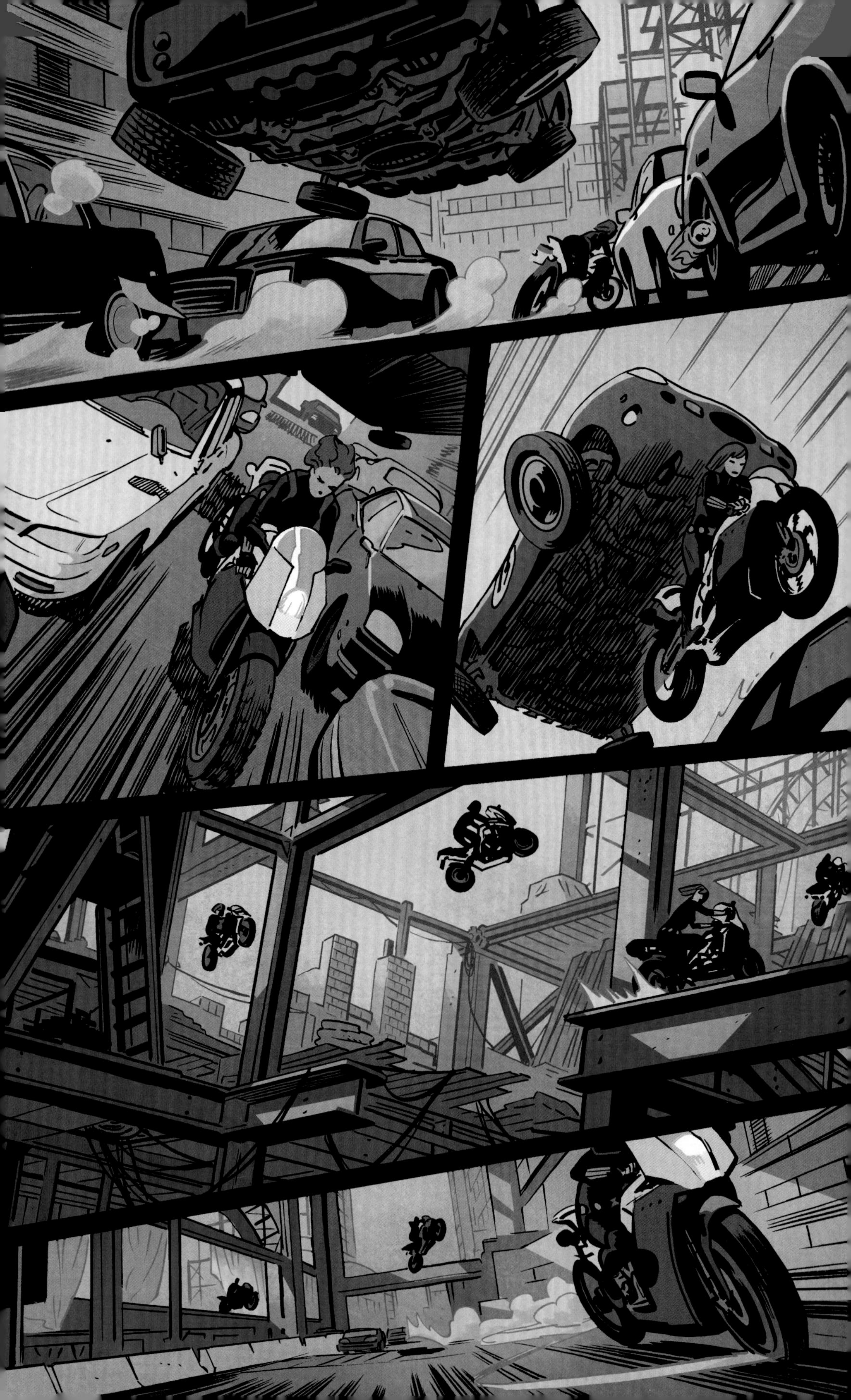

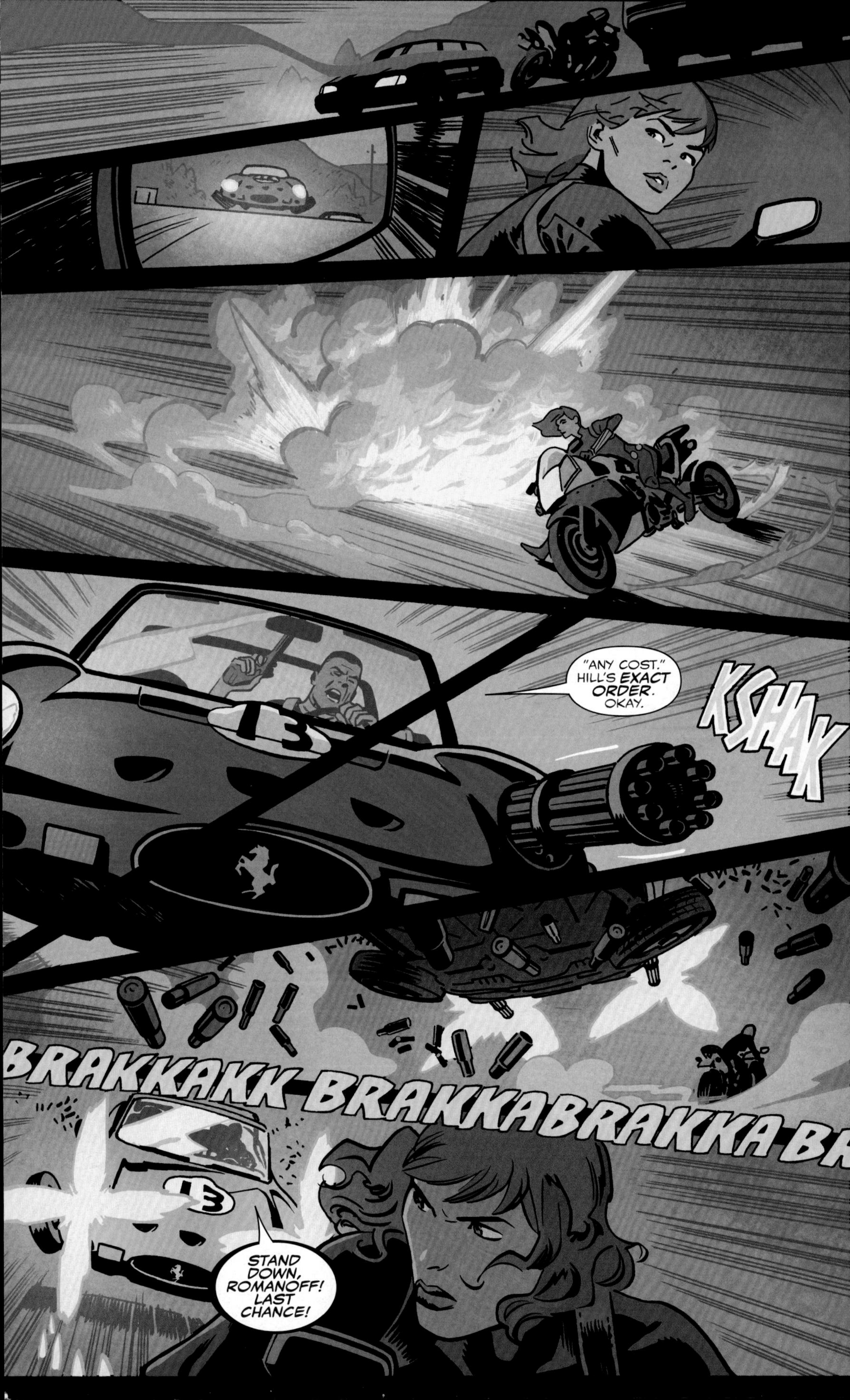
"ANY COST." HILL'S EXACT ORDER. OKAY.
KSHAK
BRAKKAKK BRAKKABRAKKA BR
STAND DOWN, ROMANOFF! LAST CHANCE!

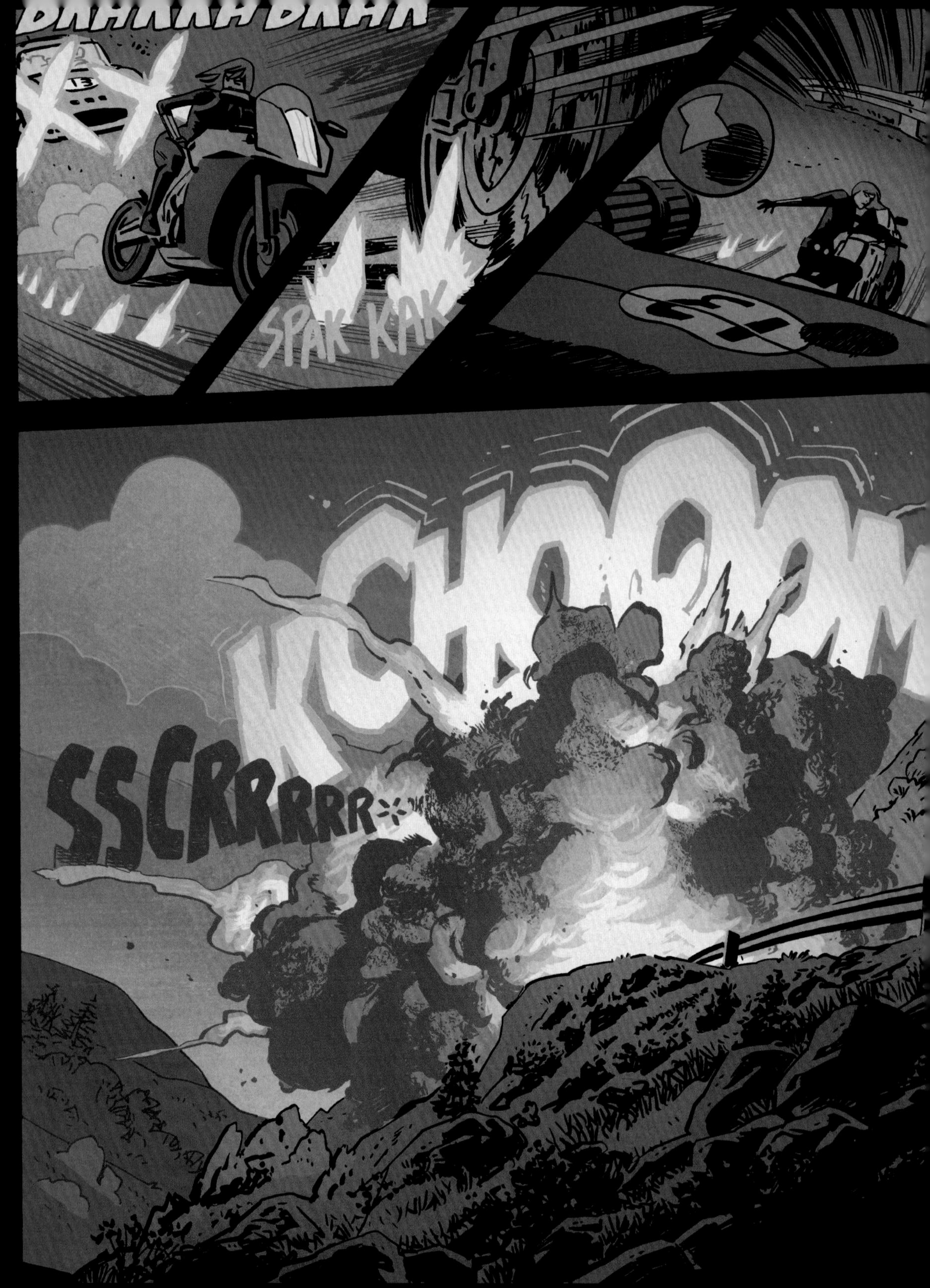
SPAK KAK
KCHOOM
SSCRRRRRR

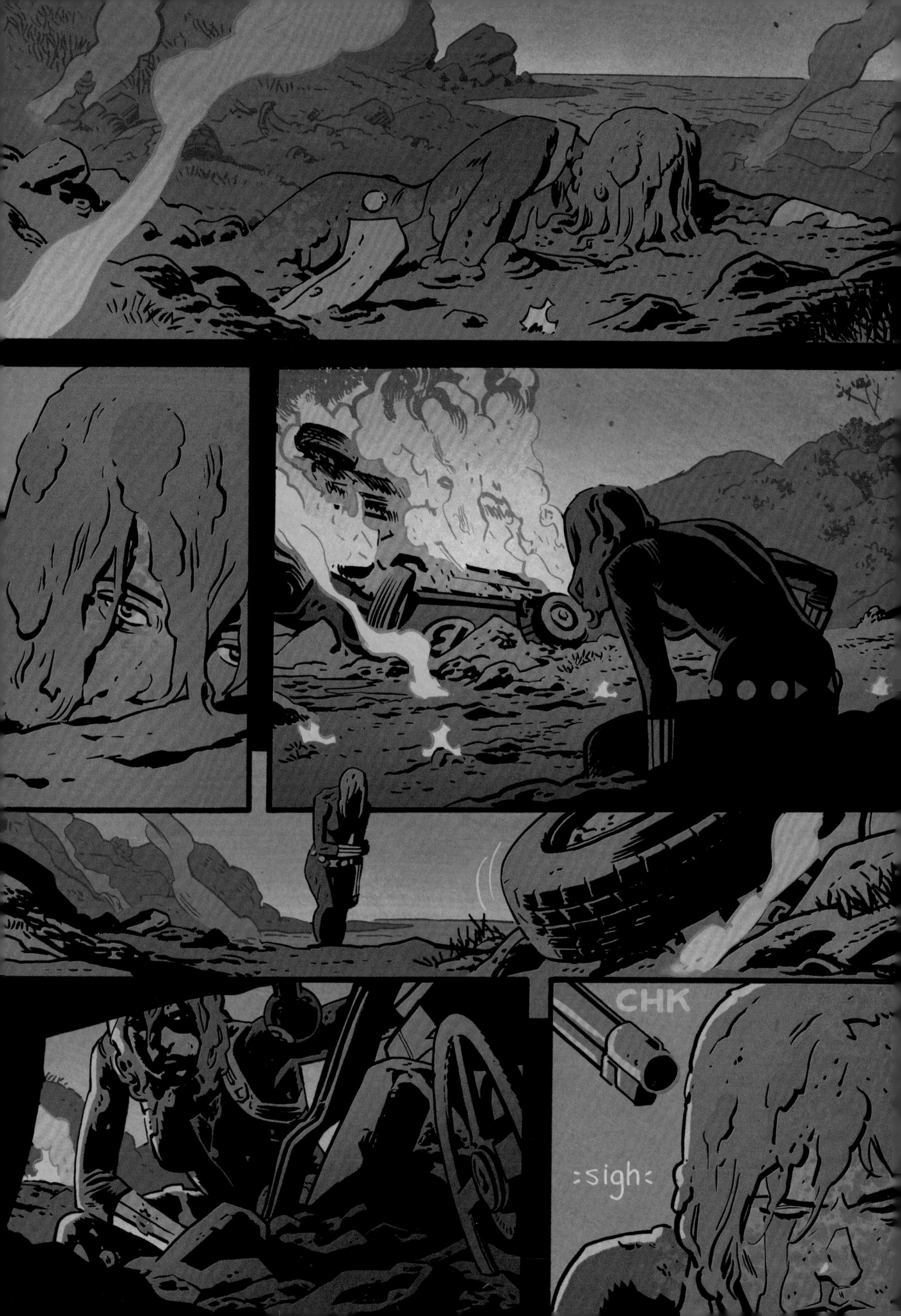
CHK
:sigh:

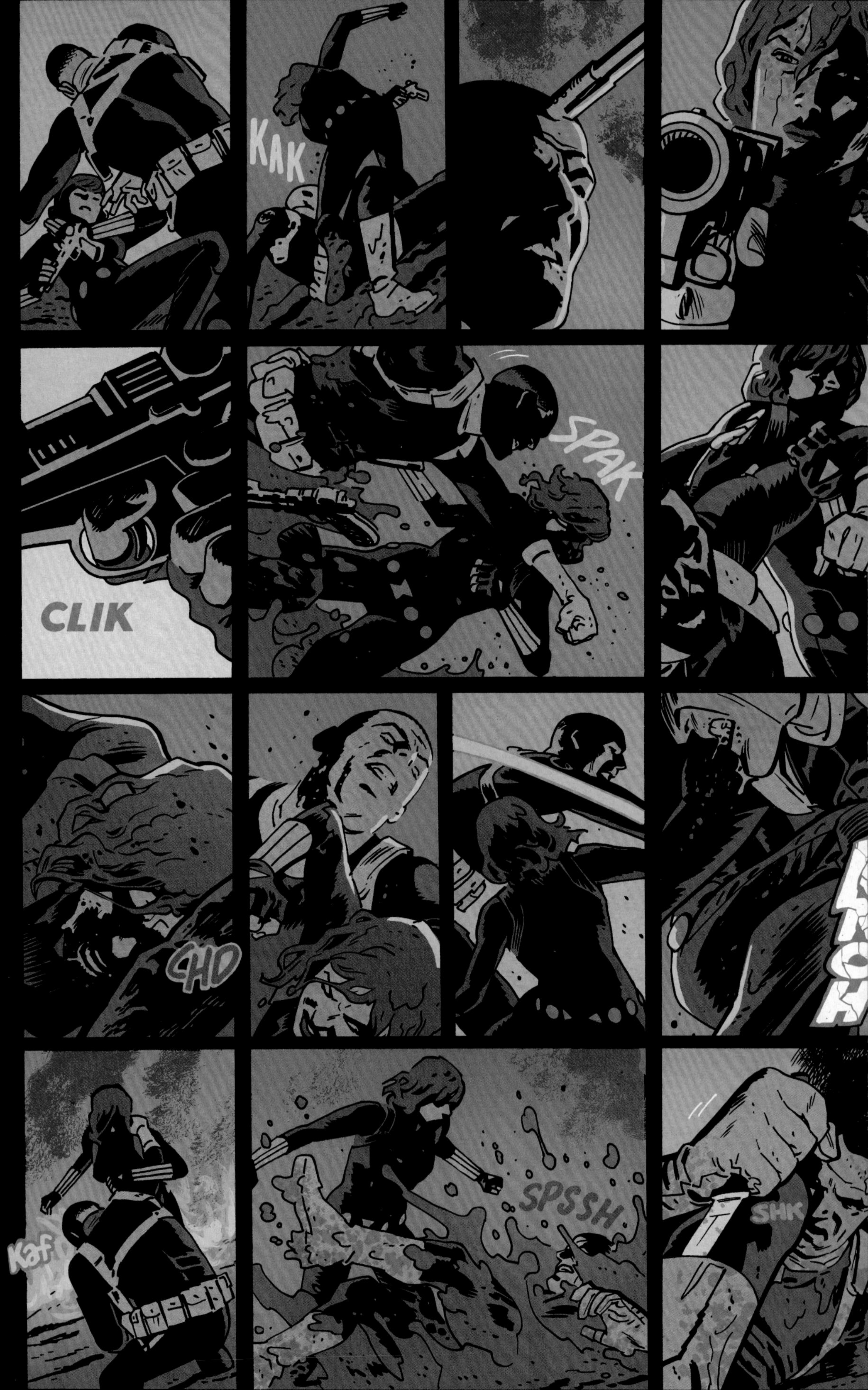
KAK
CLIK
SPAK
CHD
Kaf
SPSSH
SHK

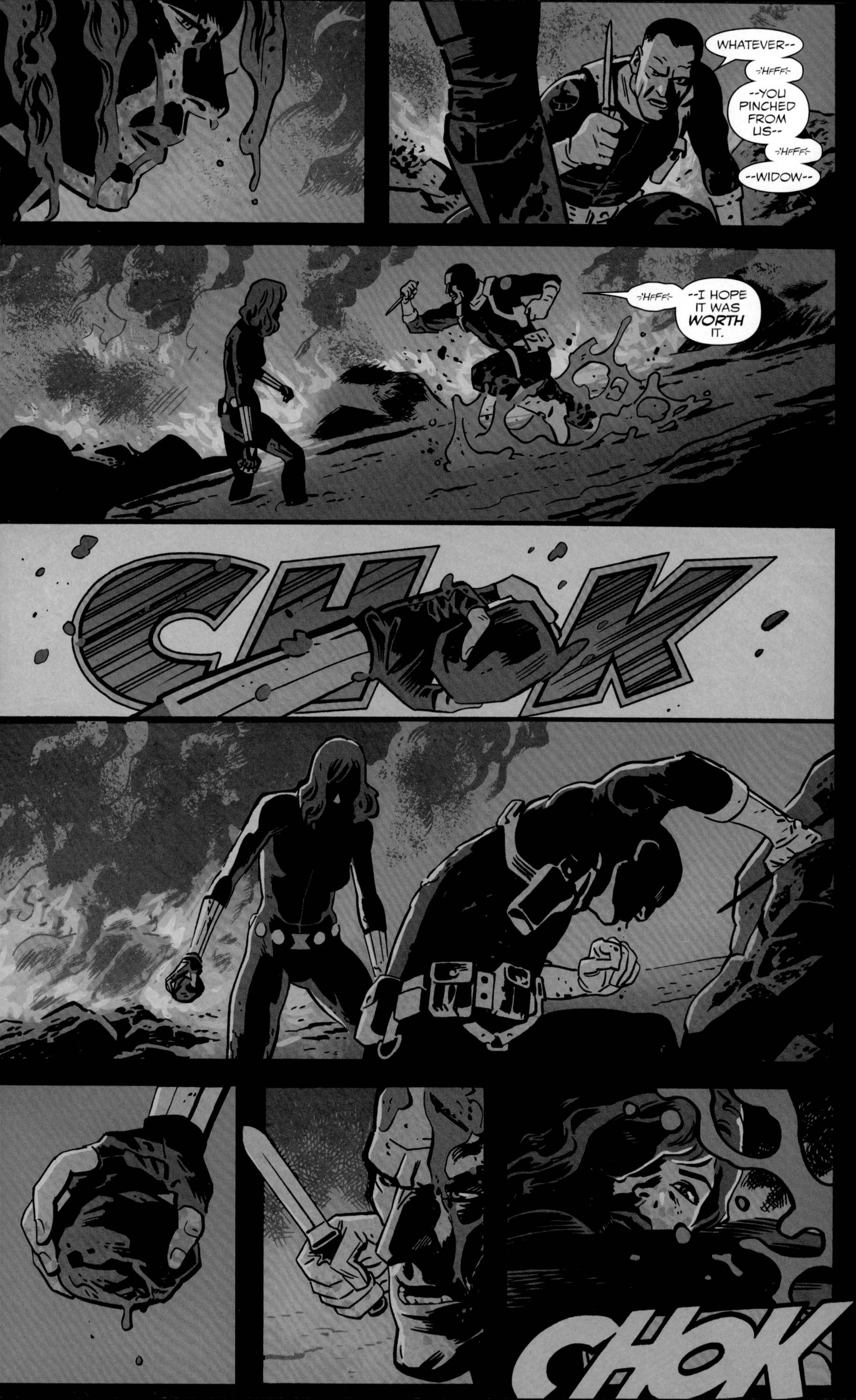
WHATEVER--
HFFF
--YOU PINCHED FROM US--
HFFF
--WIDOW--
HFFF
--I HOPE IT WAS WORTH IT.
CHK
CHOK

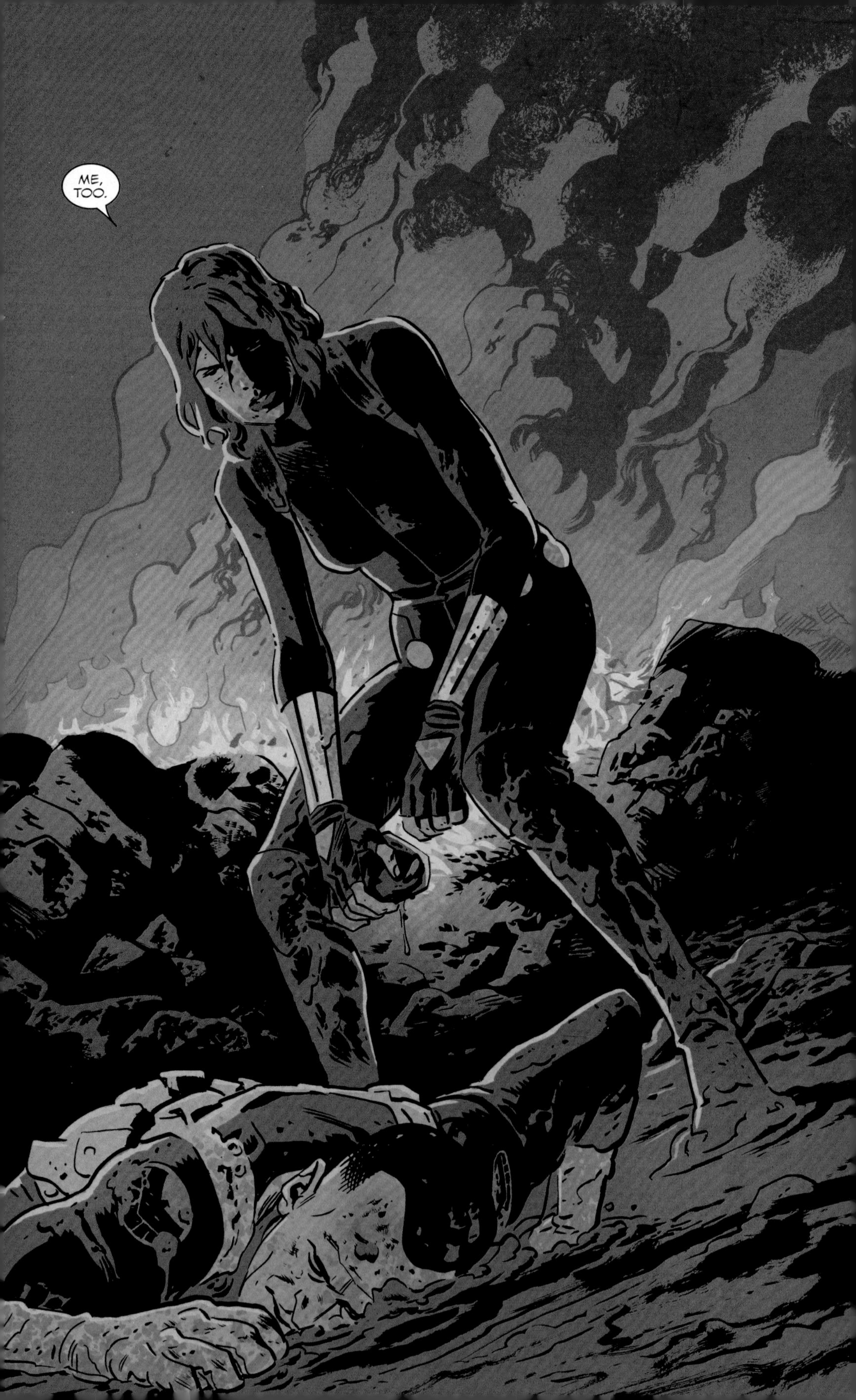
ME, TOO.

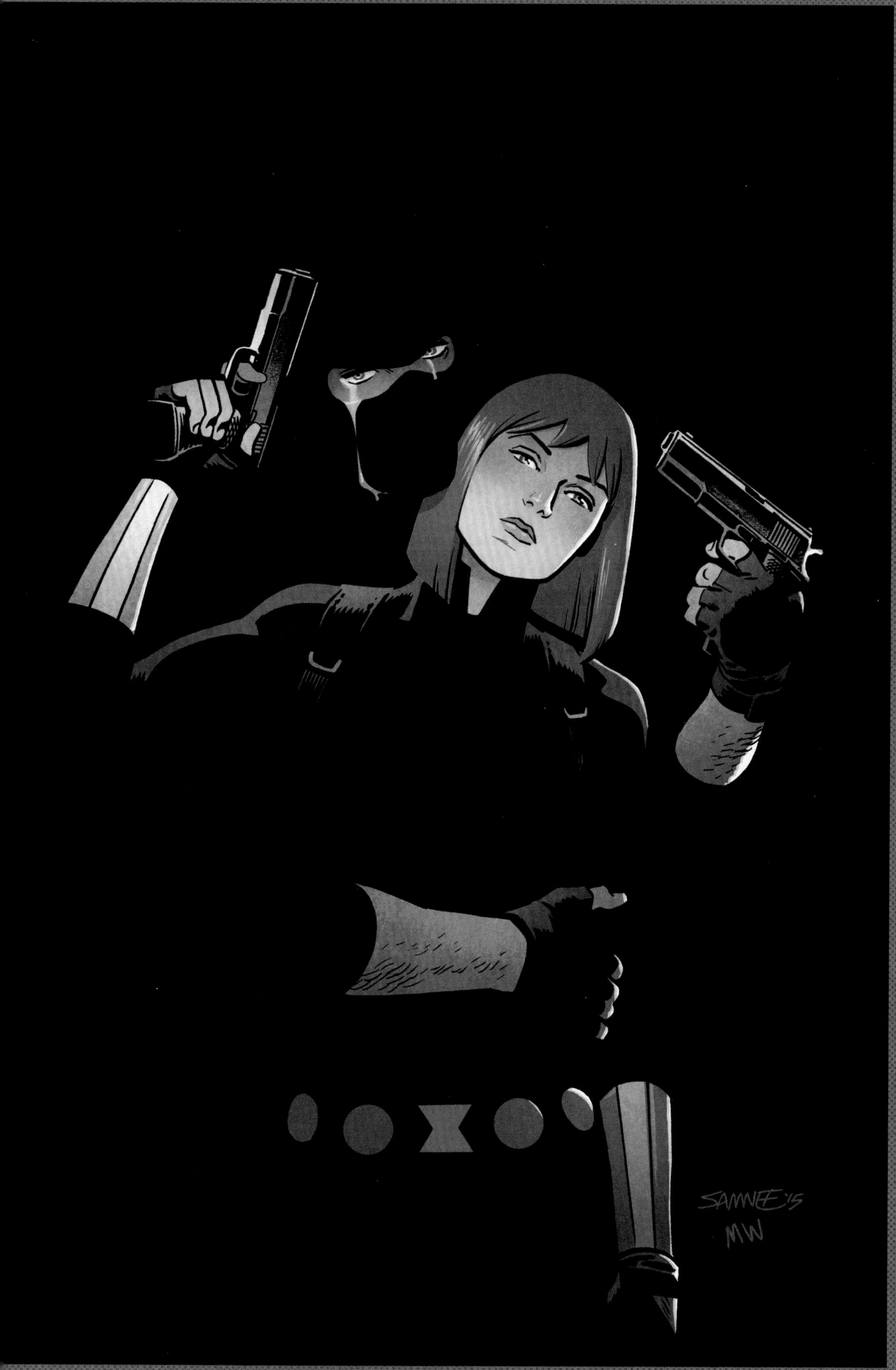
SAMNEE '15
MW

2

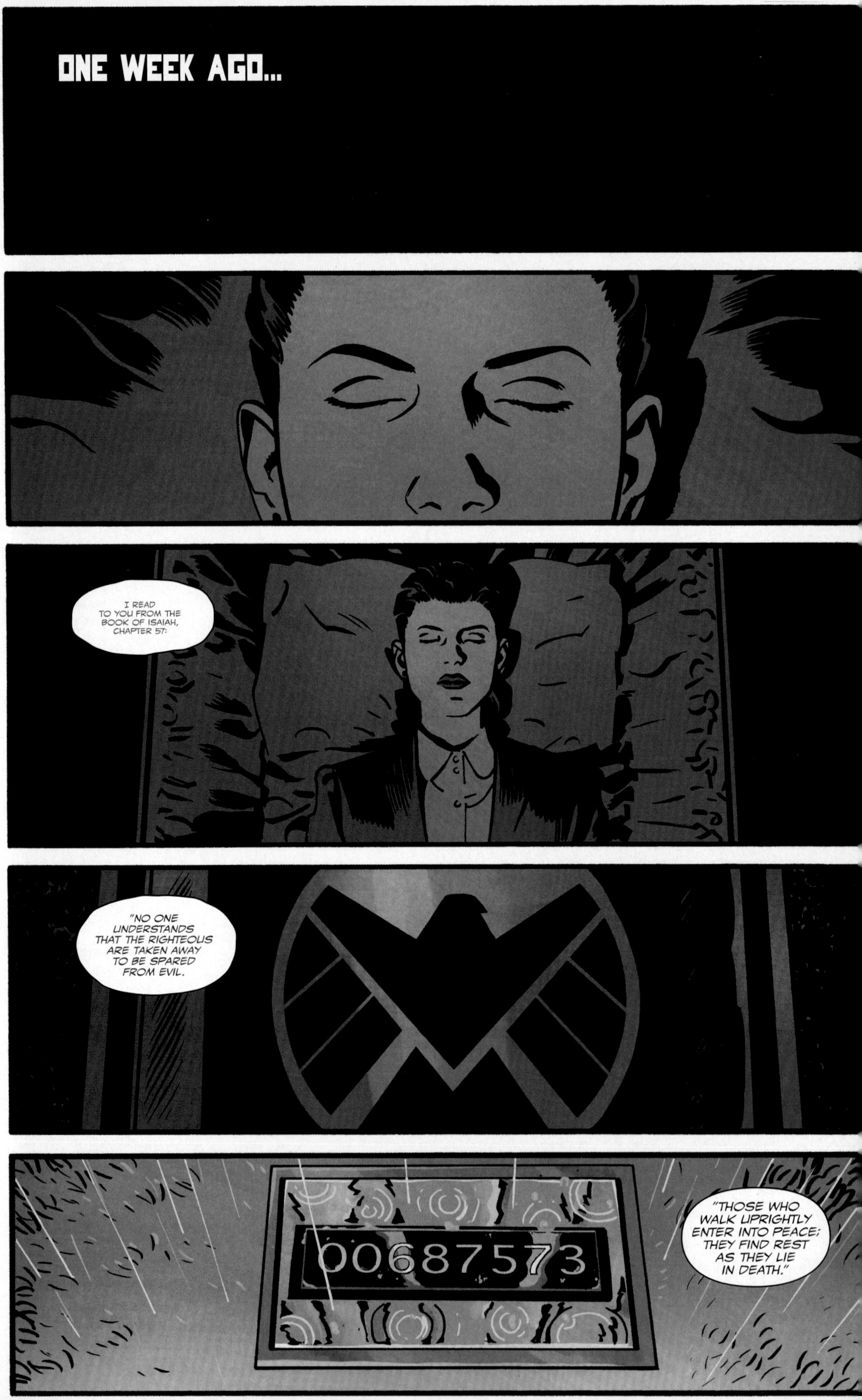
ONE WEEK AGO...
I READ TO YOU FROM THE BOOK OF ISAIAH, CHAPTER 57:
"NO ONE UNDERSTANDS THAT THE RIGHTEOUS ARE TAKEN AWAY TO BE SPARED FROM EVIL.
00687573
"THOSE WHO WALK UPRIGHTLY ENTER INTO PEACE; THEY FIND REST AS THEY LIE IN DEATH."

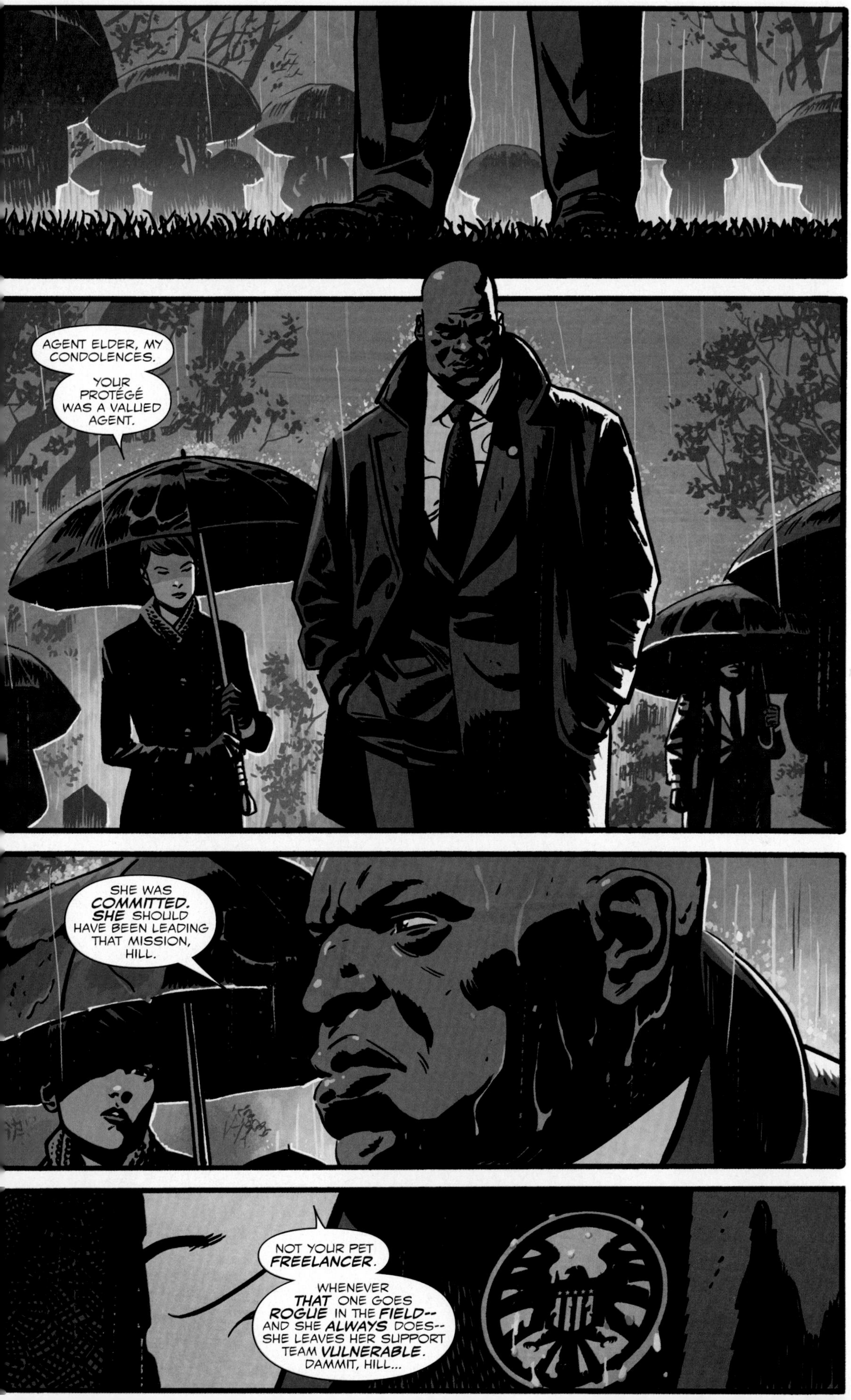
AGENT ELDER, MY CONDOLENCES.
YOUR PROTÉGÉ WAS A VALUED AGENT.
SHE WAS COMMITTED. SHE SHOULD HAVE BEEN LEADING THAT MISSION, HILL.
NOT YOUR PET FREELANCER.
WHENEVER THAT ONE GOES ROGUE IN THE FIELD-- AND SHE ALWAYS DOES-- SHE LEAVES HER SUPPORT TEAM VULNERABLE. DAMMIT, HILL...

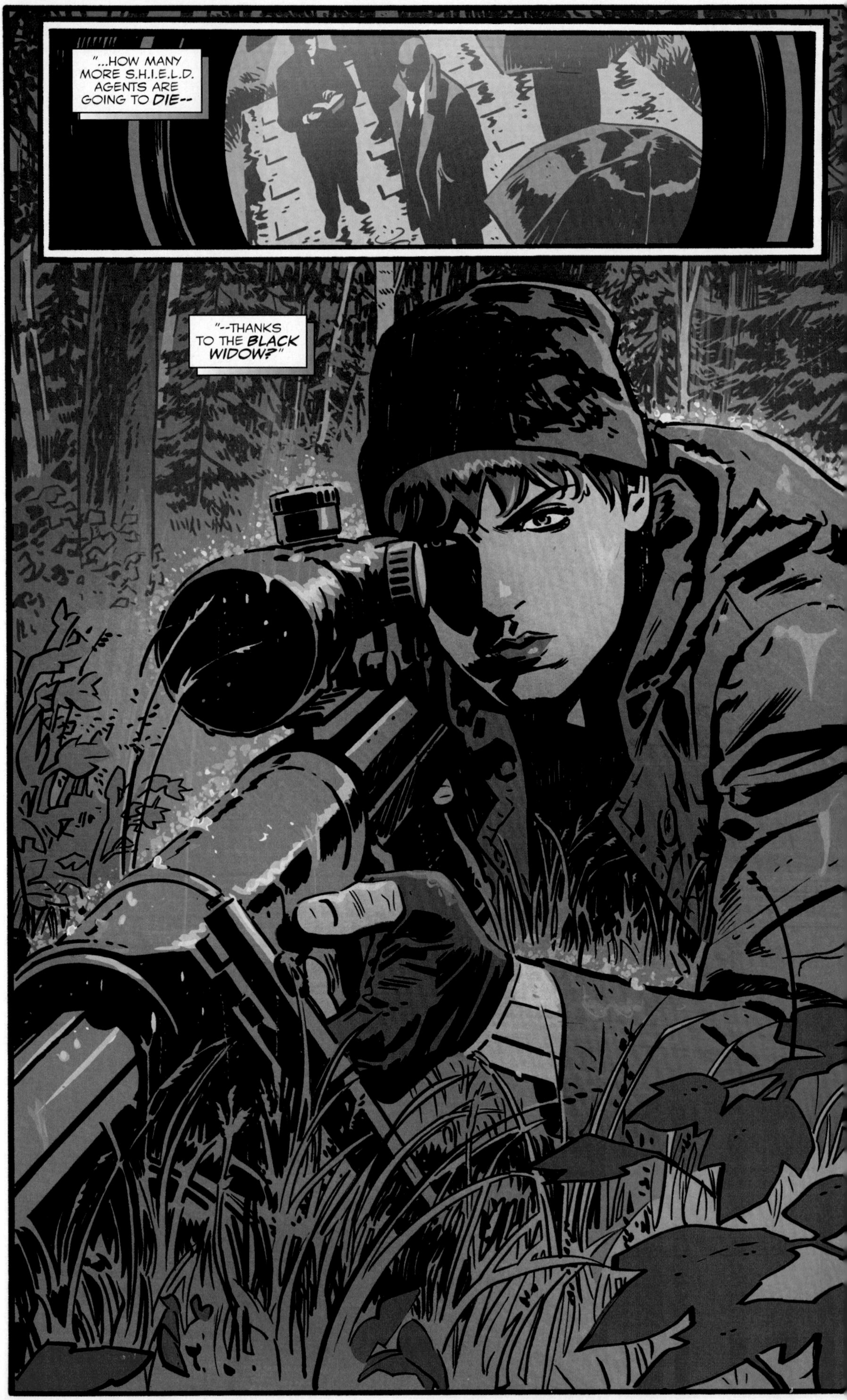
"...HOW MANY MORE S.H.I.E.L.D. AGENTS ARE GOING TO DIE--
"--THANKS TO THE BLACK WIDOW?"

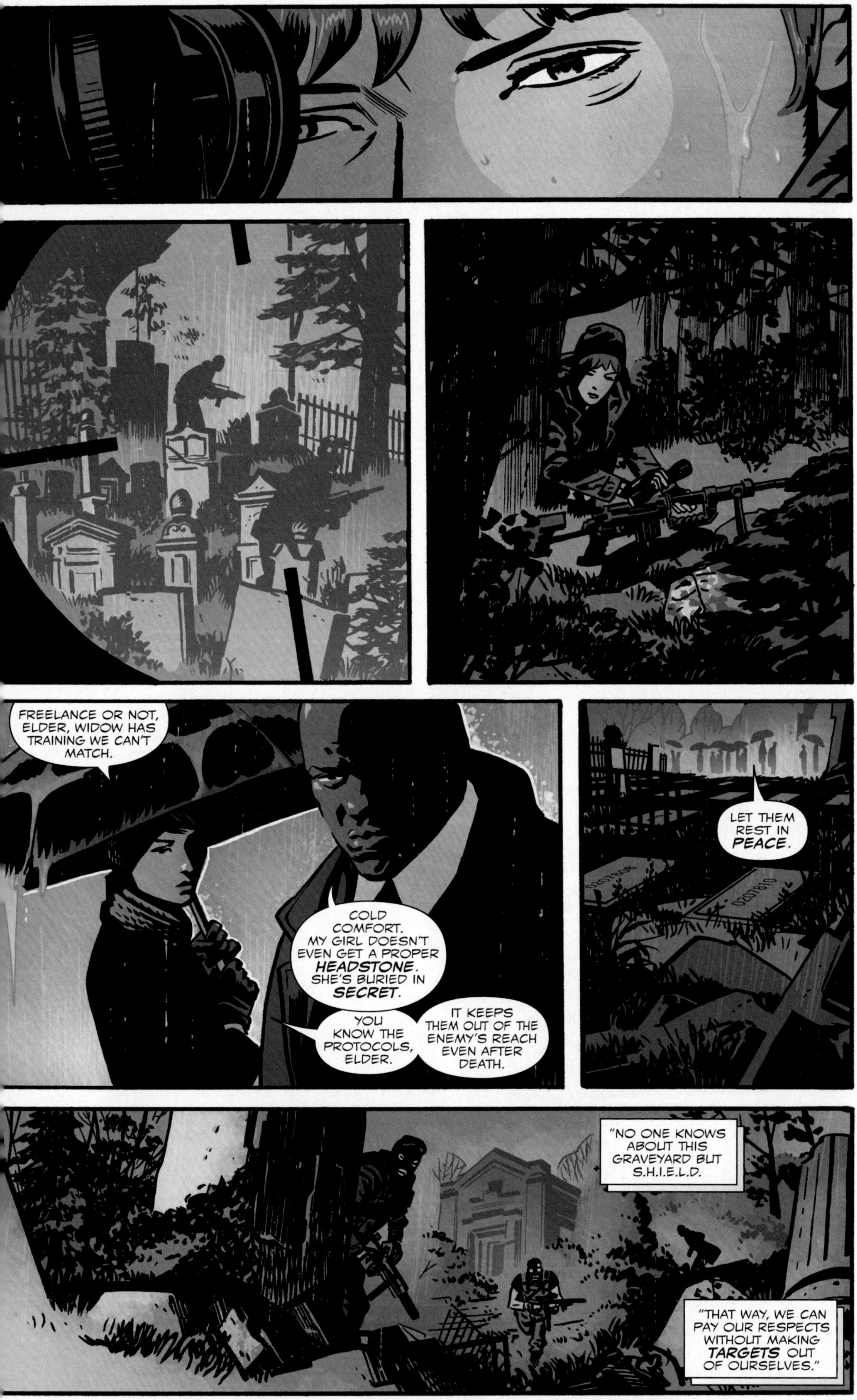
FREELANCE OR NOT, ELDER, WIDOW HAS TRAINING WE CAN'T MATCH.
COLD COMFORT. MY GIRL DOESN'T EVEN GET A PROPER HEADSTONE. SHE'S BURIED IN SECRET.
YOU KNOW THE PROTOCOLS, ELDER.
IT KEEPS THEM OUT OF THE ENEMY'S REACH EVEN AFTER DEATH.
LET THEM REST IN PEACE.
"NO ONE KNOWS ABOUT THIS GRAVEYARD BUT S.H.I.E.L.D.
"THAT WAY, WE CAN PAY OUR RESPECTS WITHOUT MAKING TARGETS OUT OF OURSELVES."

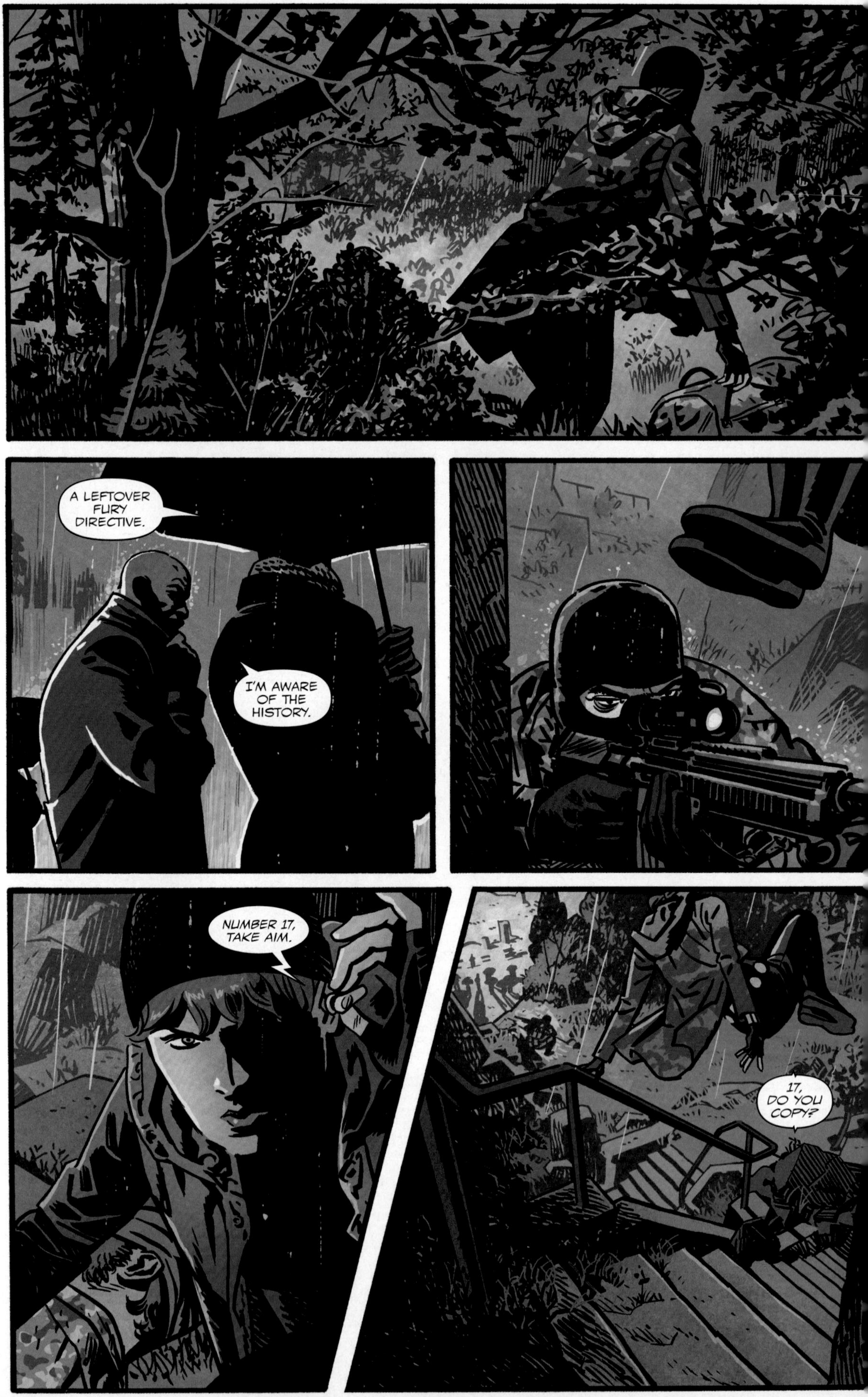
A LEFTOVER FURY DIRECTIVE.
I'M AWARE OF THE HISTORY.
NUMBER 17, TAKE AIM.
17, DO YOU COPY?

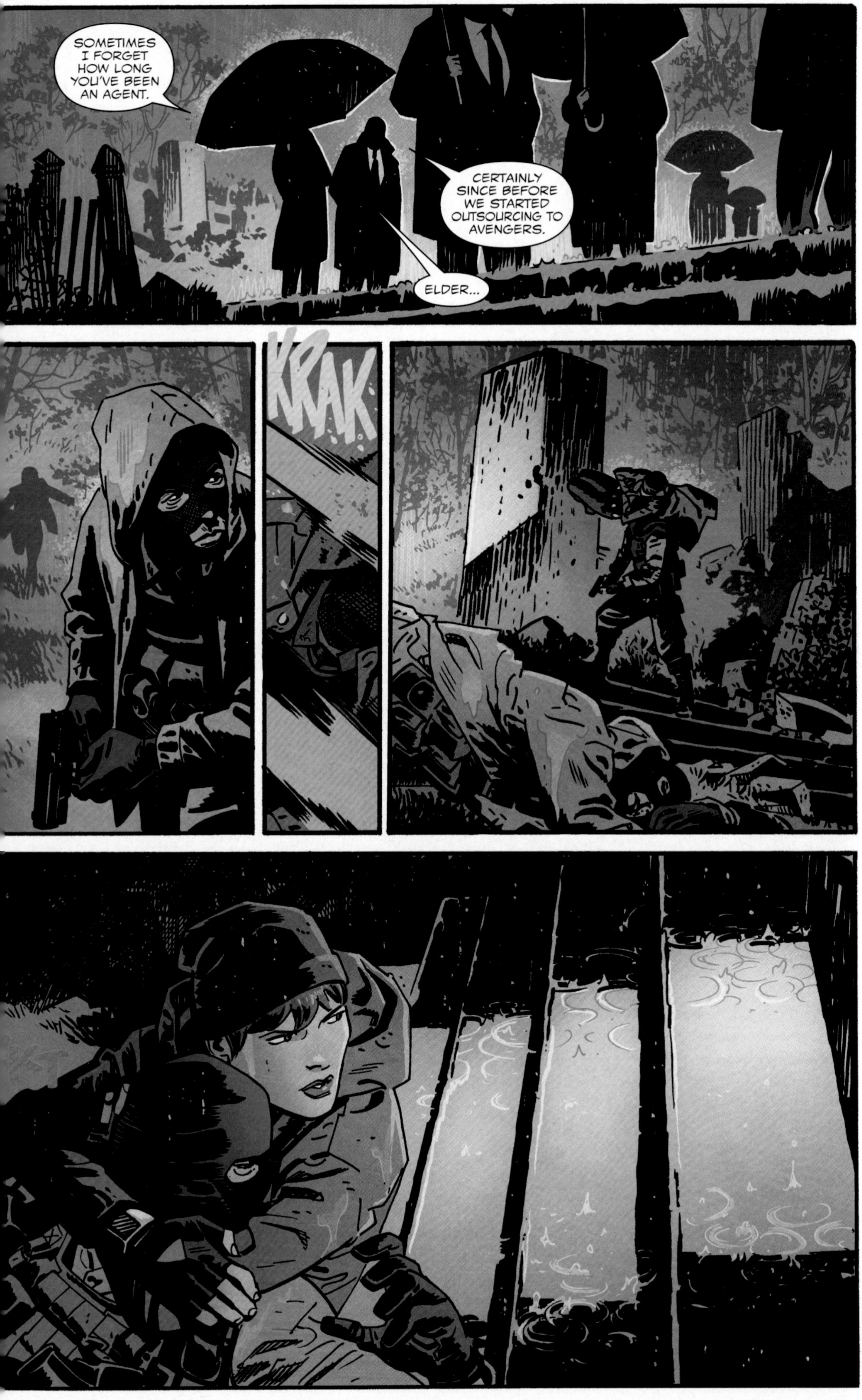
SOMETIMES I FORGET HOW LONG YOU'VE BEEN AN AGENT.
CERTAINLY SINCE BEFORE WE STARTED OUTSOURCING TO AVENGERS.
ELDER...
KRAK

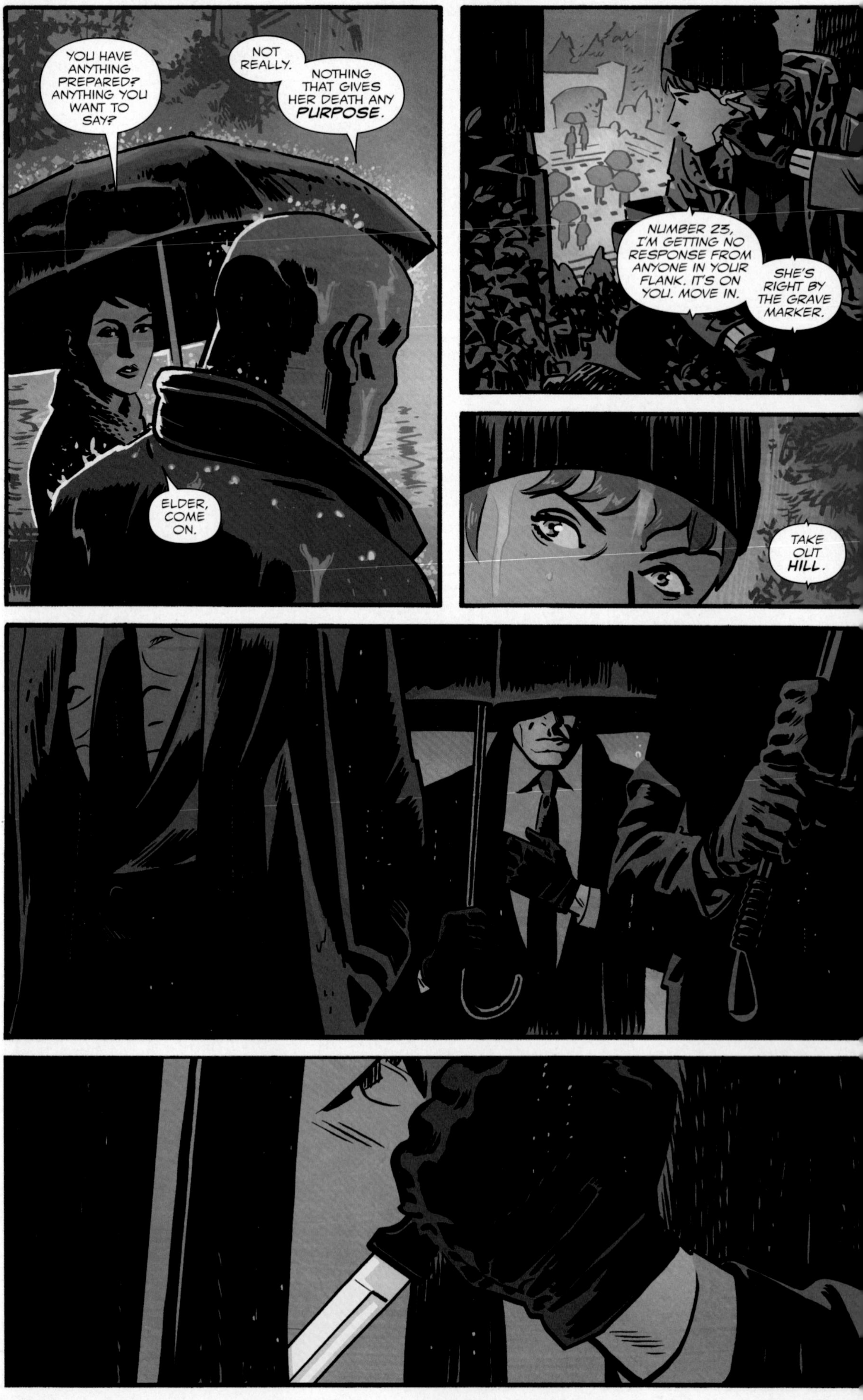
YOU HAVE ANYTHING PREPARED? ANYTHING YOU WANT TO SAY?
NOT REALLY.
NOTHING THAT GIVES HER DEATH ANY PURPOSE.
ELDER, COME ON.
NUMBER 23, I'M GETTING NO RESPONSE FROM ANYONE IN YOUR FLANK. IT'S ON YOU. MOVE IN.
SHE'S RIGHT BY THE GRAVE MARKER.
TAKE OUT HILL.

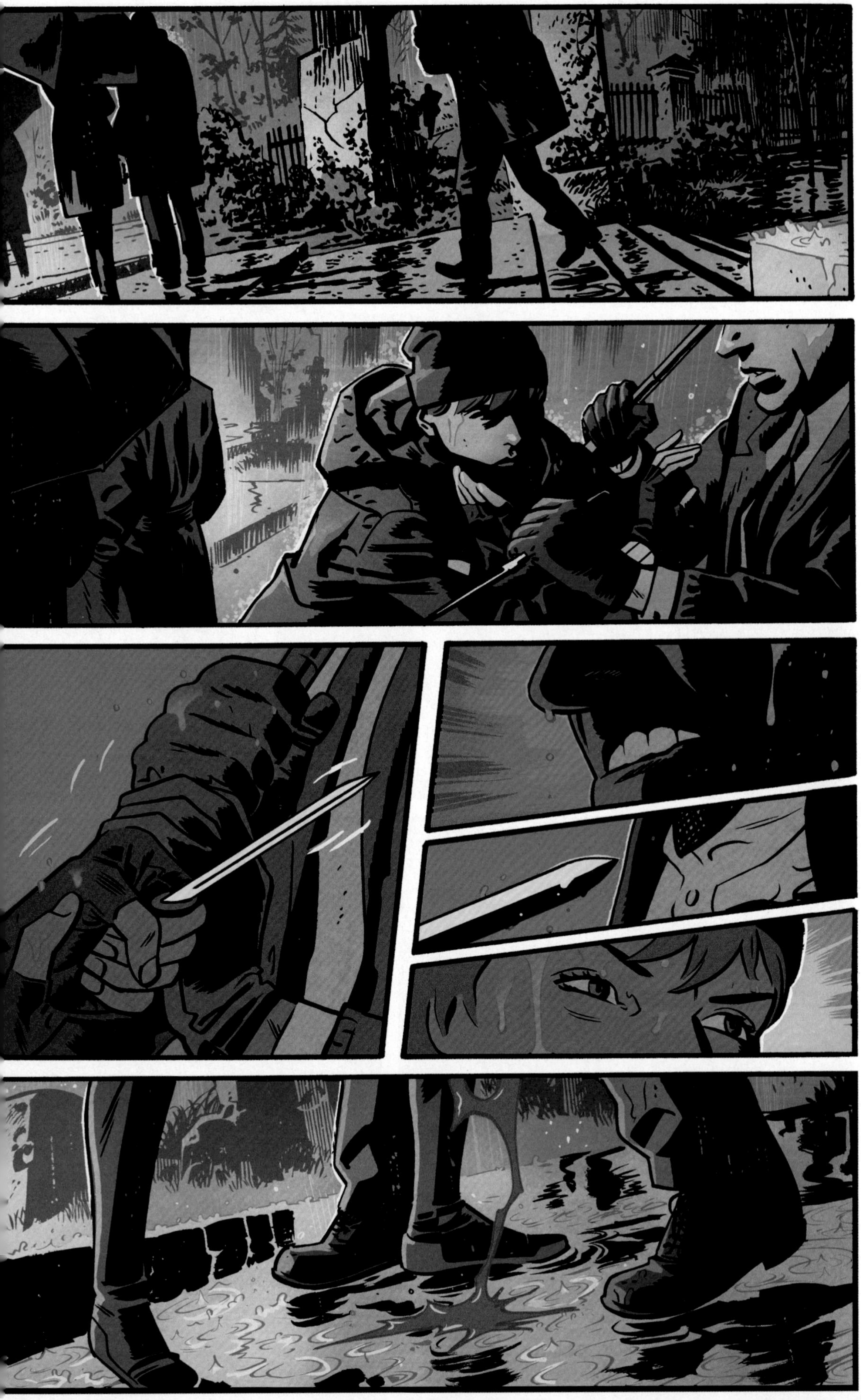

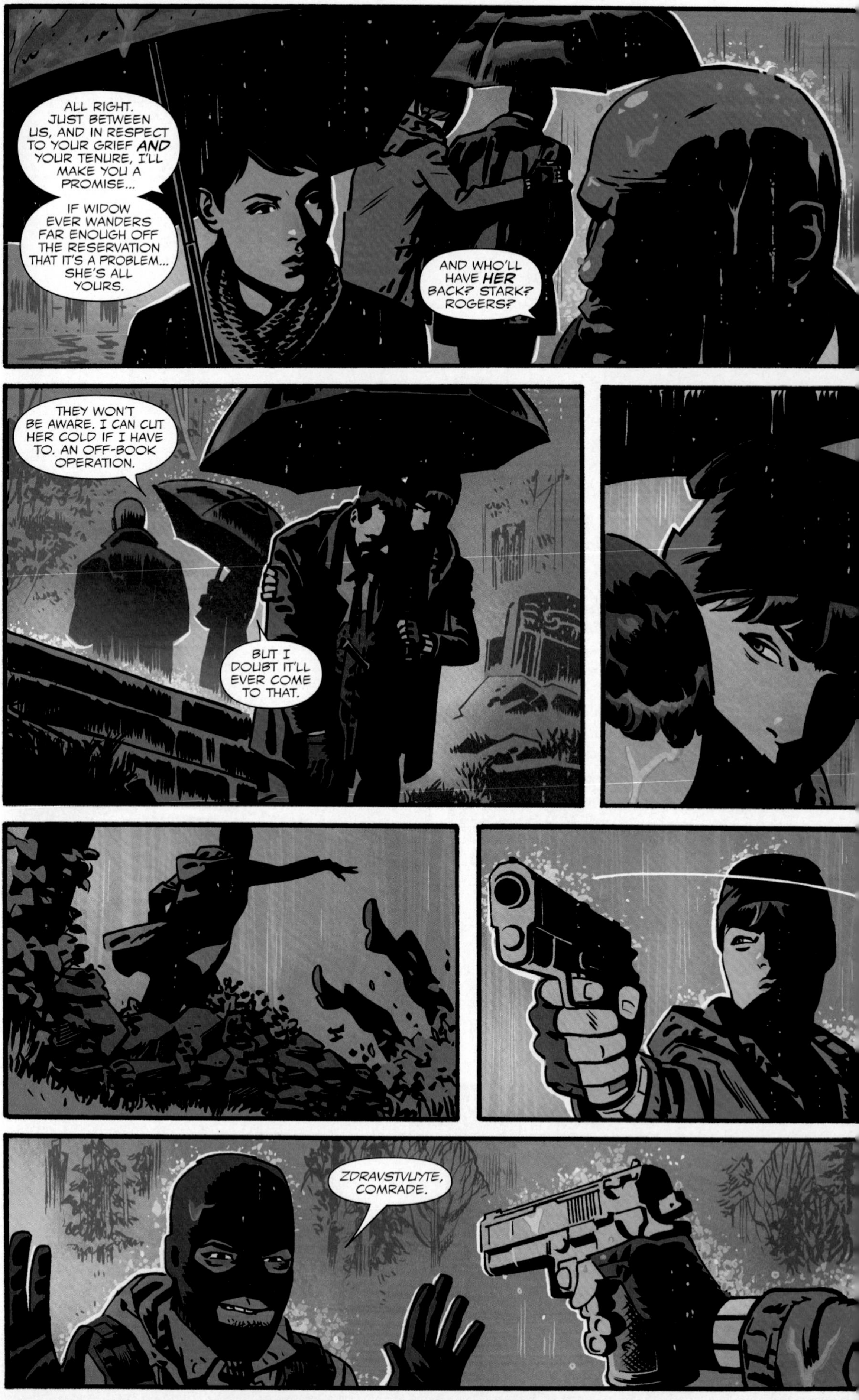
ALL RIGHT. JUST BETWEEN US, AND IN RESPECT TO YOUR GRIEF **AND** YOUR TENURE, I'LL MAKE YOU A PROMISE...
IF WIDOW EVER WANDERS FAR ENOUGH OFF THE RESERVATION THAT IT'S A PROBLEM... SHE'S ALL YOURS.
AND WHO'LL HAVE **HER** BACK? STARK? ROGERS?
THEY WON'T BE AWARE. I CAN CUT HER COLD IF I HAVE TO. AN OFF-BOOK OPERATION.
BUT I DOUBT IT'LL EVER COME TO THAT.
ZDRAVSTVUYTE, COMRADE.

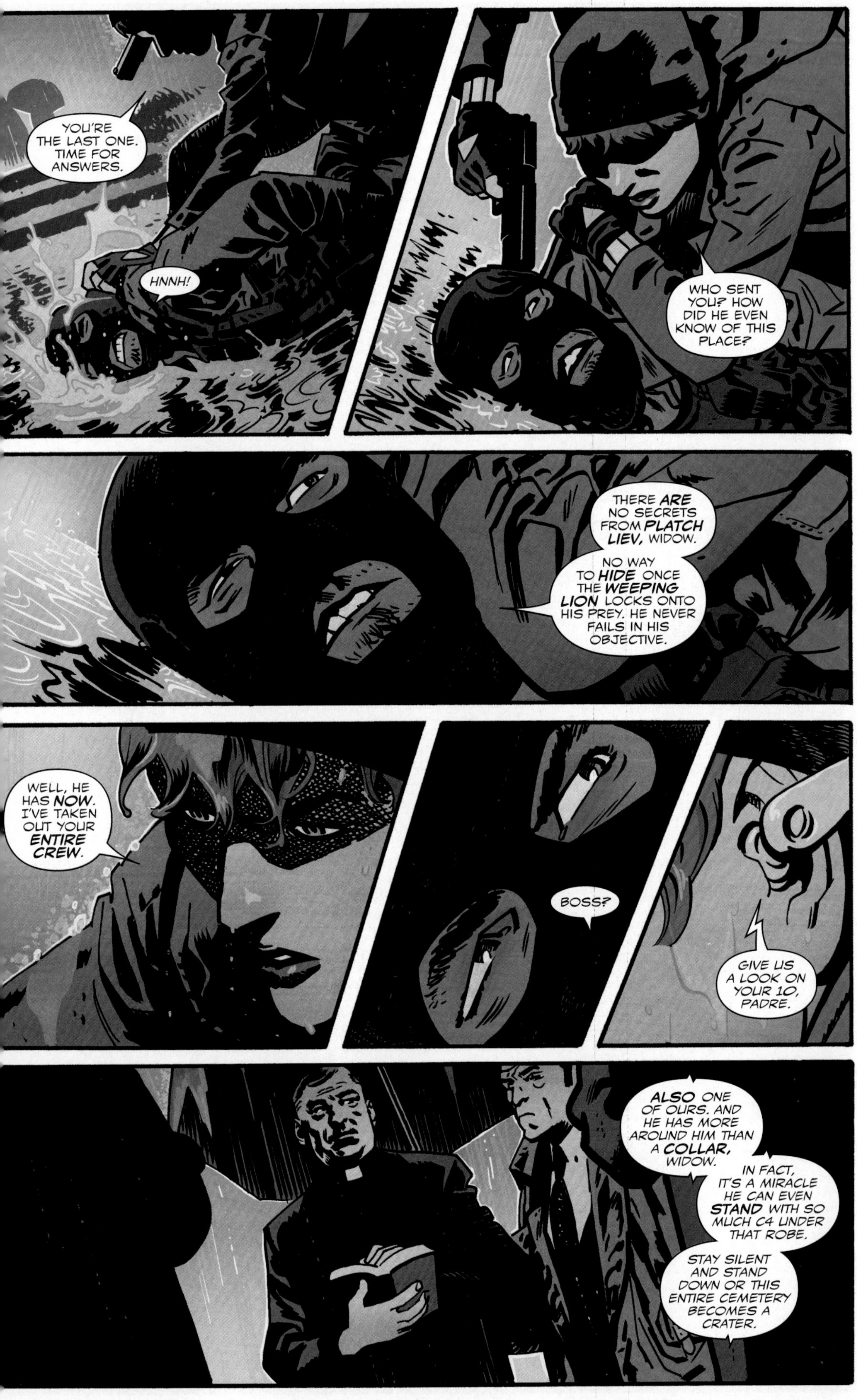
YOU'RE THE LAST ONE. TIME FOR ANSWERS.
HNNH!
WHO SENT YOU? HOW DID HE EVEN KNOW OF THIS PLACE?
THERE ARE NO SECRETS FROM PLATCH LIEV, WIDOW.
NO WAY TO HIDE ONCE THE WEEPING LION LOCKS ONTO HIS PREY. HE NEVER FAILS IN HIS OBJECTIVE.
WELL, HE HAS NOW. I'VE TAKEN OUT YOUR ENTIRE CREW.
BOSS?
GIVE US A LOOK ON YOUR 10, PADRE.
ALSO ONE OF OURS. AND HE HAS MORE AROUND HIM THAN A COLLAR, WIDOW.
IN FACT, IT'S A MIRACLE HE CAN EVEN STAND WITH SO MUCH C4 UNDER THAT ROBE.
STAY SILENT AND STAND DOWN OR THIS ENTIRE CEMETERY BECOMES A CRATER.

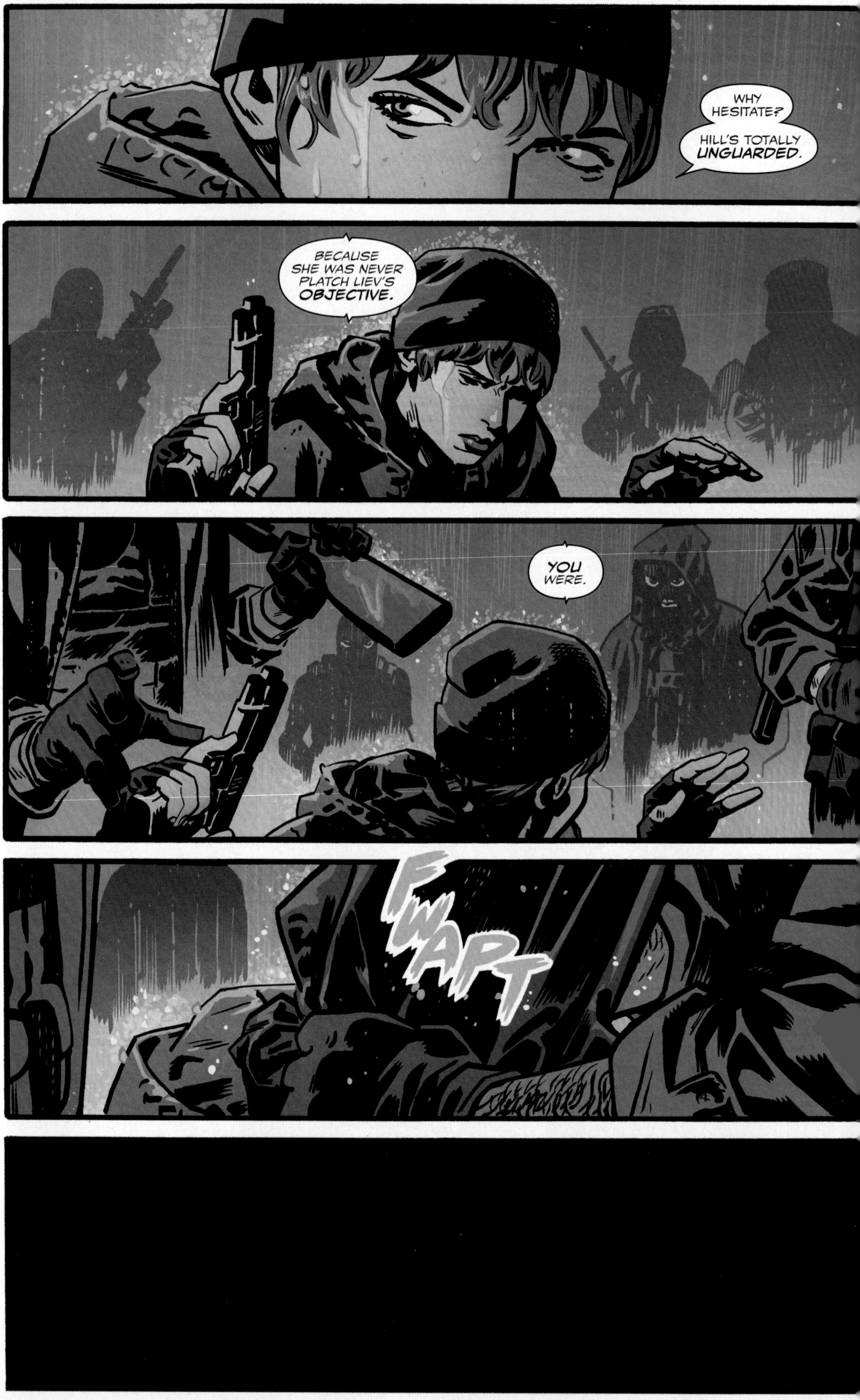
WHY HESITATE?
HILL'S TOTALLY UNGUARDED.
BECAUSE SHE WAS NEVER PLATCH LIEV'S OBJECTIVE.
YOU WERE.
FWAPT

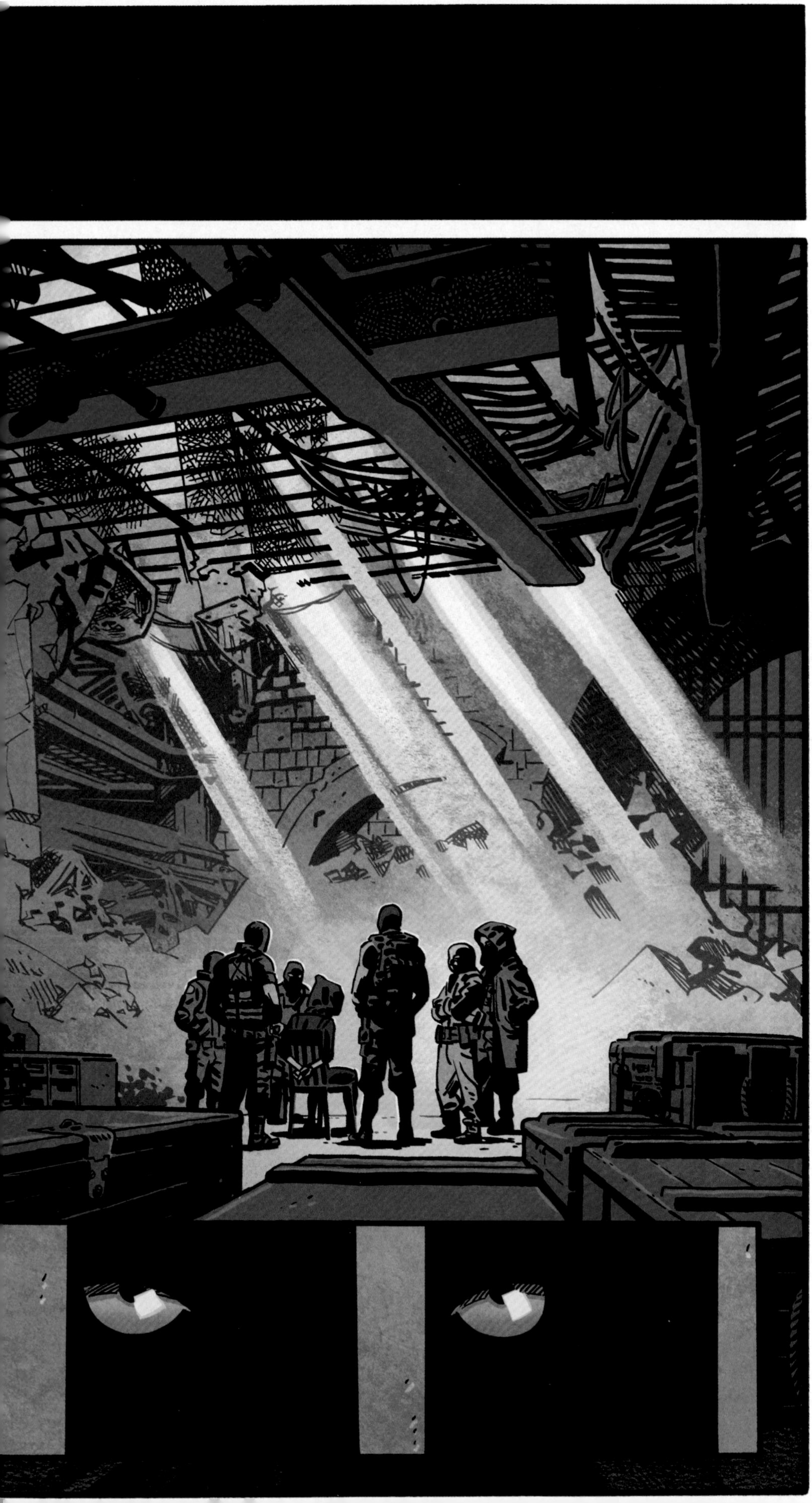

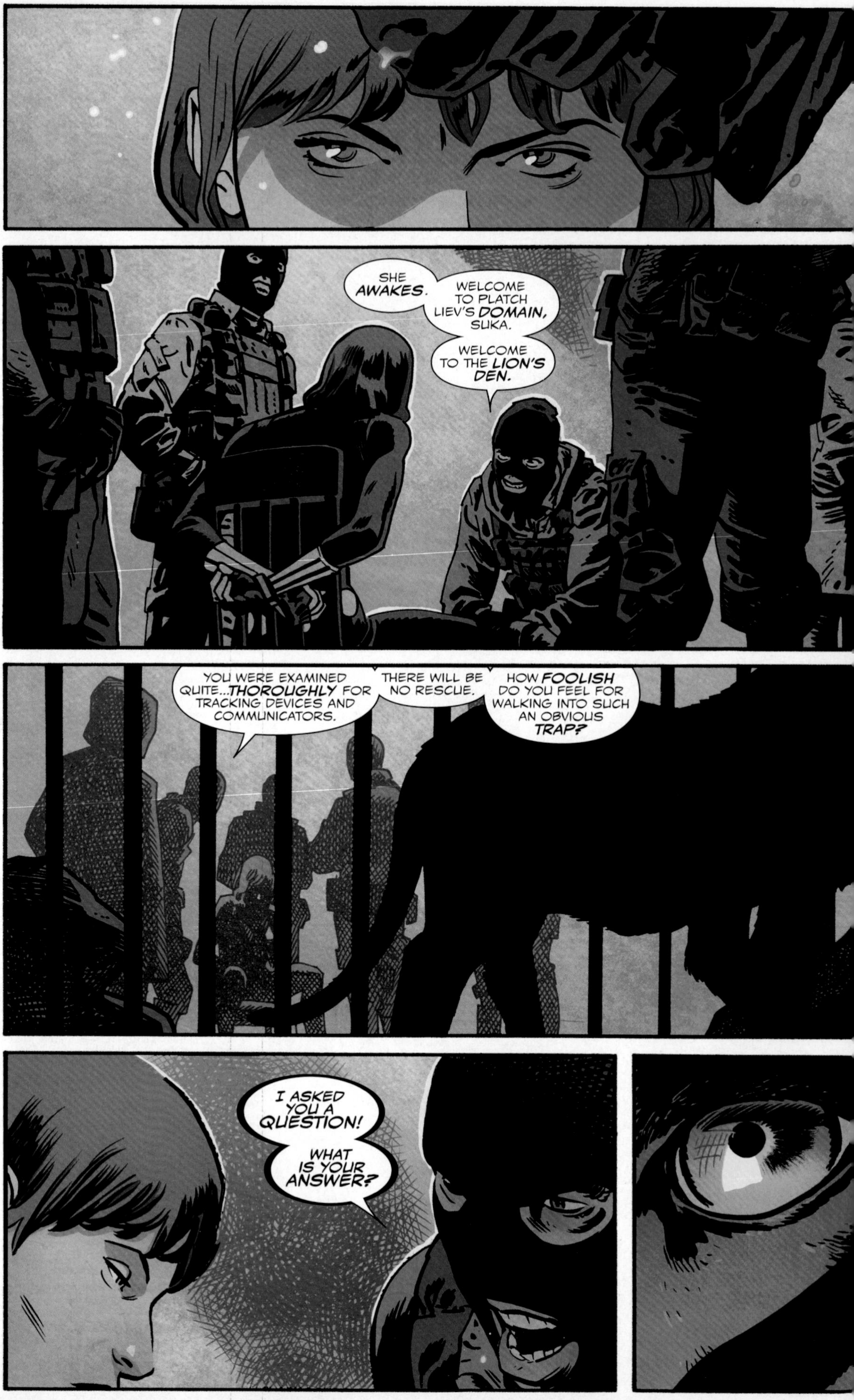

SHE AWAKES.
WELCOME TO PLATCH LIEV'S DOMAIN, SUKA.
WELCOME TO THE LION'S DEN.
YOU WERE EXAMINED QUITE...THOROUGHLY FOR TRACKING DEVICES AND COMMUNICATORS.
THERE WILL BE NO RESCUE.
HOW FOOLISH DO YOU FEEL FOR WALKING INTO SUCH AN OBVIOUS TRAP?
I ASKED YOU A QUESTION!
WHAT IS YOUR ANSWER?

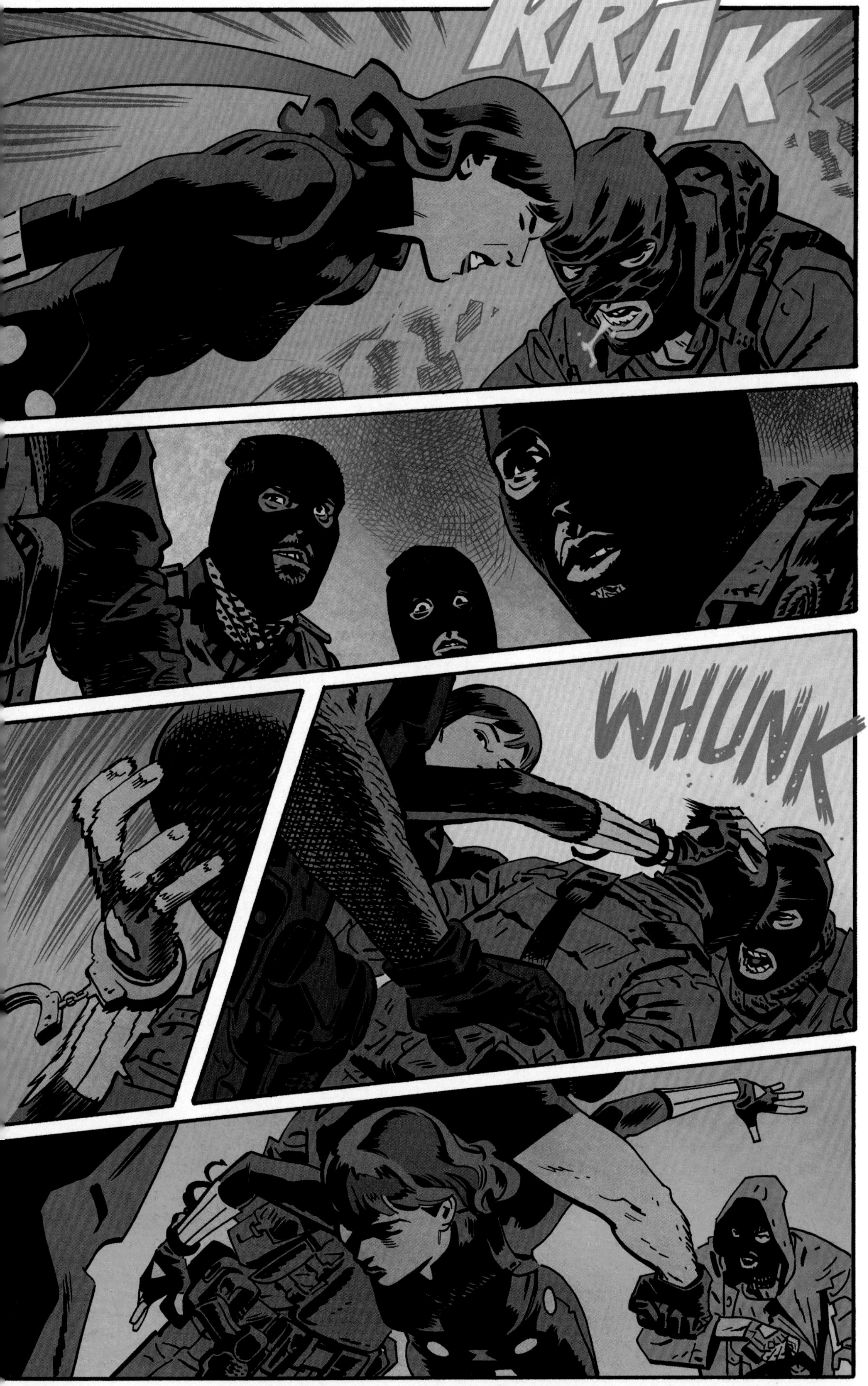
KRAK
WHUNK

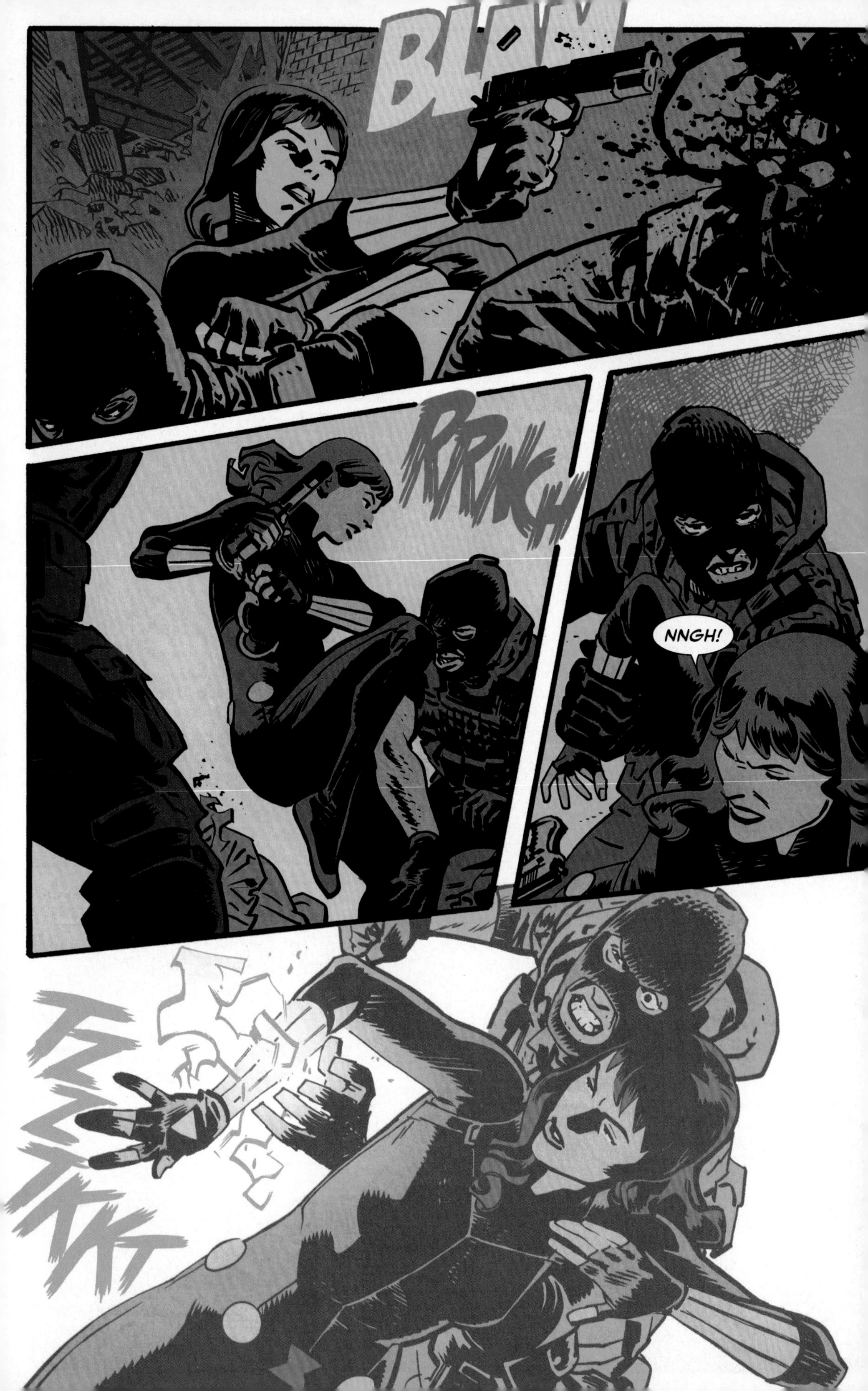
BLAM
NNGH!
FZZTKKT

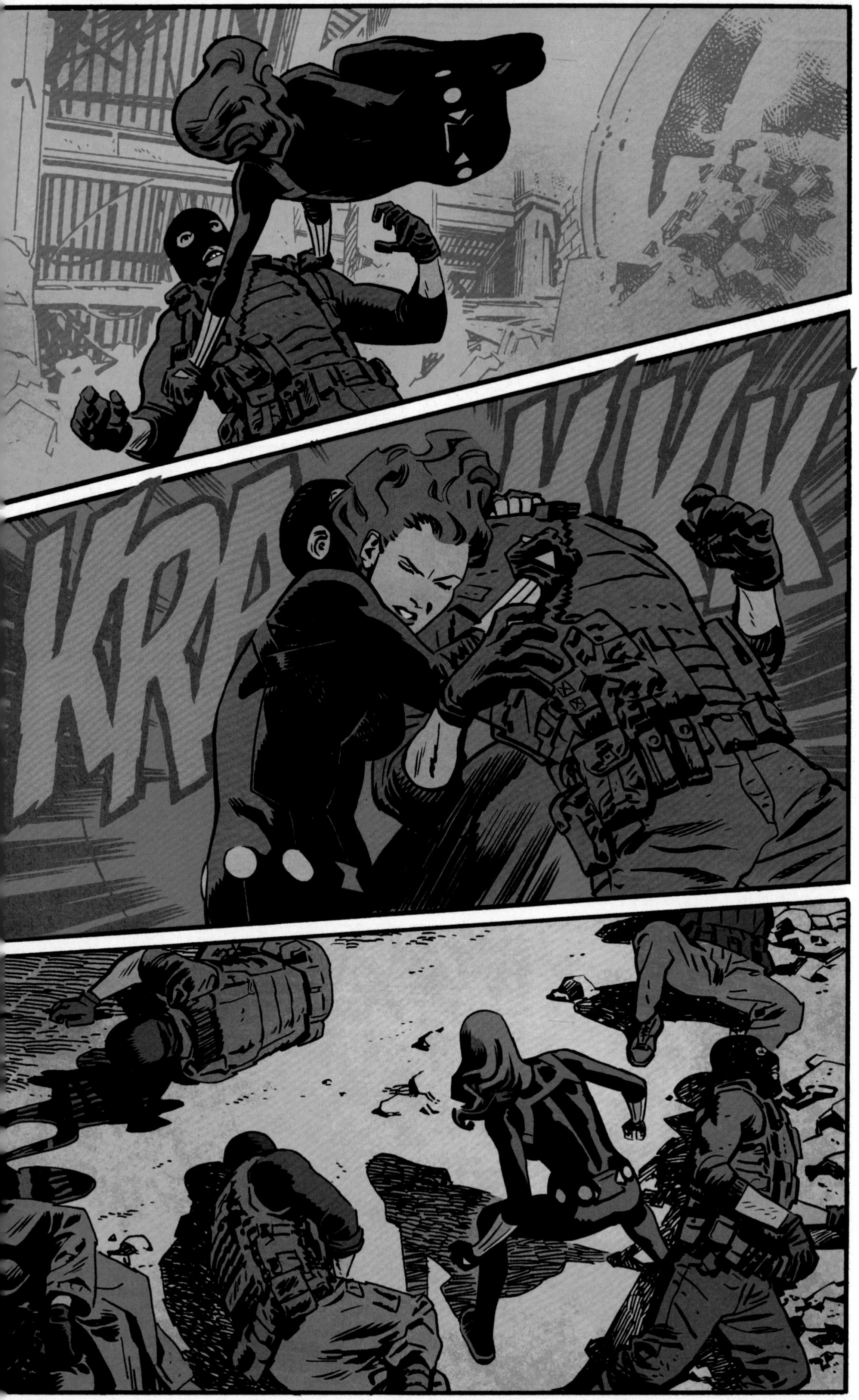
KRA

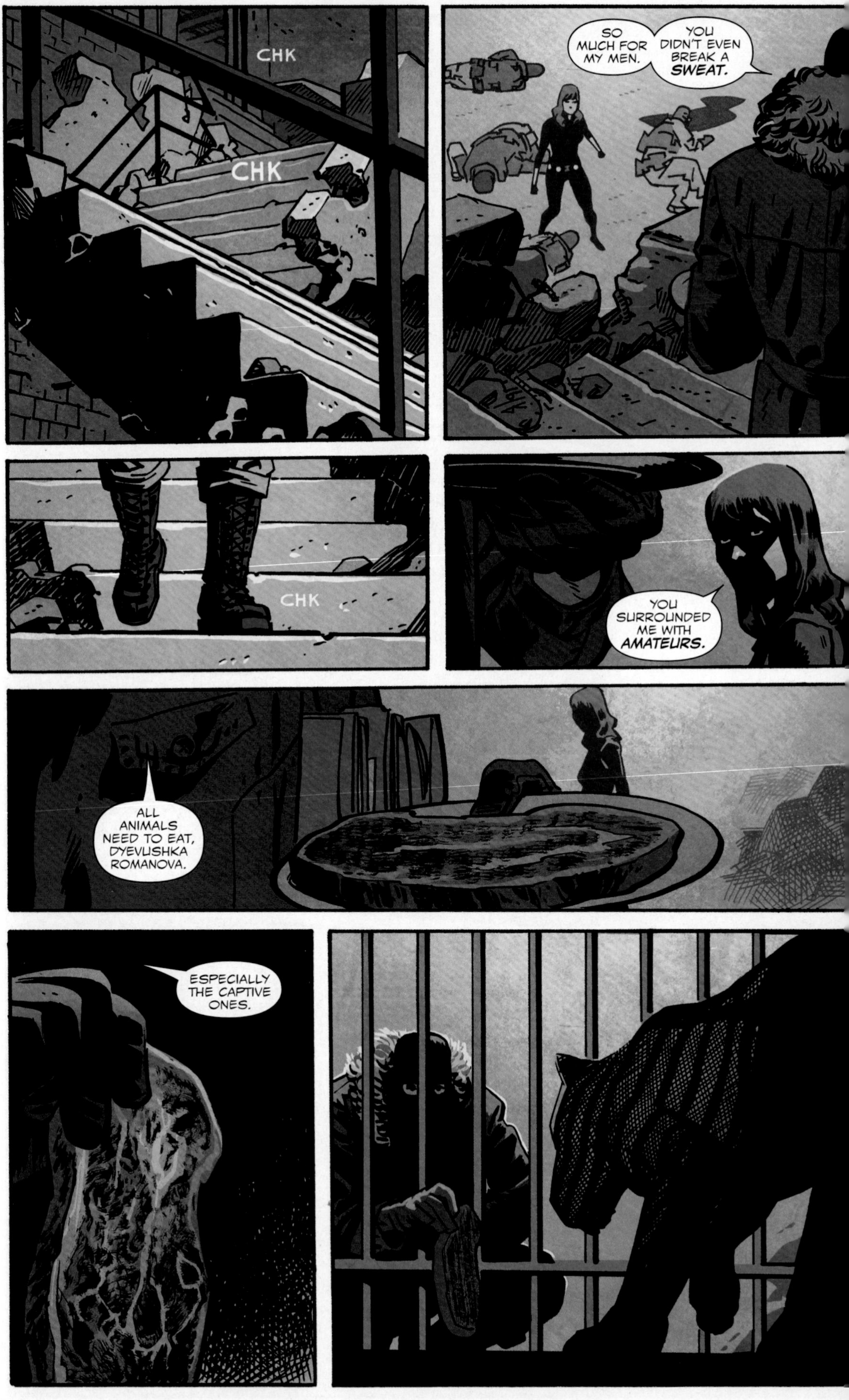
CHK
CHK
SO MUCH FOR MY MEN.
YOU DIDN'T EVEN BREAK A SWEAT.
CHK
YOU SURROUNDED ME WITH AMATEURS.
ALL ANIMALS NEED TO EAT, DYEVUSHKA ROMANOVA.
ESPECIALLY THE CAPTIVE ONES.

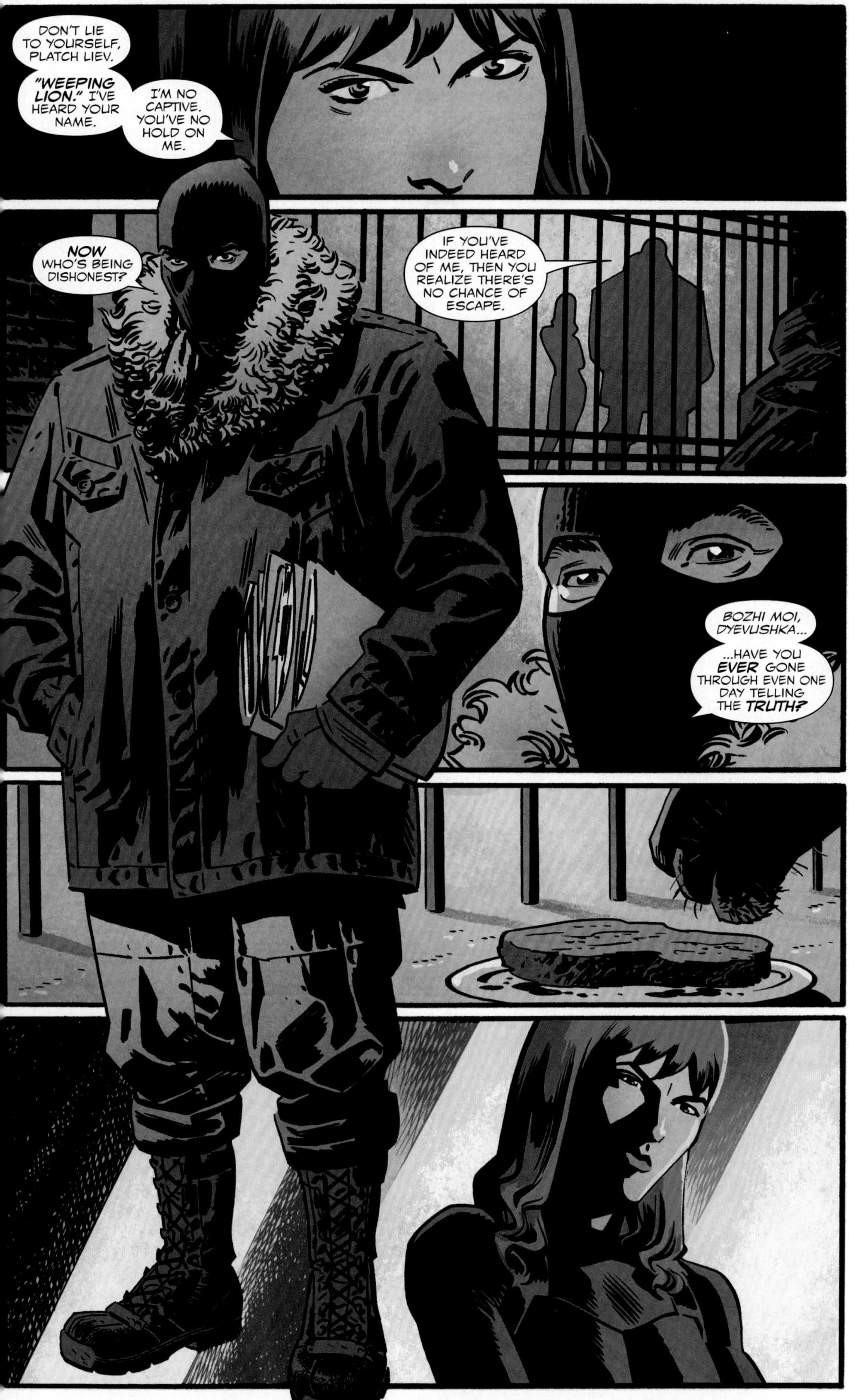
DON'T LIE TO YOURSELF, PLATCH LIEV.
"WEEPING LION." I'VE HEARD YOUR NAME.
I'M NO CAPTIVE. YOU'VE NO HOLD ON ME.
NOW WHO'S BEING DISHONEST?
IF YOU'VE INDEED HEARD OF ME, THEN YOU REALIZE THERE'S NO CHANCE OF ESCAPE.
BOZHI MOI, DYEVUSHKA...
...HAVE YOU EVER GONE THROUGH EVEN ONE DAY TELLING THE TRUTH?

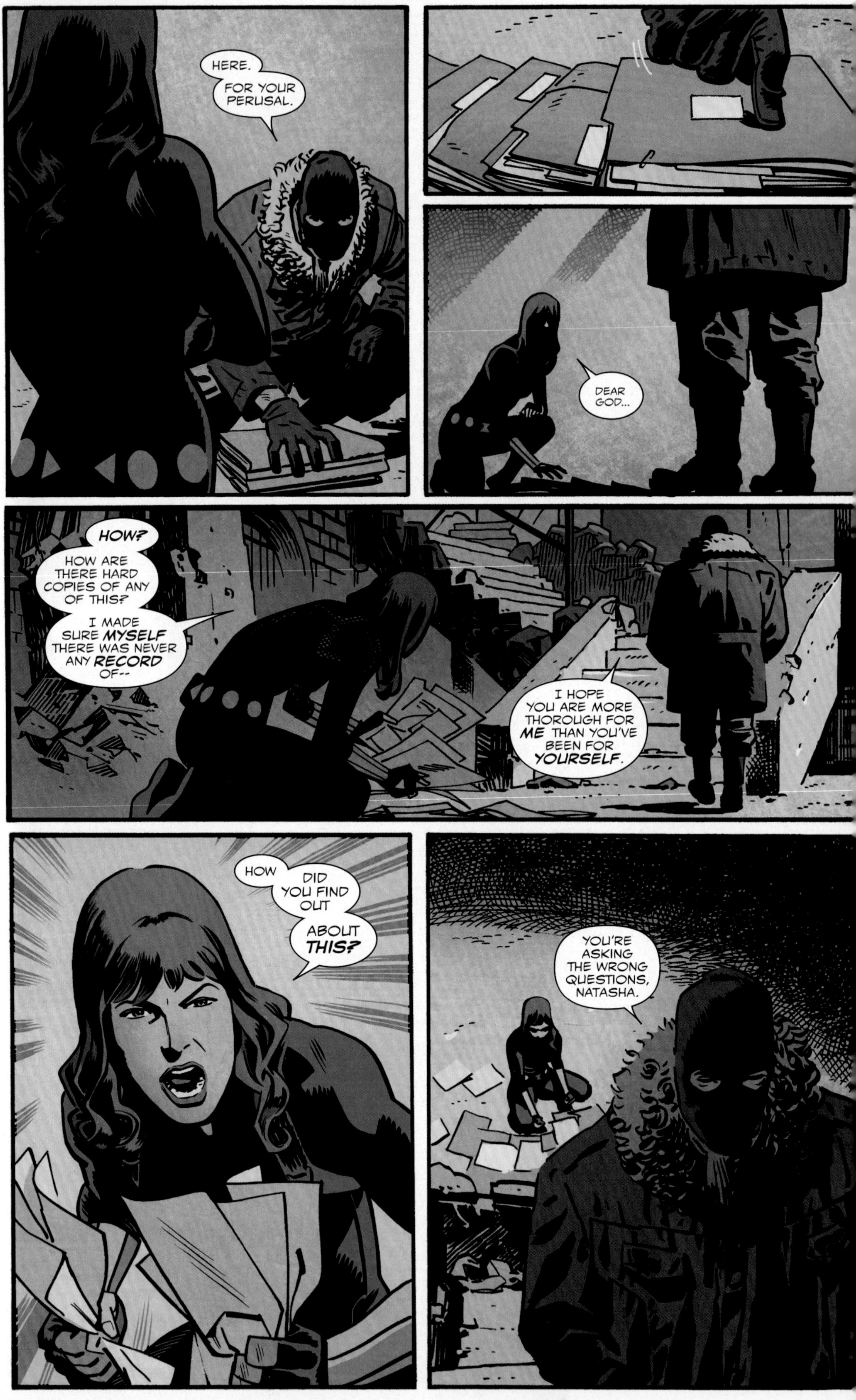
HERE.
FOR YOUR PERUSAL.
DEAR GOD...
HOW?
HOW ARE THERE HARD COPIES OF ANY OF THIS?
I MADE SURE MYSELF THERE WAS NEVER ANY RECORD OF--
I HOPE YOU ARE MORE THOROUGH FOR ME THAN YOU'VE BEEN FOR YOURSELF.
HOW
DID YOU FIND OUT
ABOUT THIS?
YOU'RE ASKING THE WRONG QUESTIONS, NATASHA.

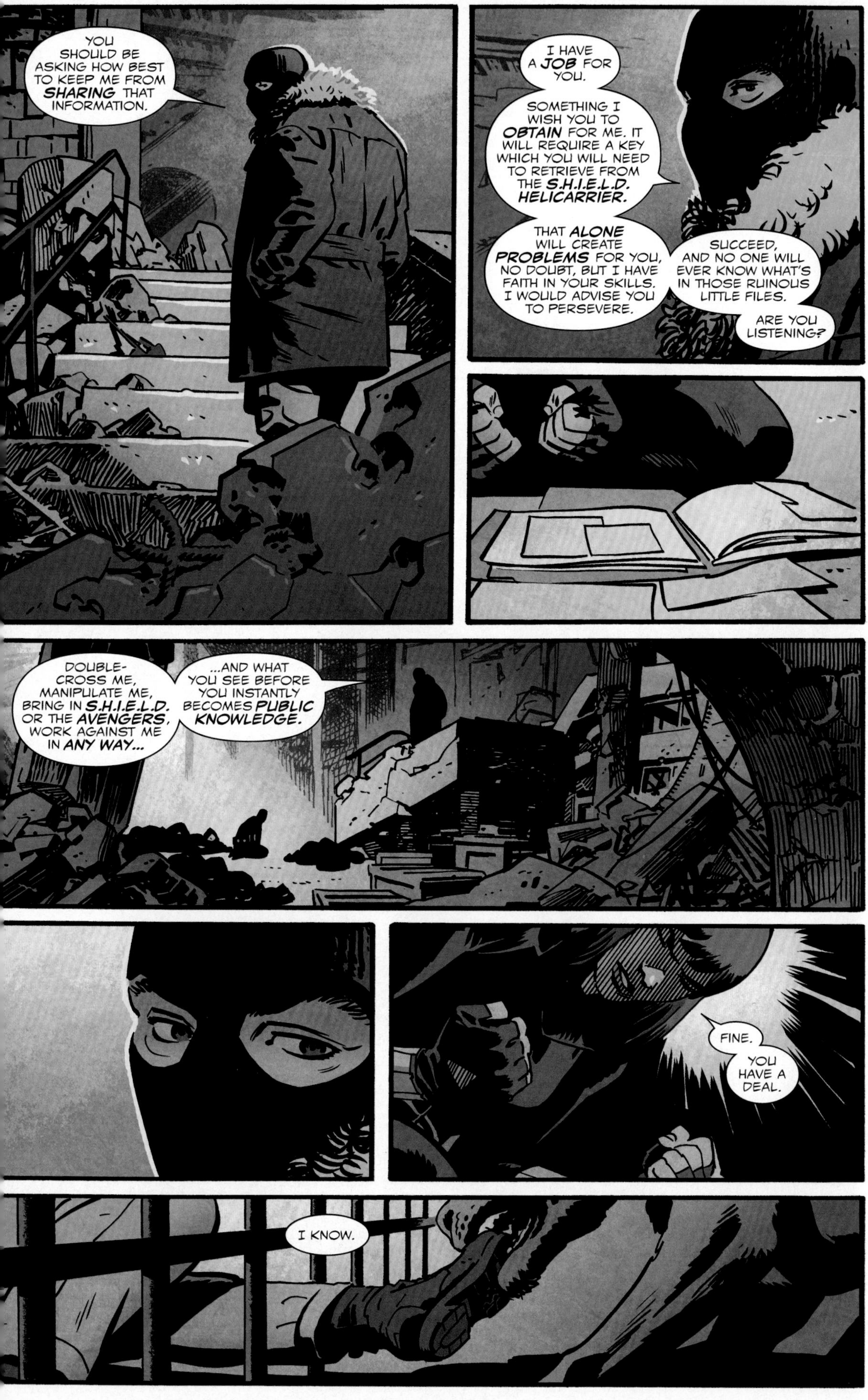
YOU SHOULD BE ASKING HOW BEST TO KEEP ME FROM SHARING THAT INFORMATION.
I HAVE A JOB FOR YOU.
SOMETHING I WISH YOU TO OBTAIN FOR ME. IT WILL REQUIRE A KEY WHICH YOU WILL NEED TO RETRIEVE FROM THE S.H.I.E.L.D. HELICARRIER.
THAT ALONE WILL CREATE PROBLEMS FOR YOU, NO DOUBT, BUT I HAVE FAITH IN YOUR SKILLS. I WOULD ADVISE YOU TO PERSEVERE.
SUCCEED, AND NO ONE WILL EVER KNOW WHAT'S IN THOSE RUINOUS LITTLE FILES.
ARE YOU LISTENING?
DOUBLE-CROSS ME, MANIPULATE ME, BRING IN S.H.I.E.L.D. OR THE AVENGERS, WORK AGAINST ME IN ANY WAY...
...AND WHAT YOU SEE BEFORE YOU INSTANTLY BECOMES PUBLIC KNOWLEDGE.
FINE.
YOU HAVE A DEAL.
I KNOW.

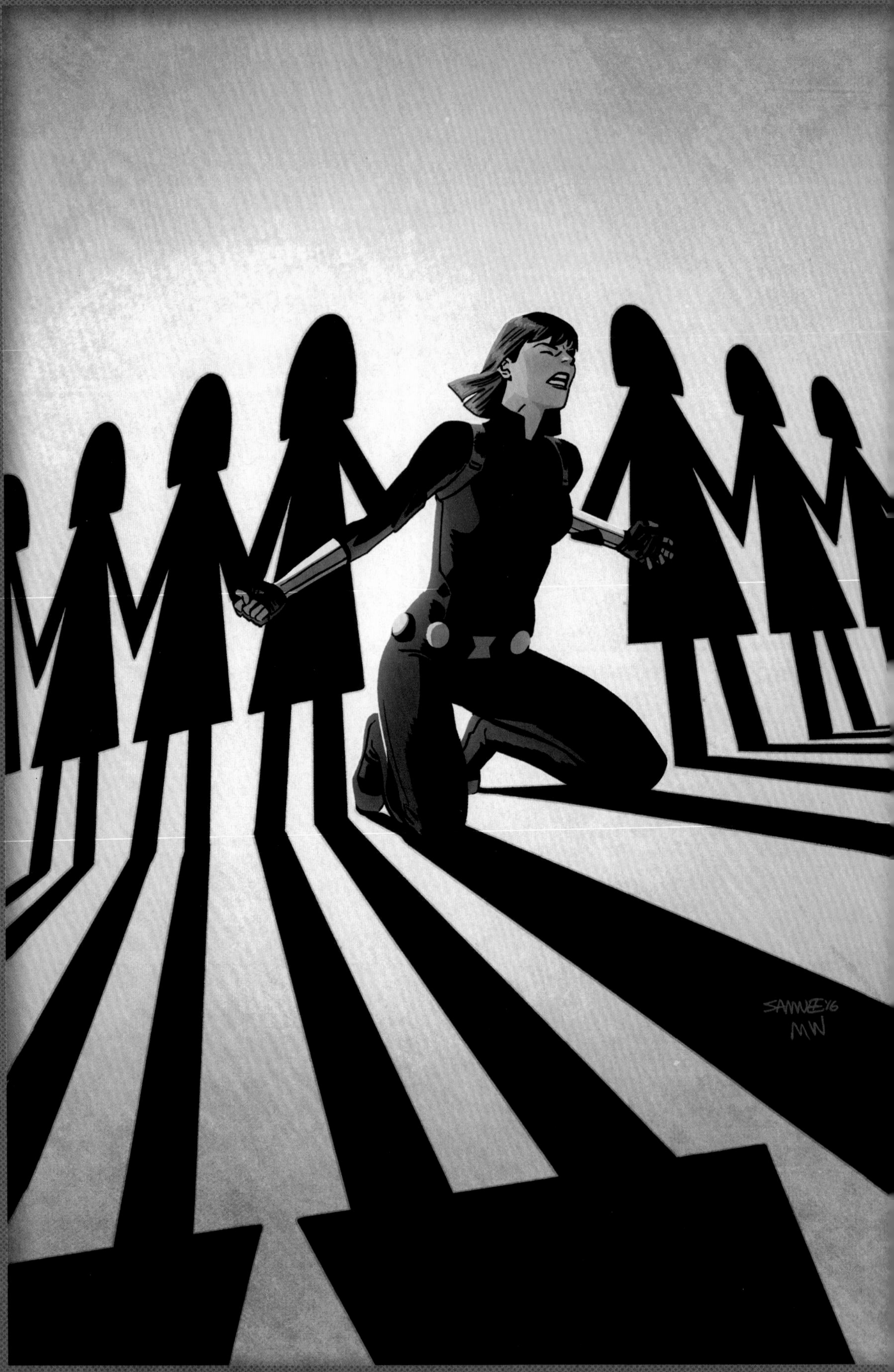
SAMNEE '16
MW

3

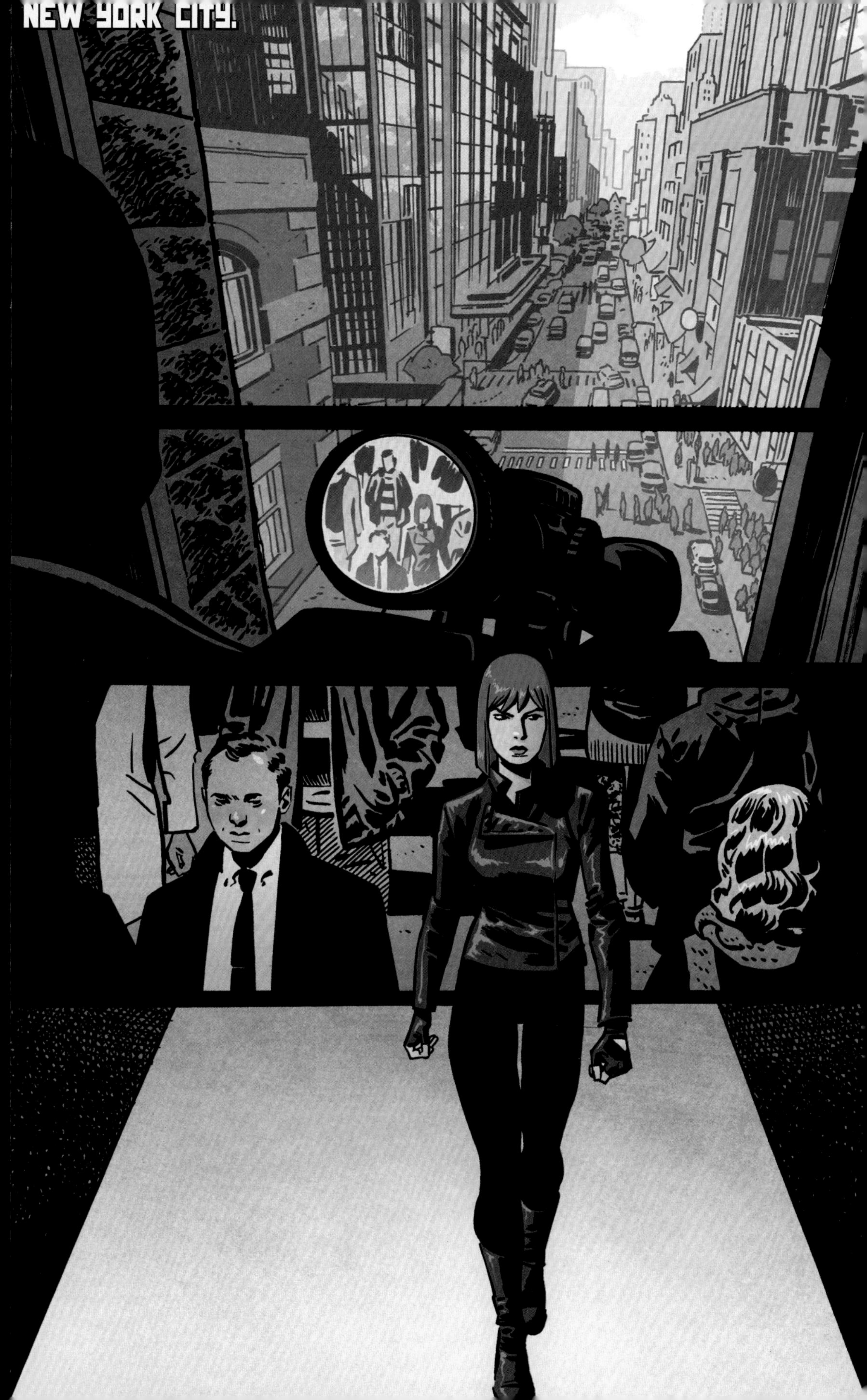
NEW YORK CITY.

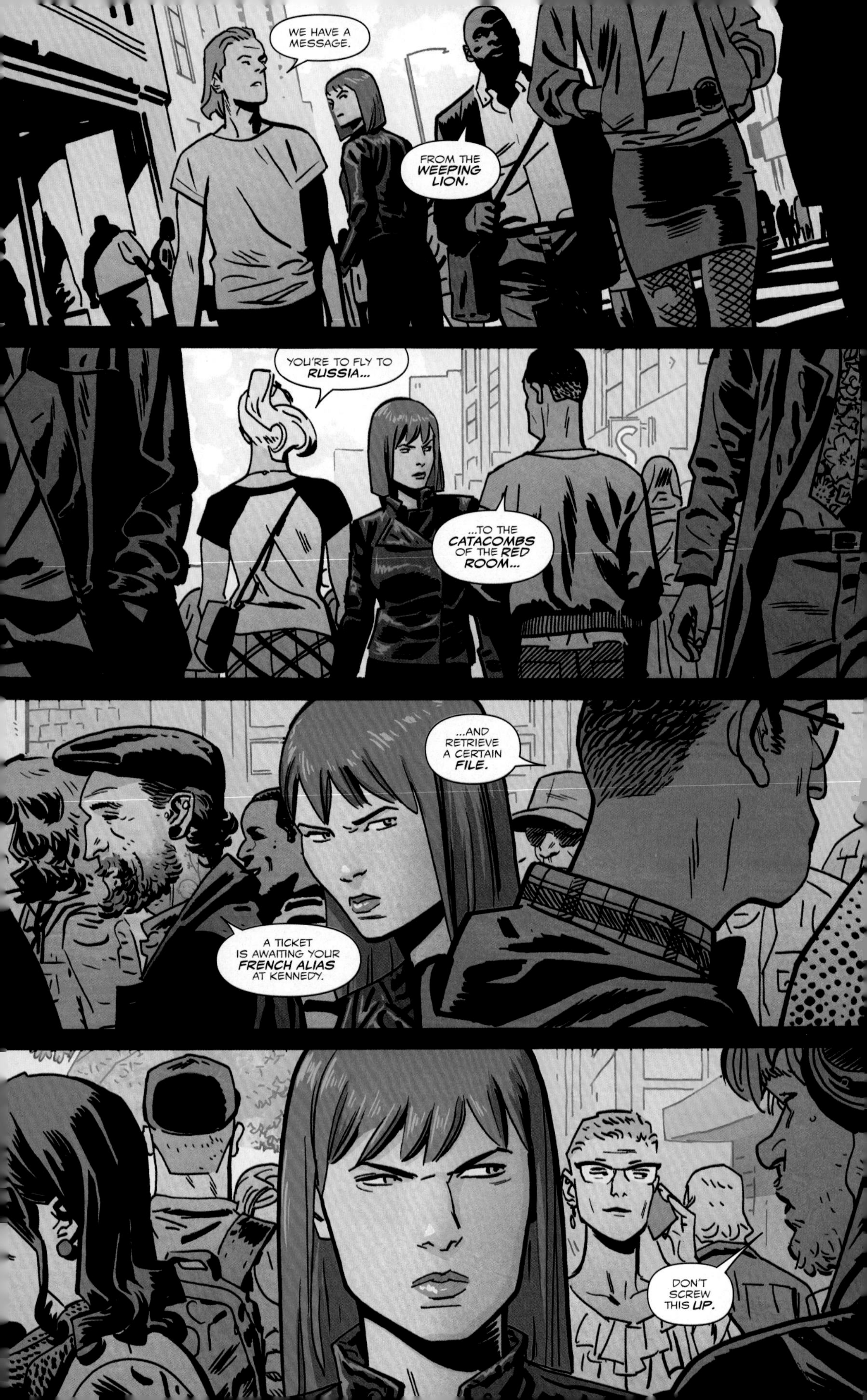
WE HAVE A MESSAGE.
FROM THE WEEPING LION.
YOU'RE TO FLY TO RUSSIA...
...TO THE CATACOMBS OF THE RED ROOM...
...AND RETRIEVE A CERTAIN FILE.
A TICKET IS AWAITING YOUR FRENCH ALIAS AT KENNEDY.
DON'T SCREW THIS UP.

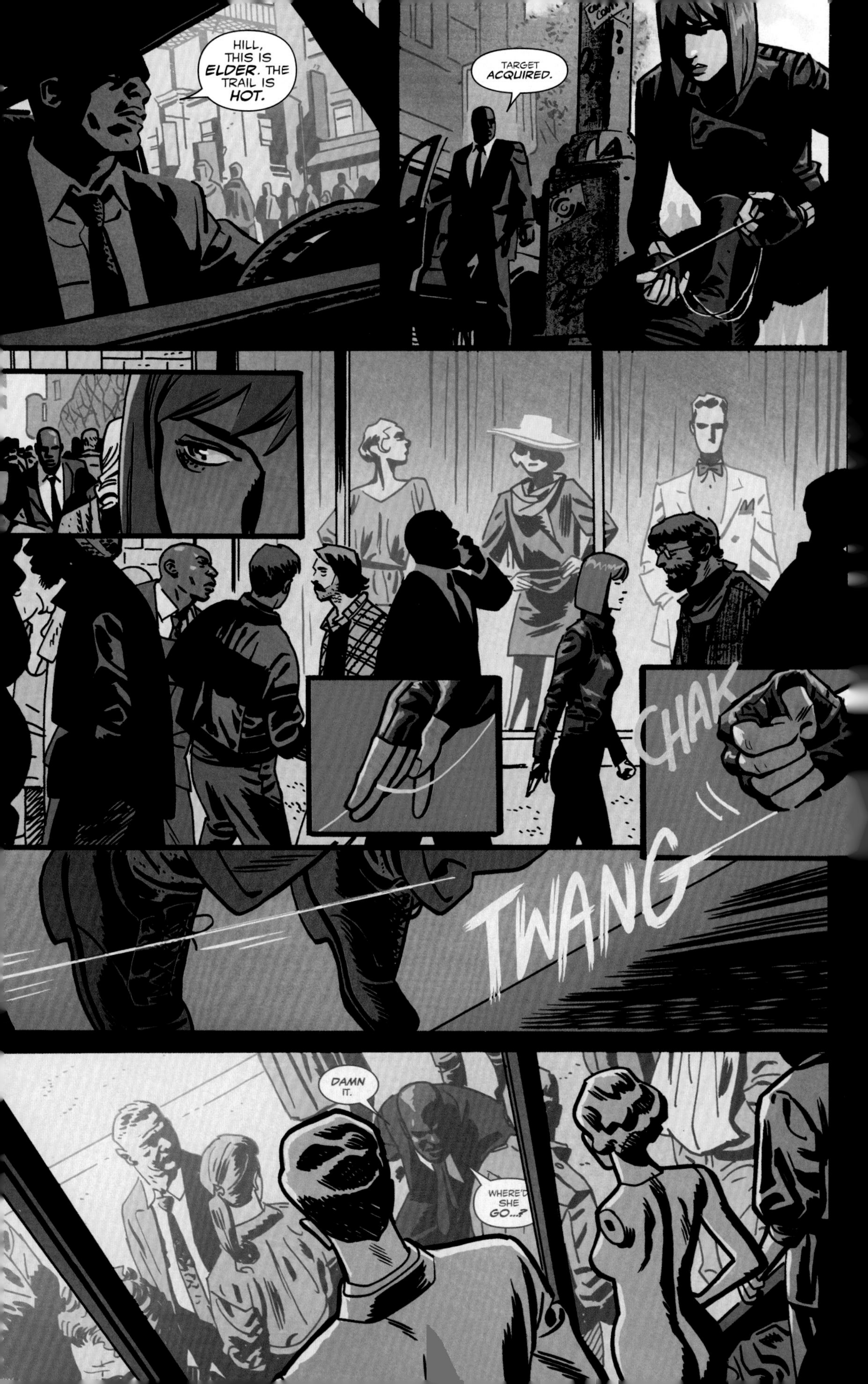
HILL, THIS IS ELDER. THE TRAIL IS HOT.
TARGET ACQUIRED.
CHAK
TWANG
DAMN IT.
WHERE'D SHE GO...?

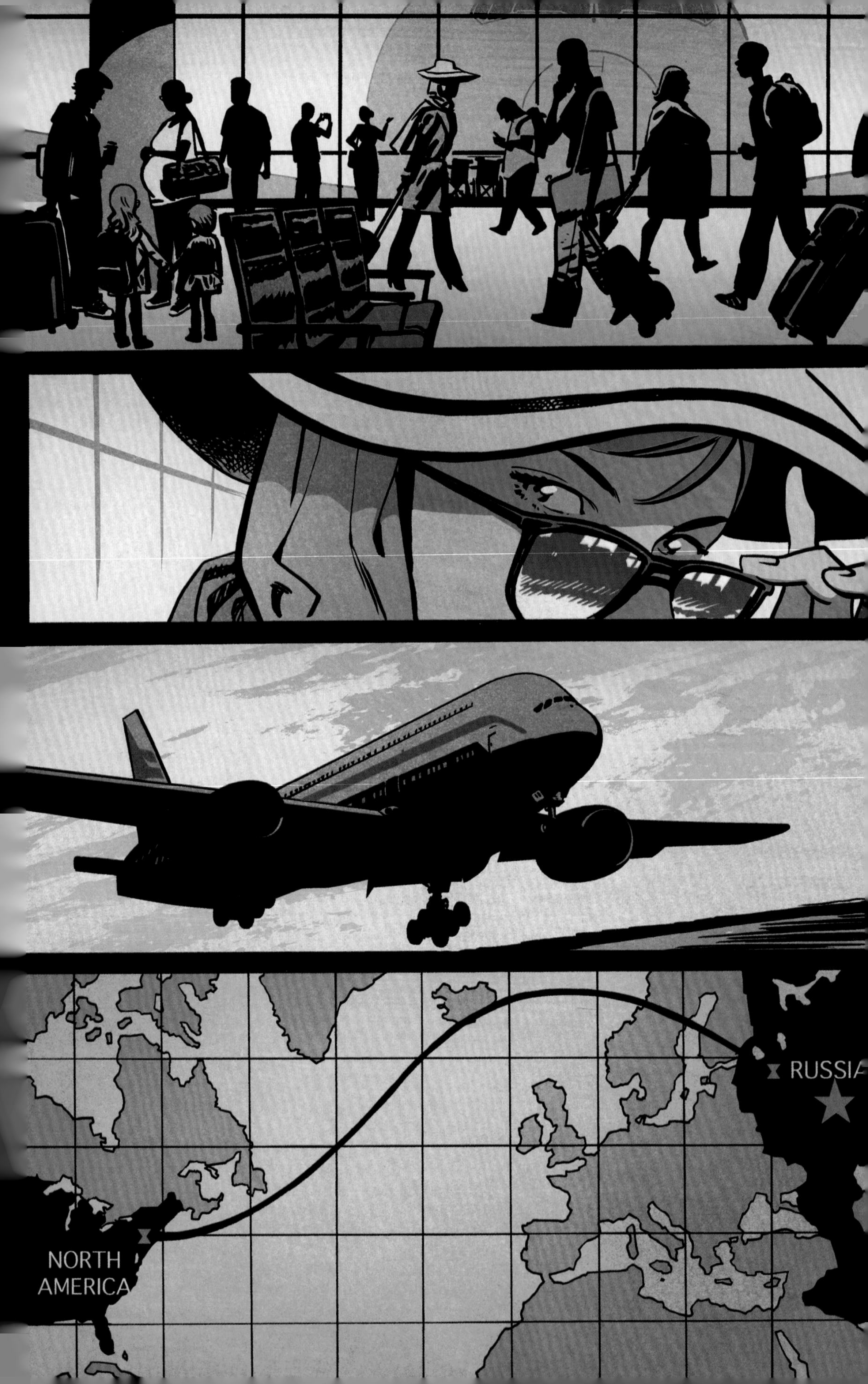
RUSSIA
NORTH AMERICA

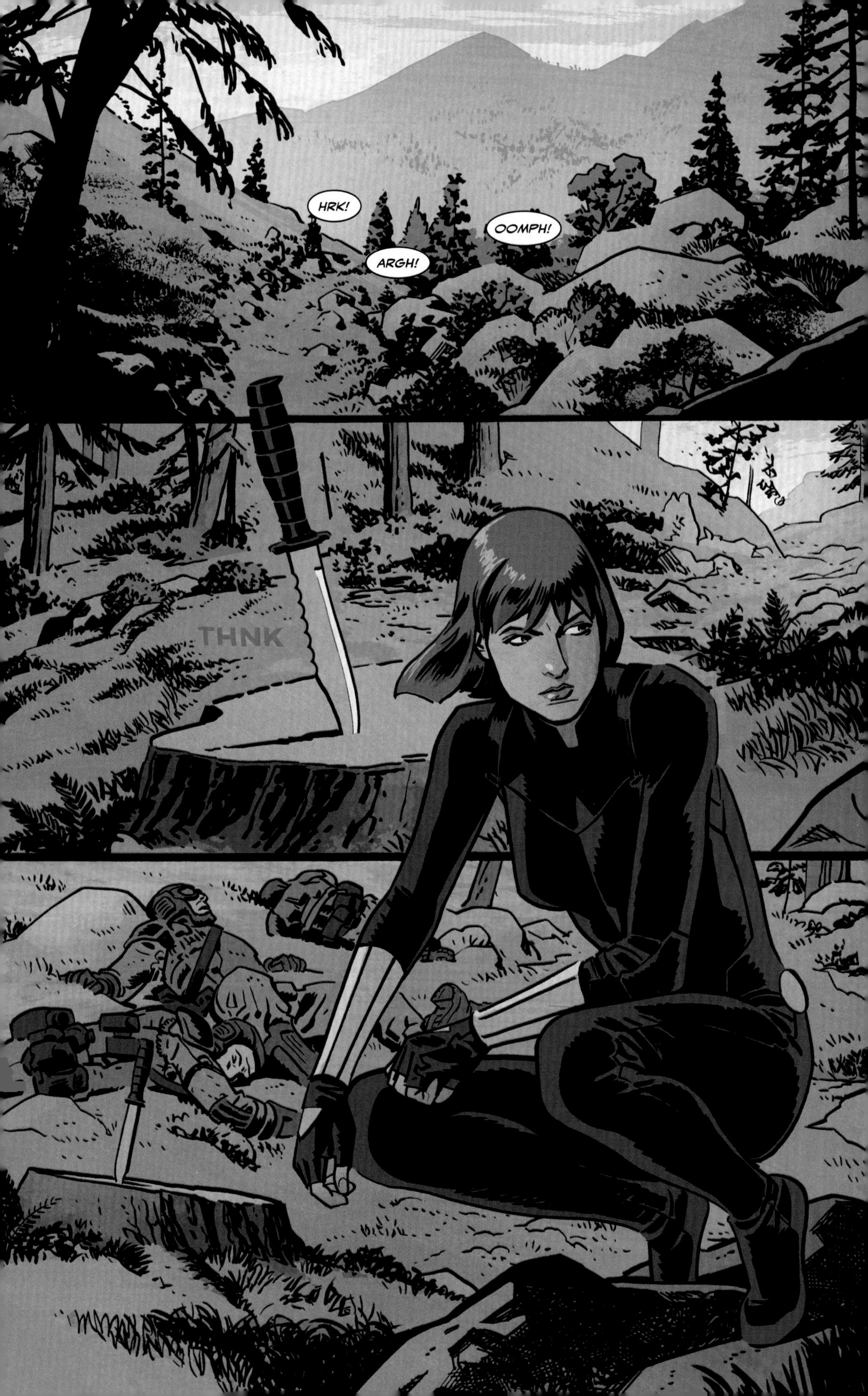
HRK!
ARGH!
OOMPH!
THNK

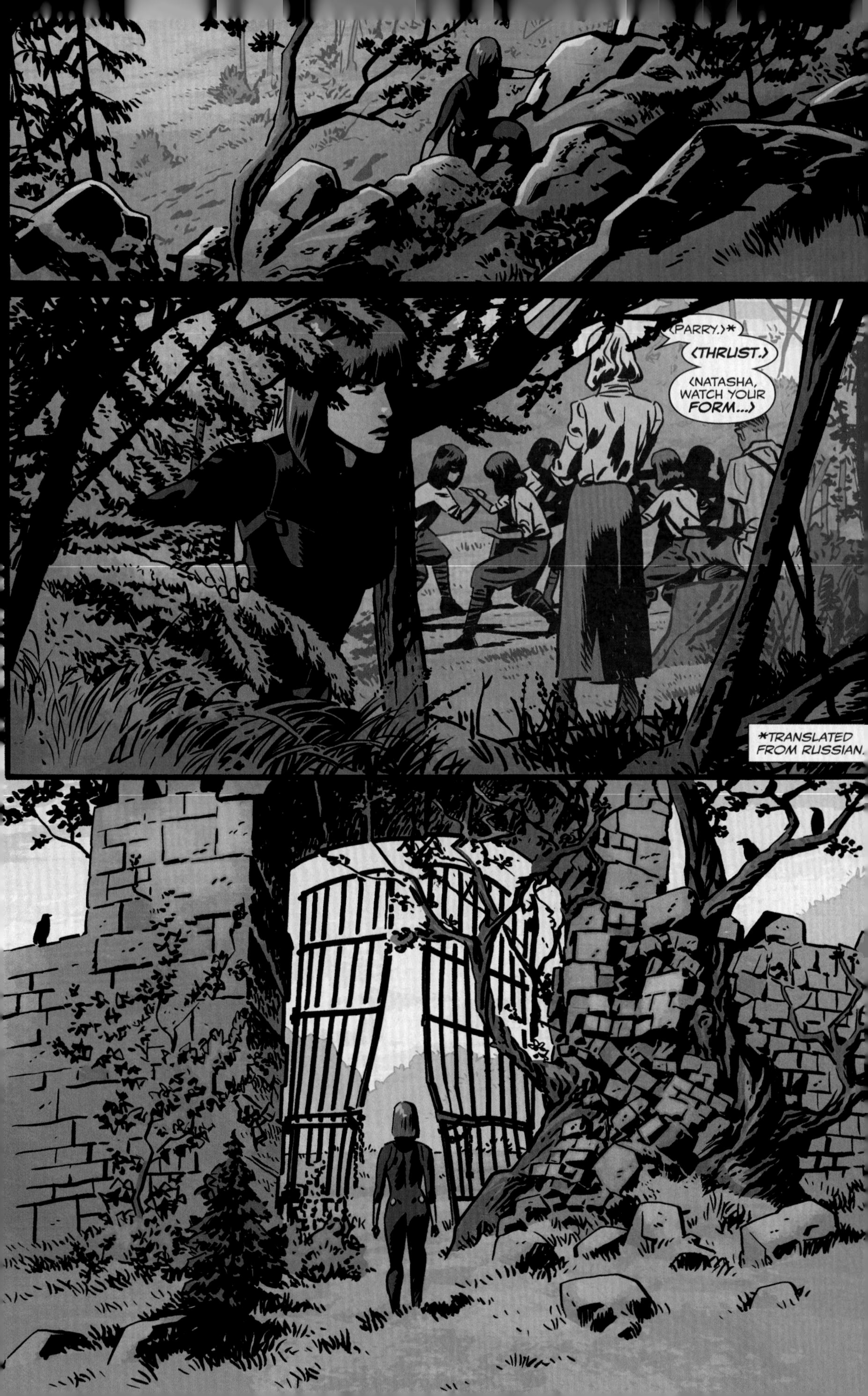
‹PARRY.›*
‹THRUST.›
‹NATASHA, WATCH YOUR FORM...›
*TRANSLATED FROM RUSSIAN.

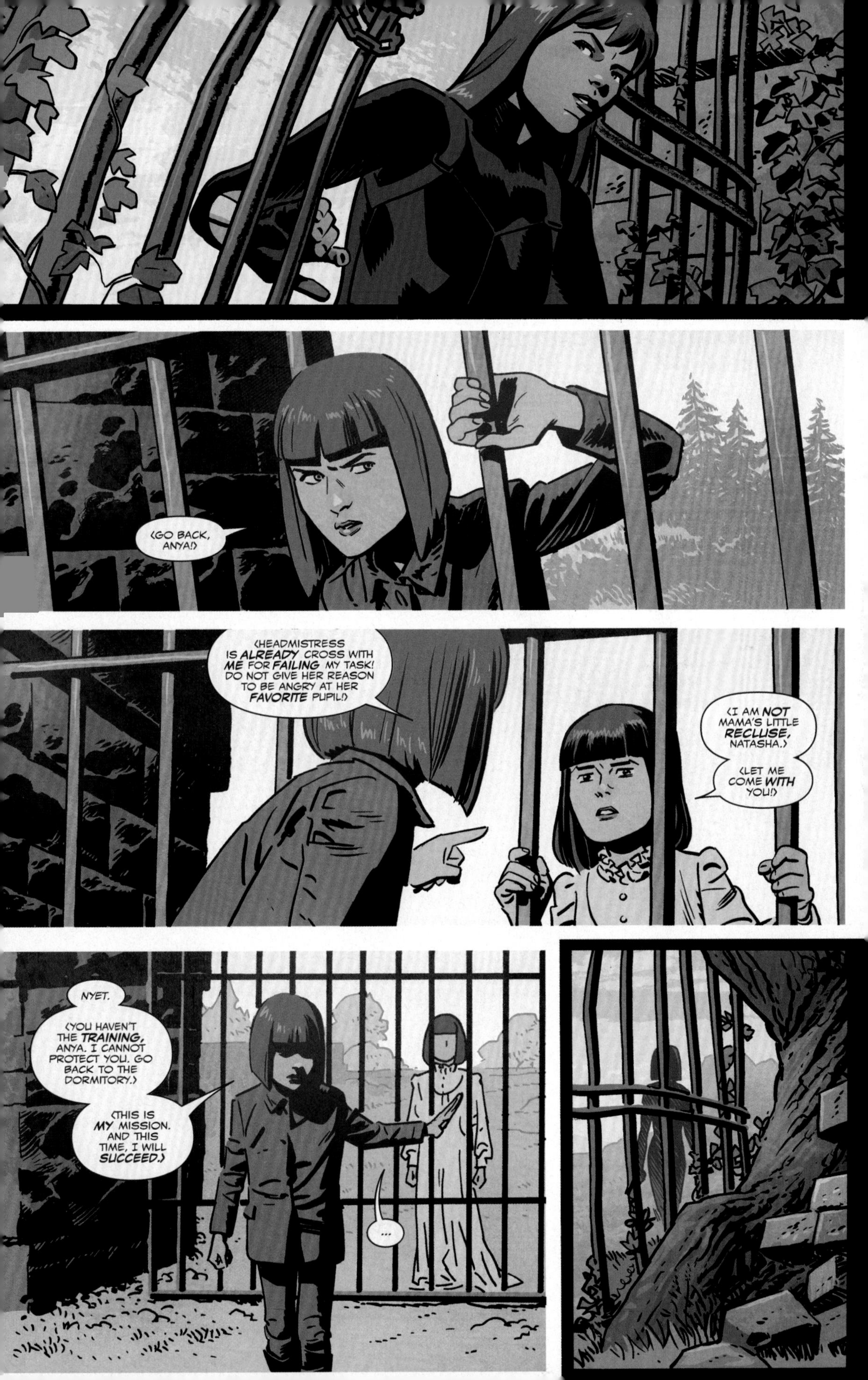
‹GO BACK, ANYA!›
‹HEADMISTRESS IS ALREADY CROSS WITH ME FOR FAILING MY TASK! DO NOT GIVE HER REASON TO BE ANGRY AT HER FAVORITE PUPIL!›
‹I AM NOT MAMA'S LITTLE RECLUSE, NATASHA.›
‹LET ME COME WITH YOU!›
NYET.
‹YOU HAVEN'T THE TRAINING, ANYA. I CANNOT PROTECT YOU. GO BACK TO THE DORMITORY.›
‹THIS IS MY MISSION. AND THIS TIME, I WILL SUCCEED.›
...

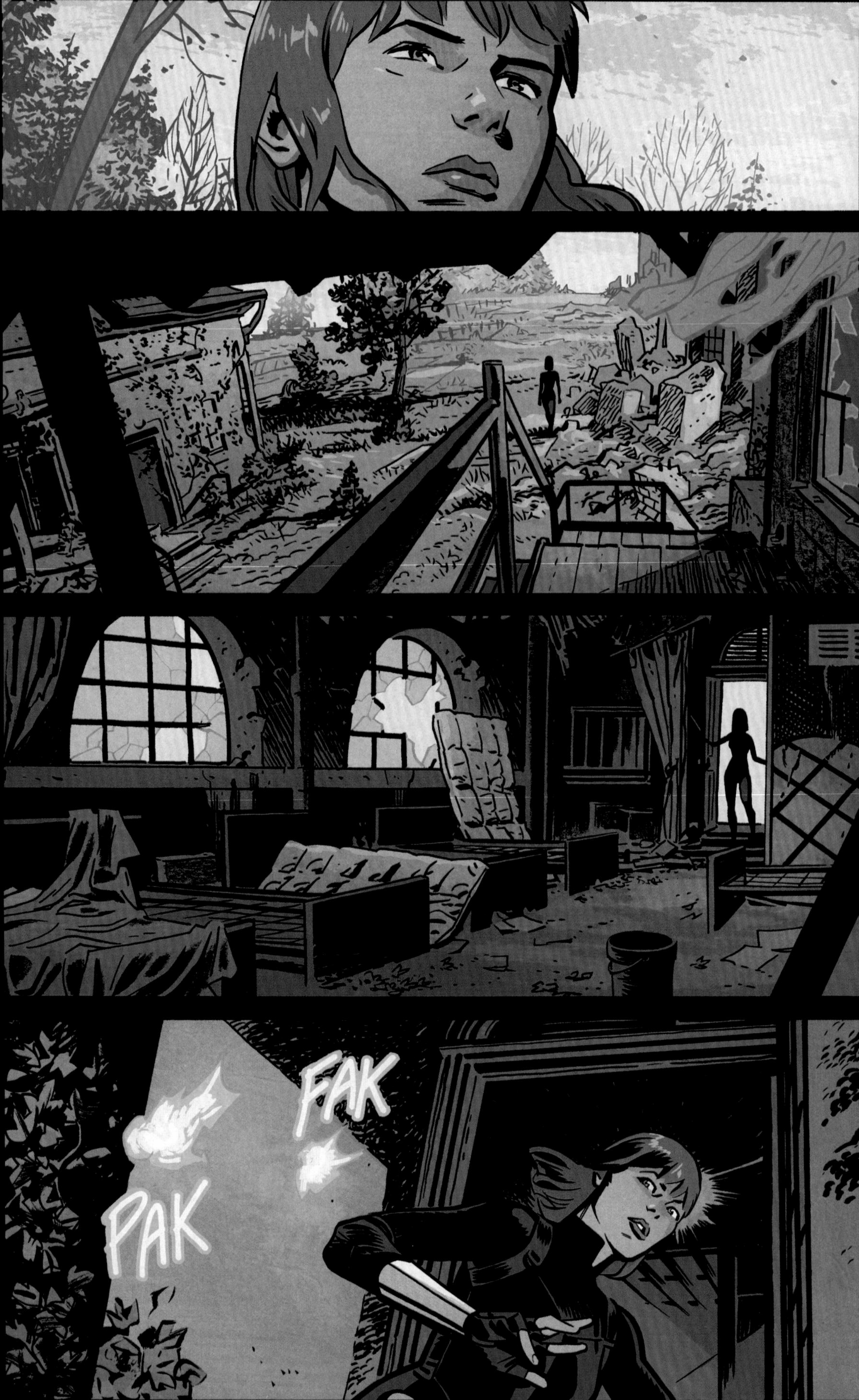
FAK
PAK

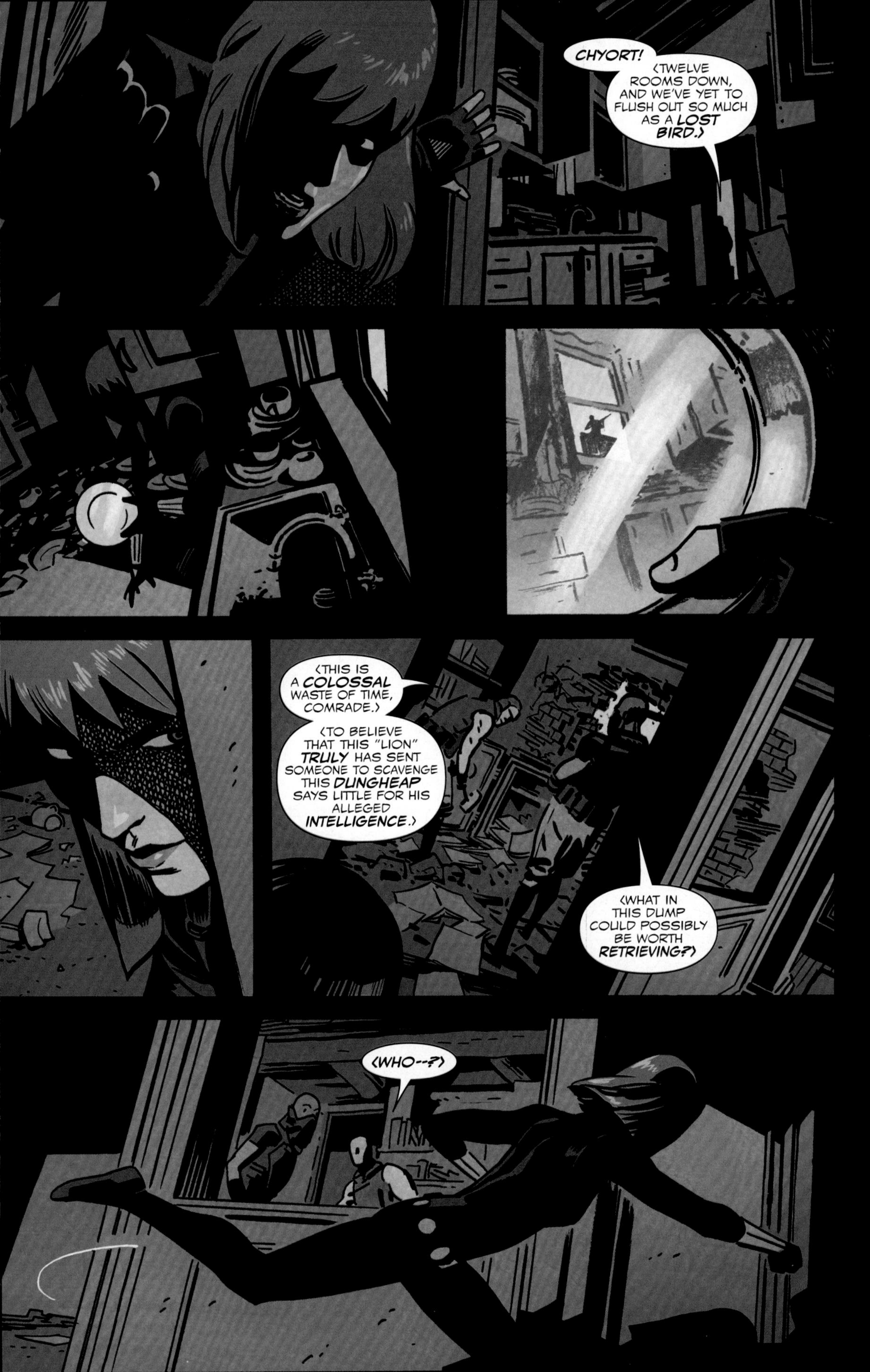
CHYORT!
‹TWELVE ROOMS DOWN, AND WE'VE YET TO FLUSH OUT SO MUCH AS A LOST BIRD.›
‹THIS IS A COLOSSAL WASTE OF TIME, COMRADE.›
‹TO BELIEVE THAT THIS "LION" TRULY HAS SENT SOMEONE TO SCAVENGE THIS DUNGHEAP SAYS LITTLE FOR HIS ALLEGED INTELLIGENCE.›
‹WHAT IN THIS DUMP COULD POSSIBLY BE WORTH RETRIEVING?›
‹WHO--?›

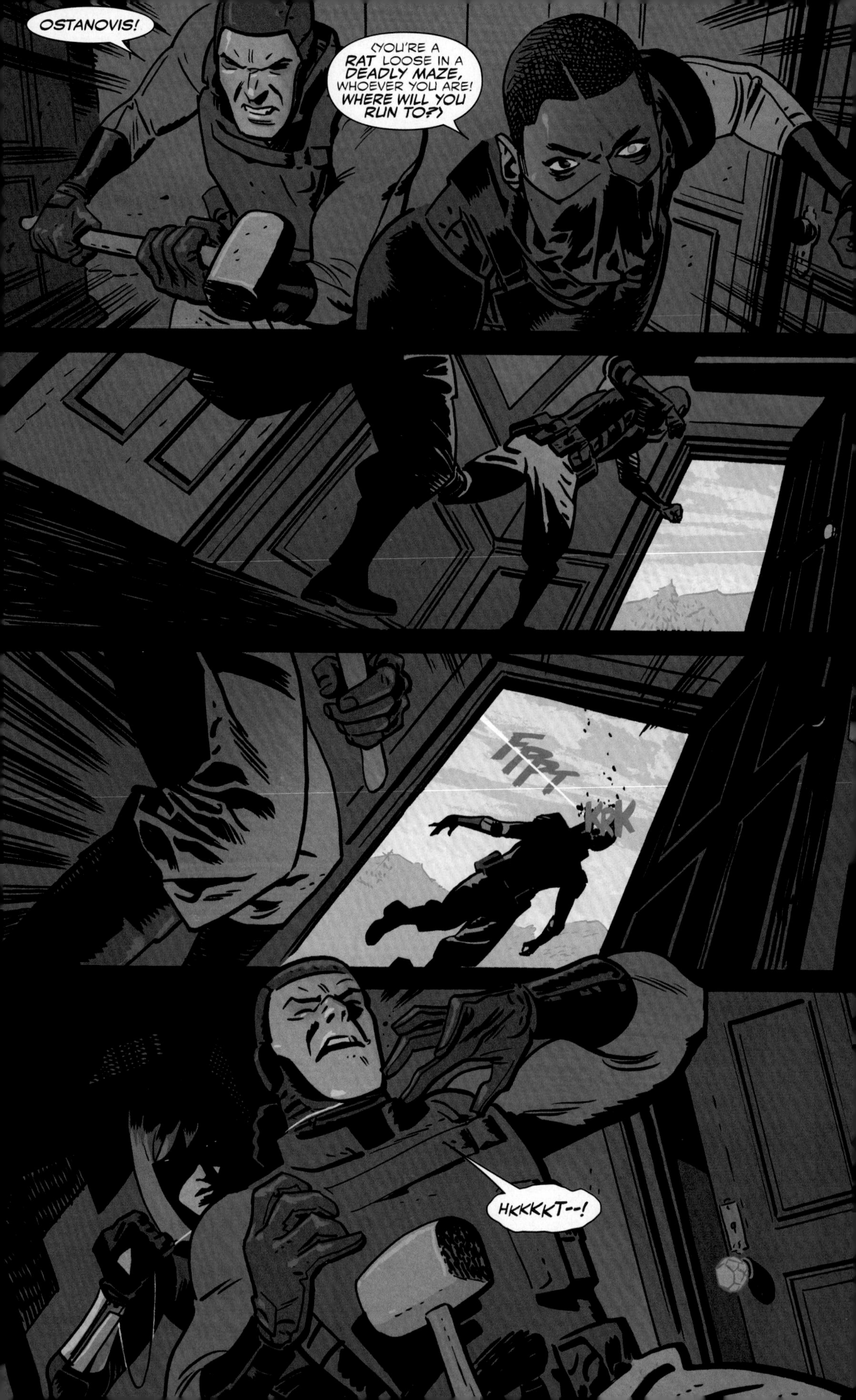
OSTANOVIS!
‹YOU'RE A RAT LOOSE IN A DEADLY MAZE, WHOEVER YOU ARE! WHERE WILL YOU RUN TO?›
HKKKKT--!

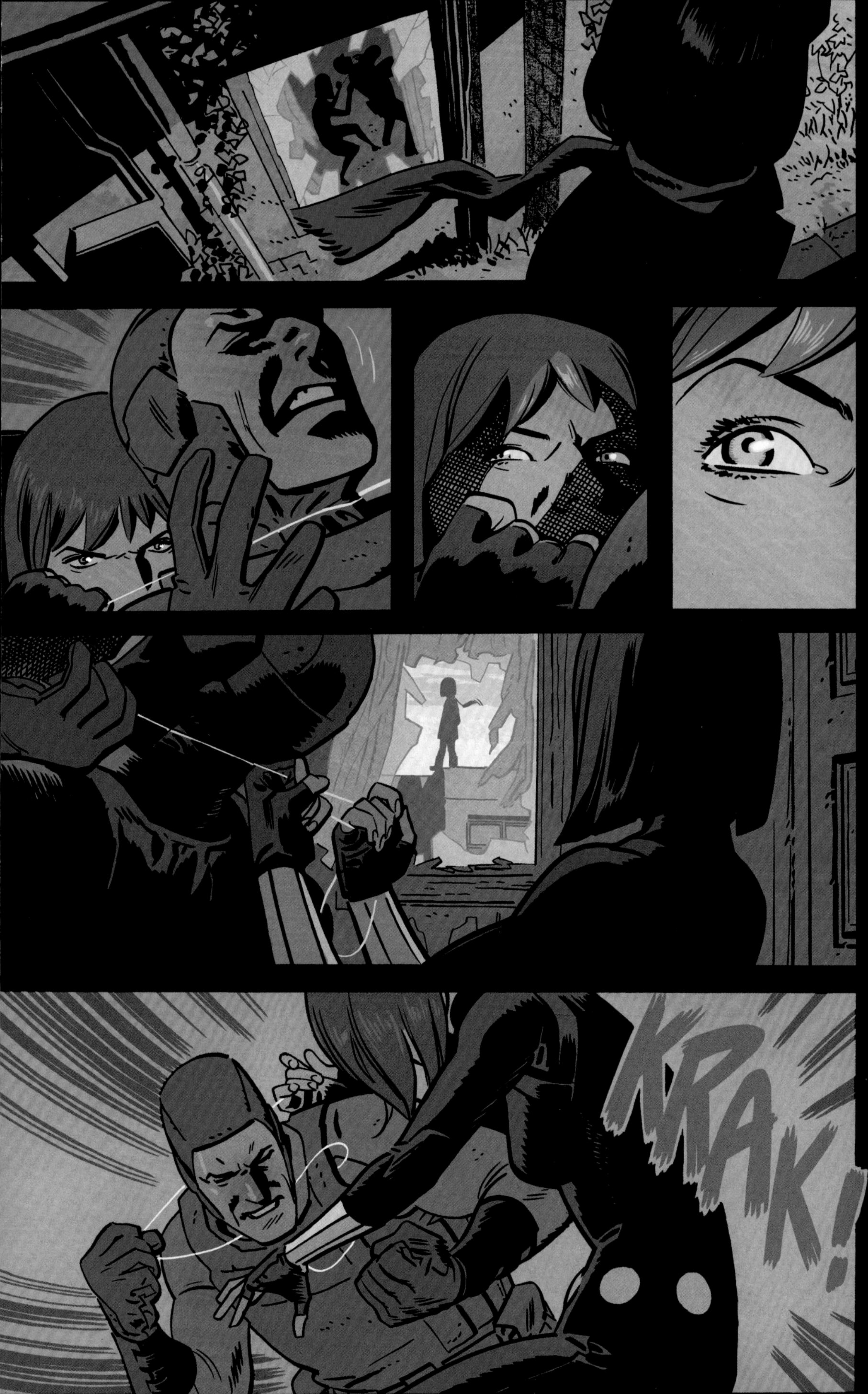
KRAK!

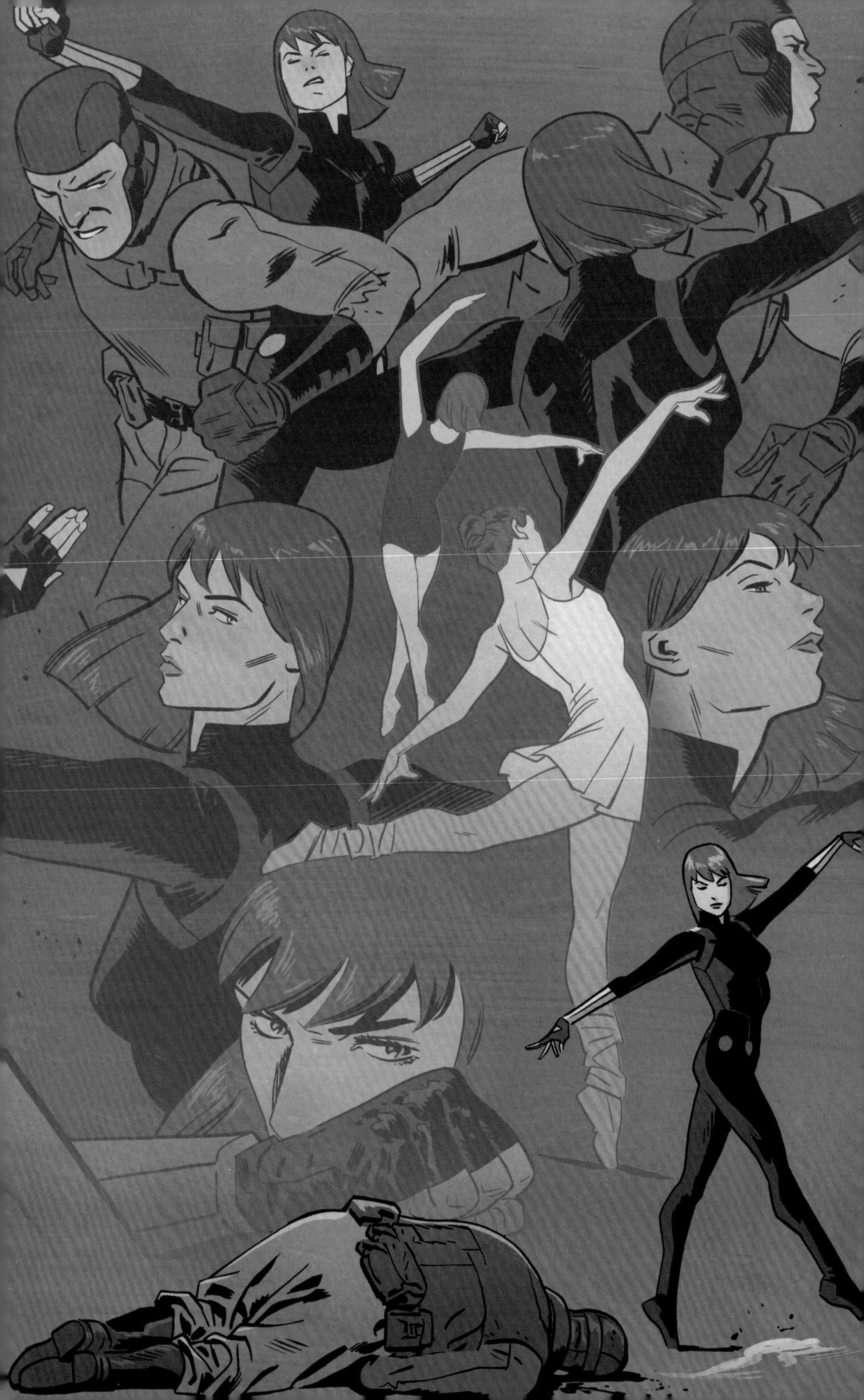

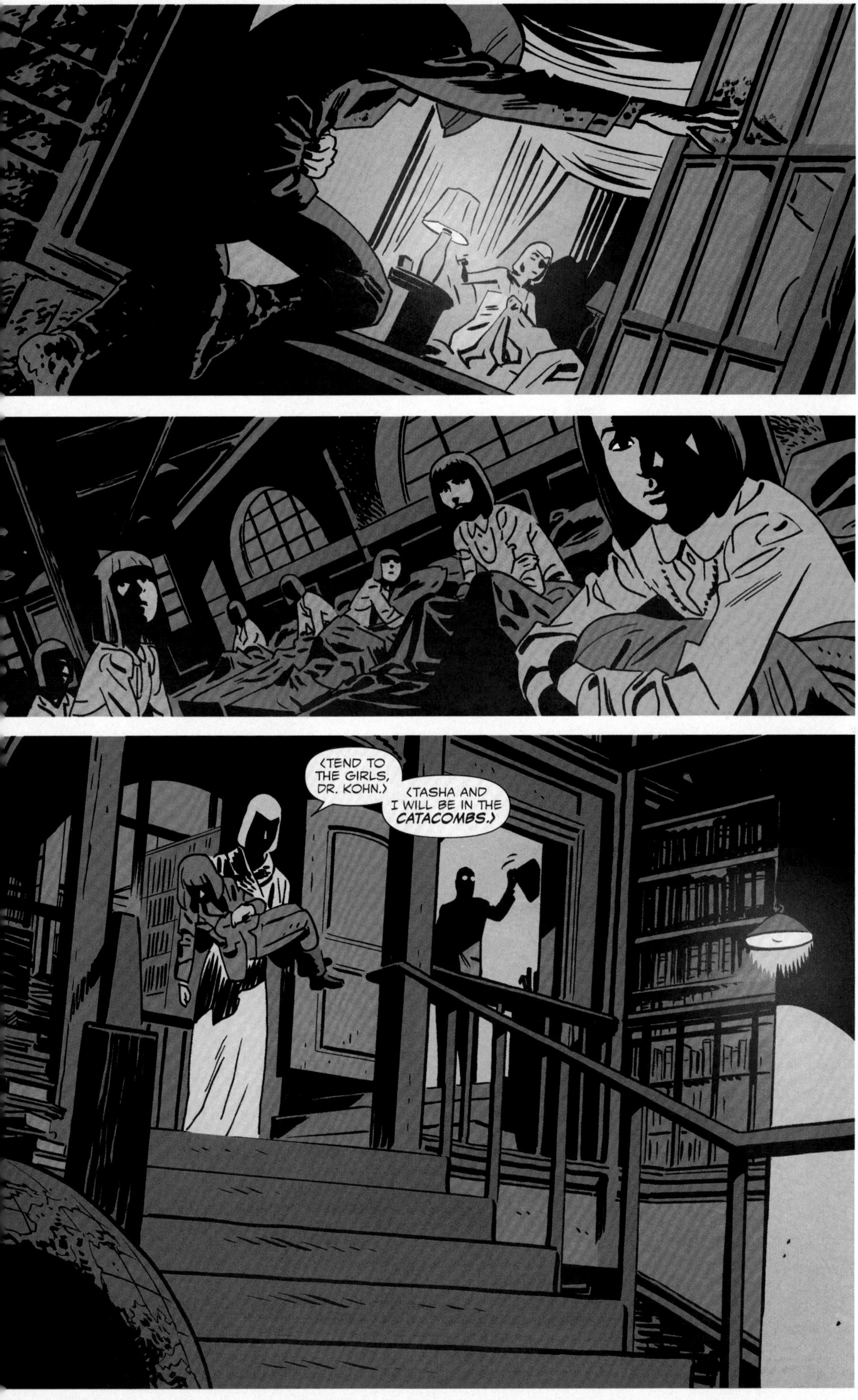

‹TEND TO THE GIRLS, DR. KOHN.›
‹TASHA AND I WILL BE IN THE CATACOMBS.›

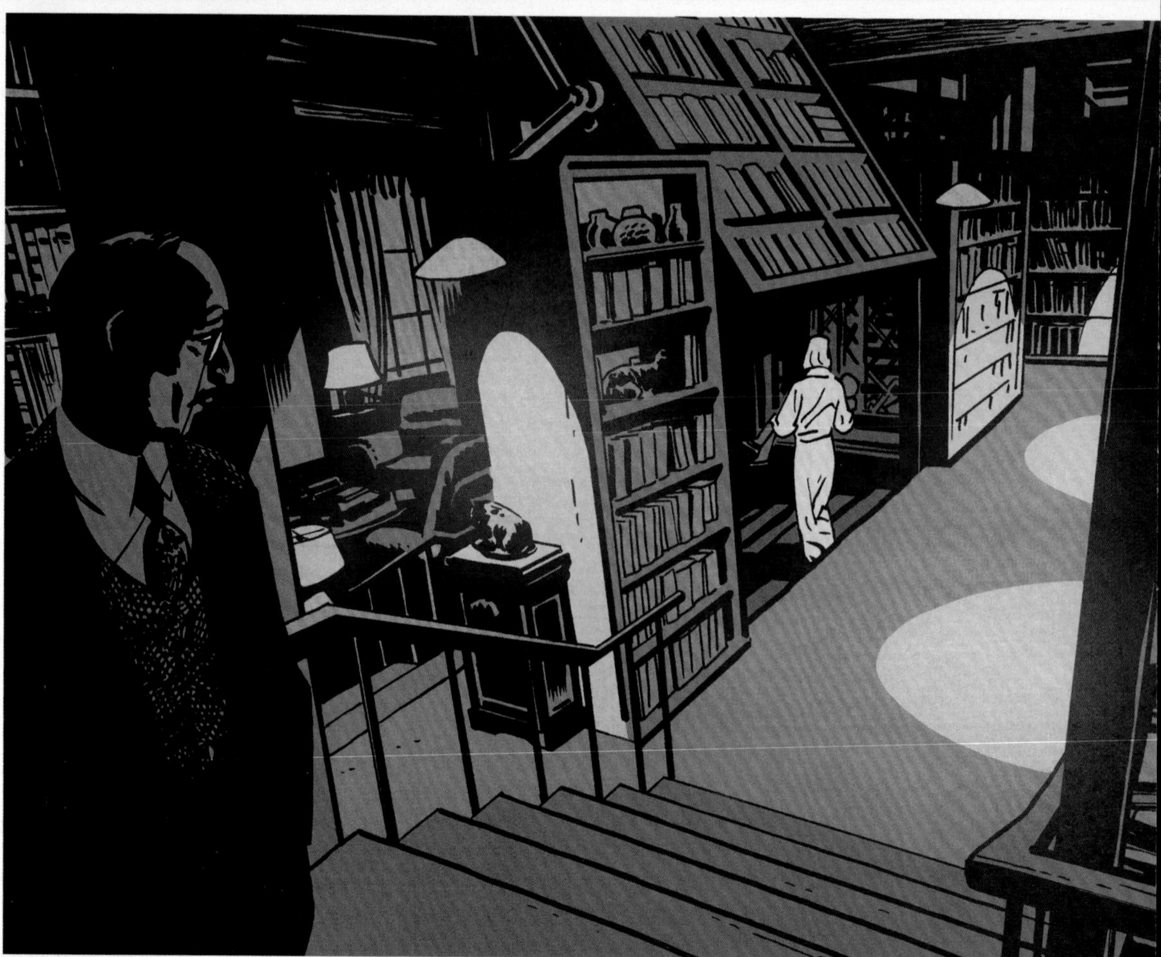
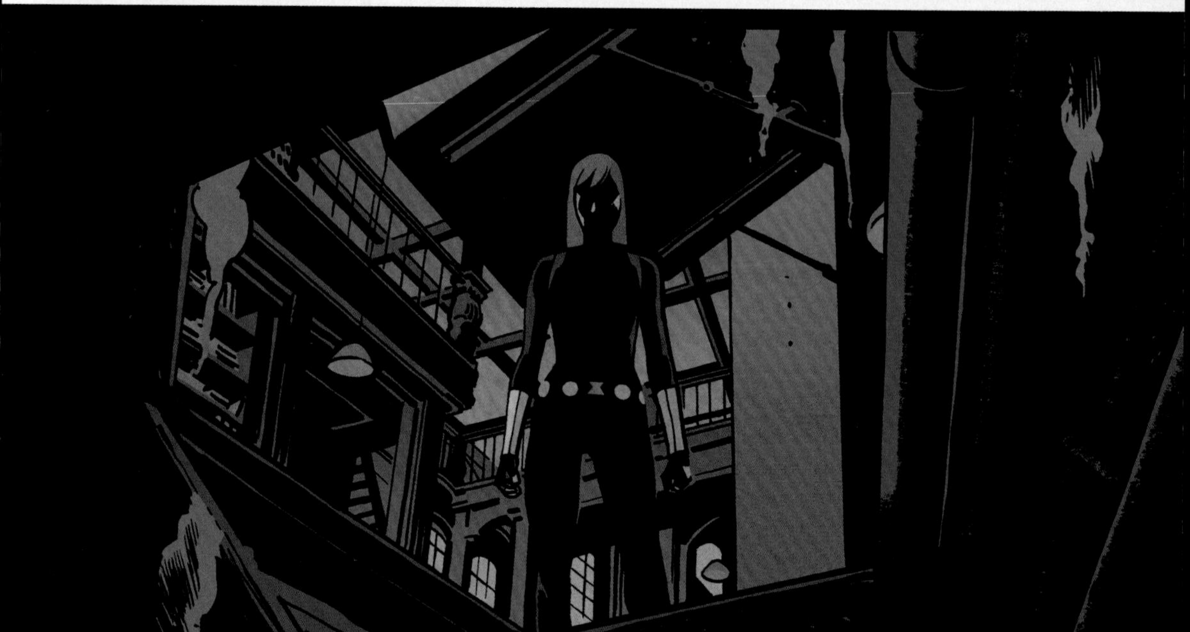

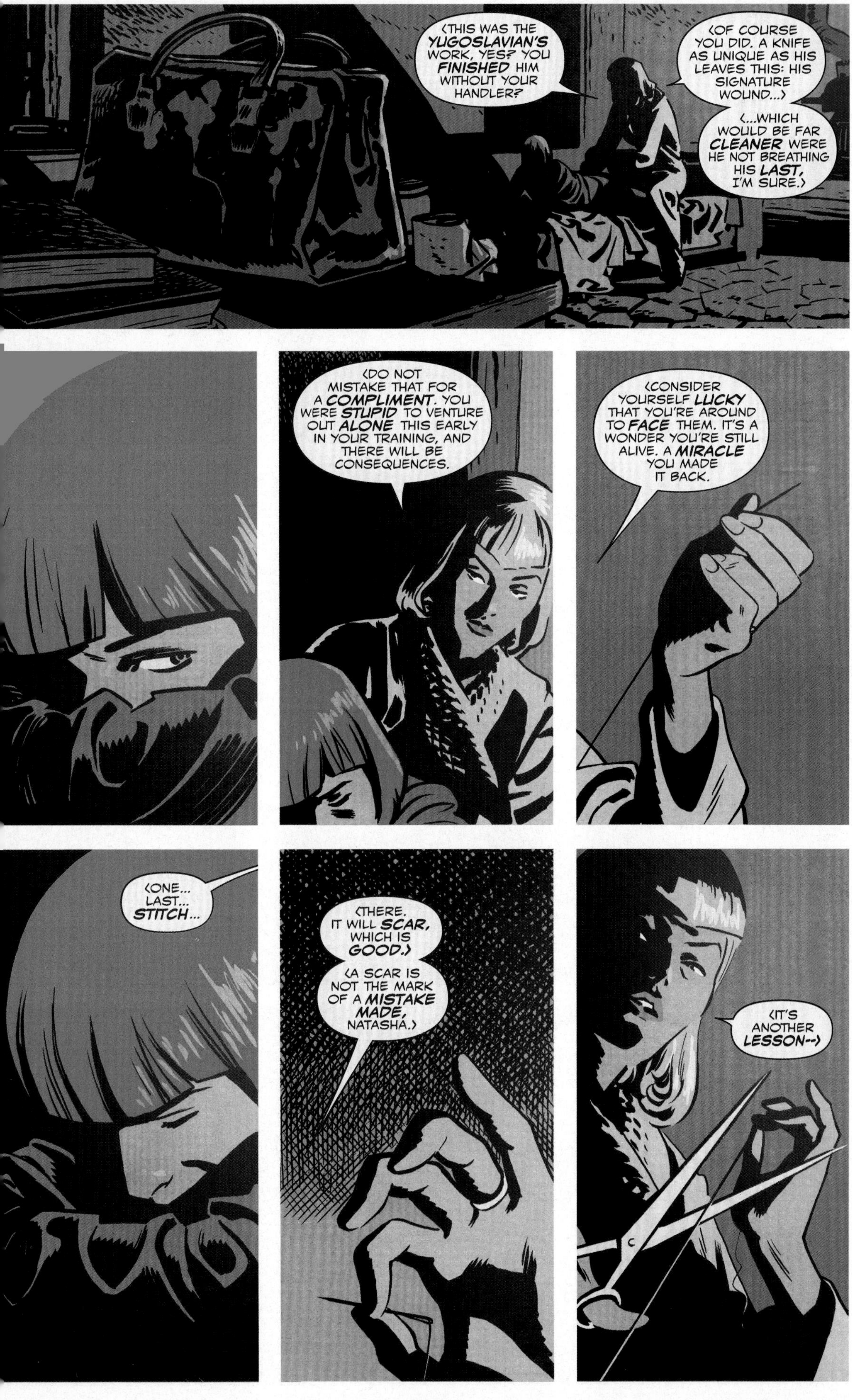

<THIS WAS THE YUGOSLAVIAN'S WORK, YES? YOU FINISHED HIM WITHOUT YOUR HANDLER?
<OF COURSE YOU DID. A KNIFE AS UNIQUE AS HIS LEAVES THIS: HIS SIGNATURE WOUND...>
<...WHICH WOULD BE FAR CLEANER WERE HE NOT BREATHING HIS LAST, I'M SURE.>
<DO NOT MISTAKE THAT FOR A COMPLIMENT. YOU WERE STUPID TO VENTURE OUT ALONE THIS EARLY IN YOUR TRAINING, AND THERE WILL BE CONSEQUENCES.
<CONSIDER YOURSELF LUCKY THAT YOU'RE AROUND TO FACE THEM. IT'S A WONDER YOU'RE STILL ALIVE. A MIRACLE YOU MADE IT BACK.
<ONE... LAST... STITCH...
<THERE. IT WILL SCAR, WHICH IS GOOD.>
<A SCAR IS NOT THE MARK OF A MISTAKE MADE, NATASHA.>
<IT'S ANOTHER LESSON-->

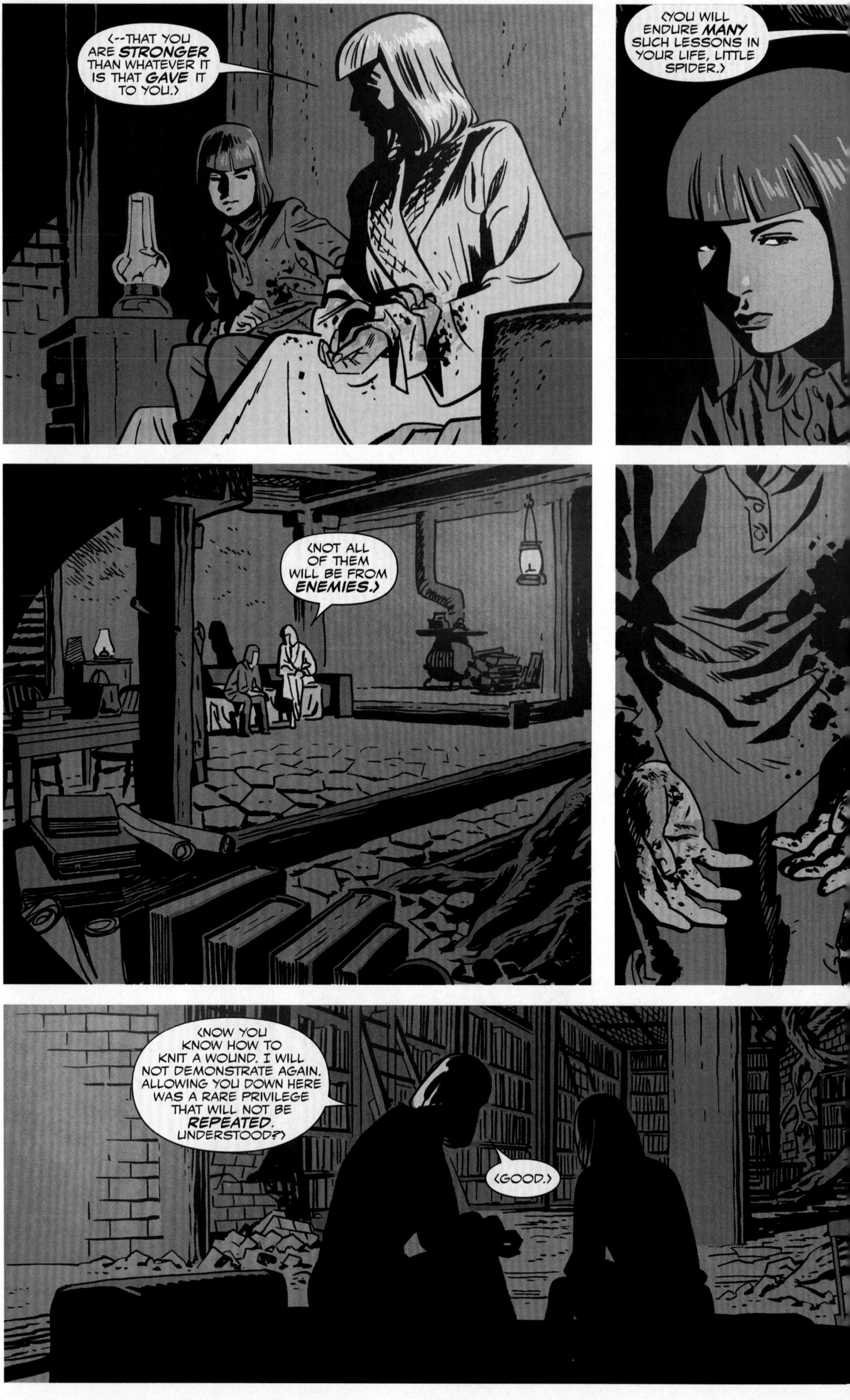

‹--THAT YOU ARE STRONGER THAN WHATEVER IT IS THAT GAVE IT TO YOU.›
‹YOU WILL ENDURE MANY SUCH LESSONS IN YOUR LIFE, LITTLE SPIDER.›
‹NOT ALL OF THEM WILL BE FROM ENEMIES.›
‹NOW YOU KNOW HOW TO KNIT A WOUND. I WILL NOT DEMONSTRATE AGAIN. ALLOWING YOU DOWN HERE WAS A RARE PRIVILEGE THAT WILL NOT BE REPEATED. UNDERSTOOD?›
‹GOOD.›

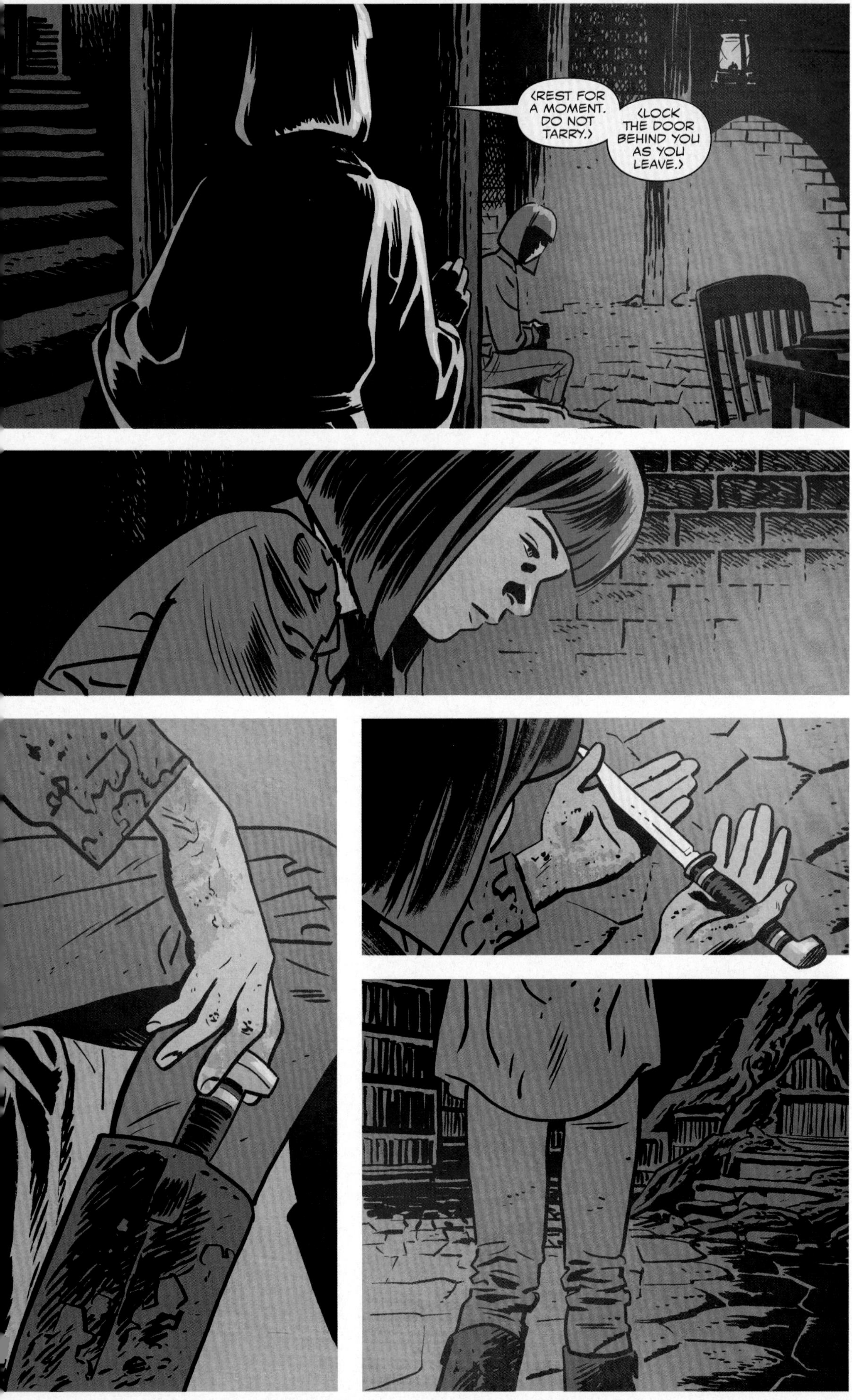
<REST FOR A MOMENT. DO NOT TARRY.>
<LOCK THE DOOR BEHIND YOU AS YOU LEAVE.>

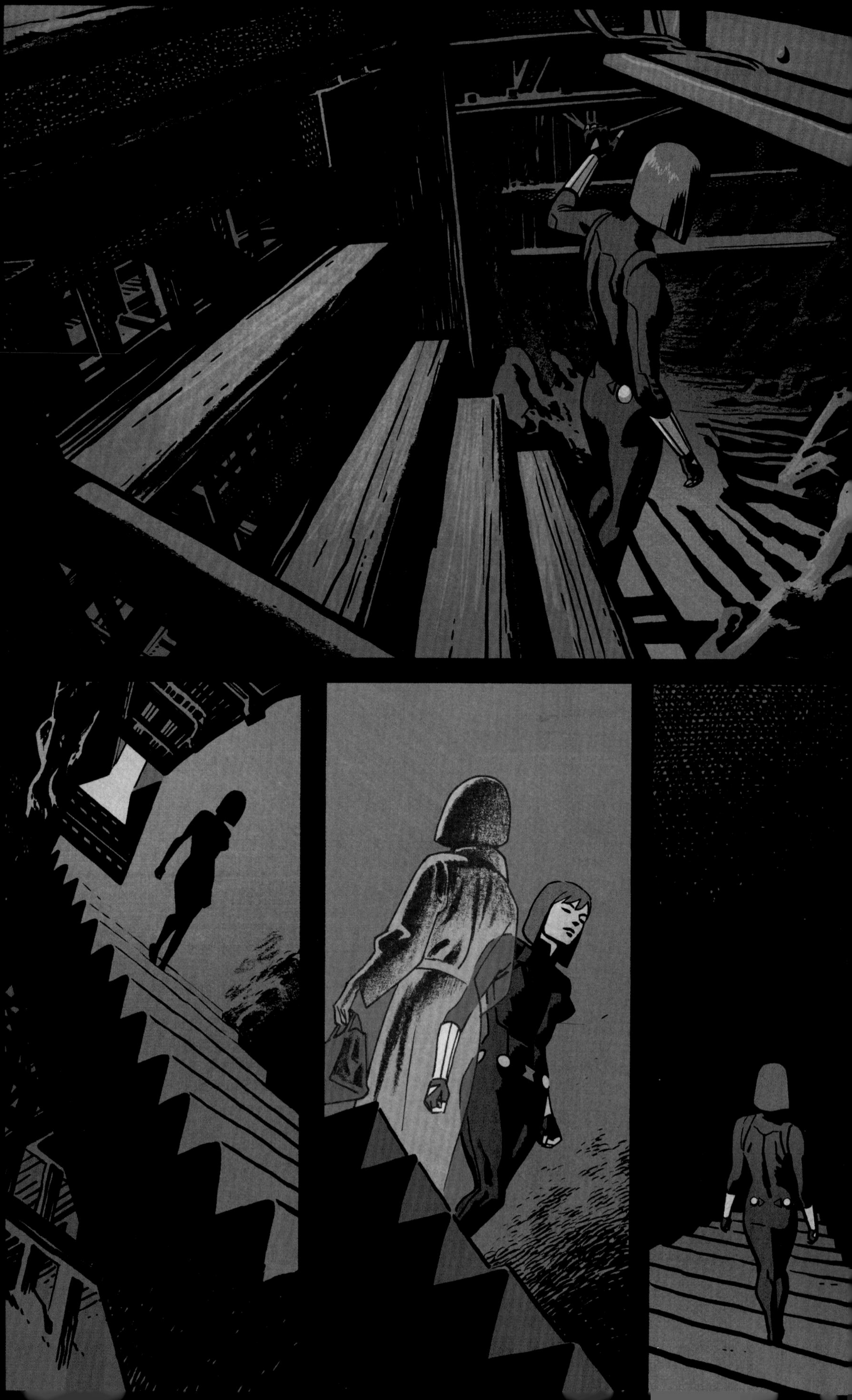

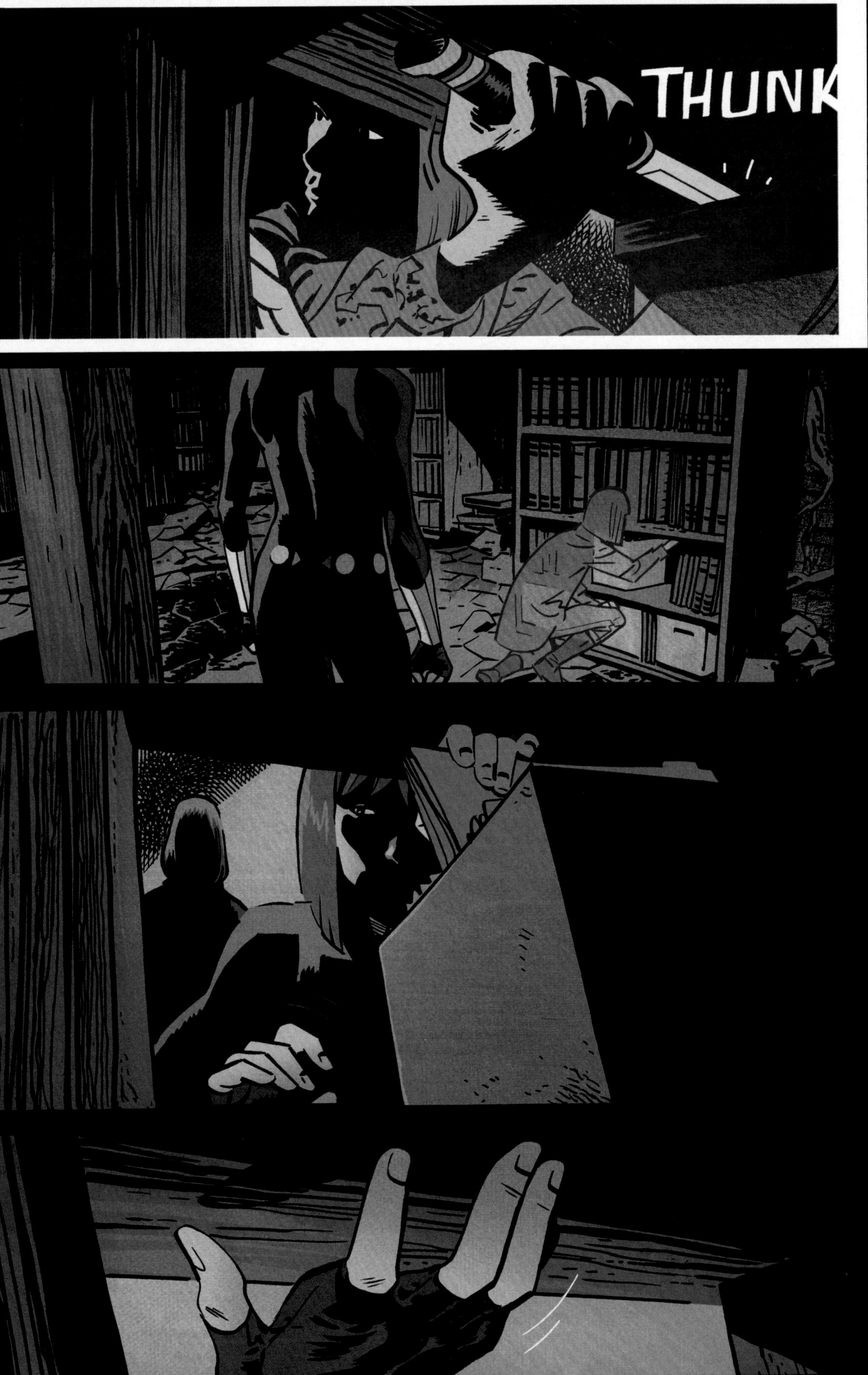
THUNK

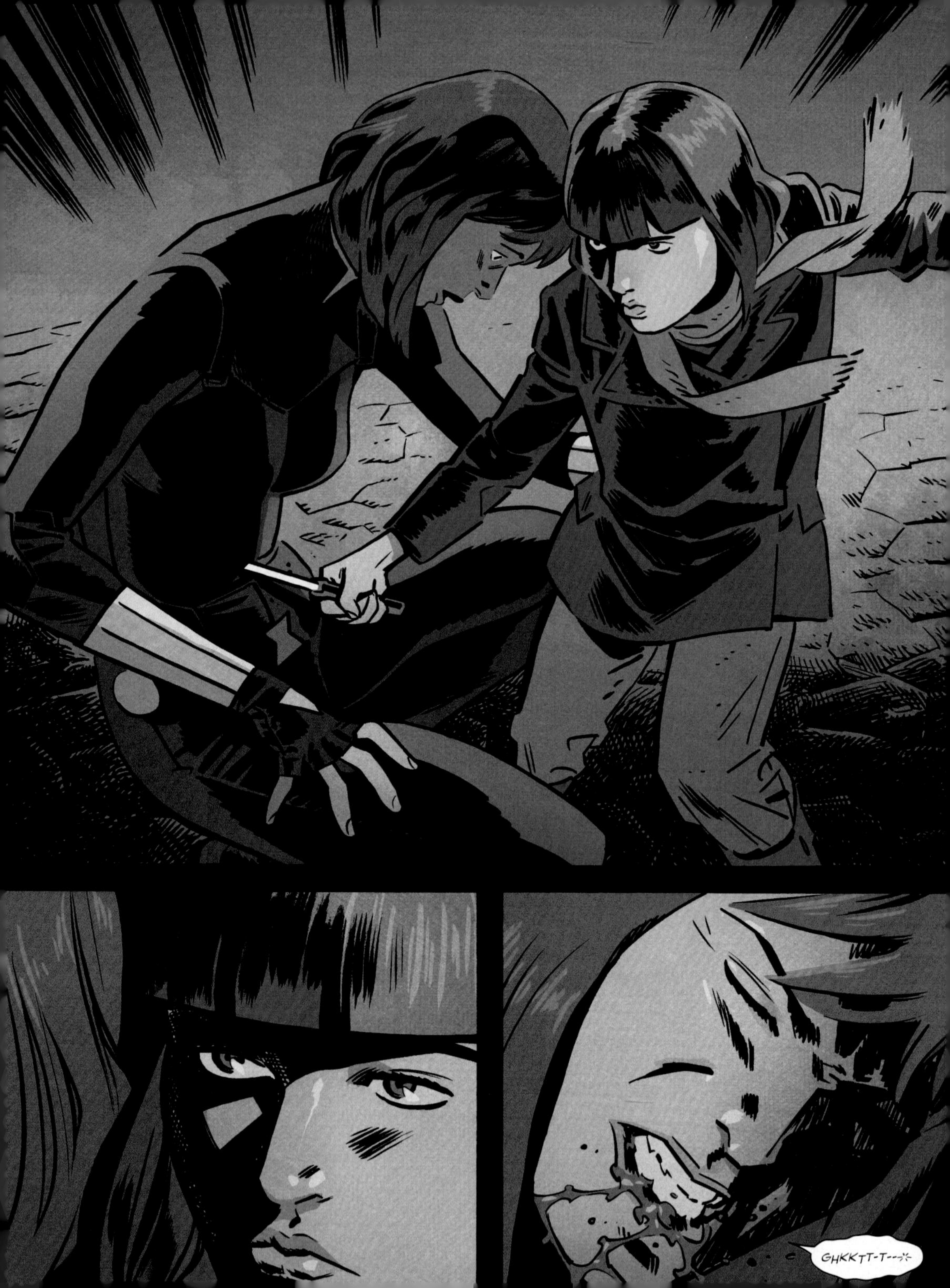
GHKKTT-T--

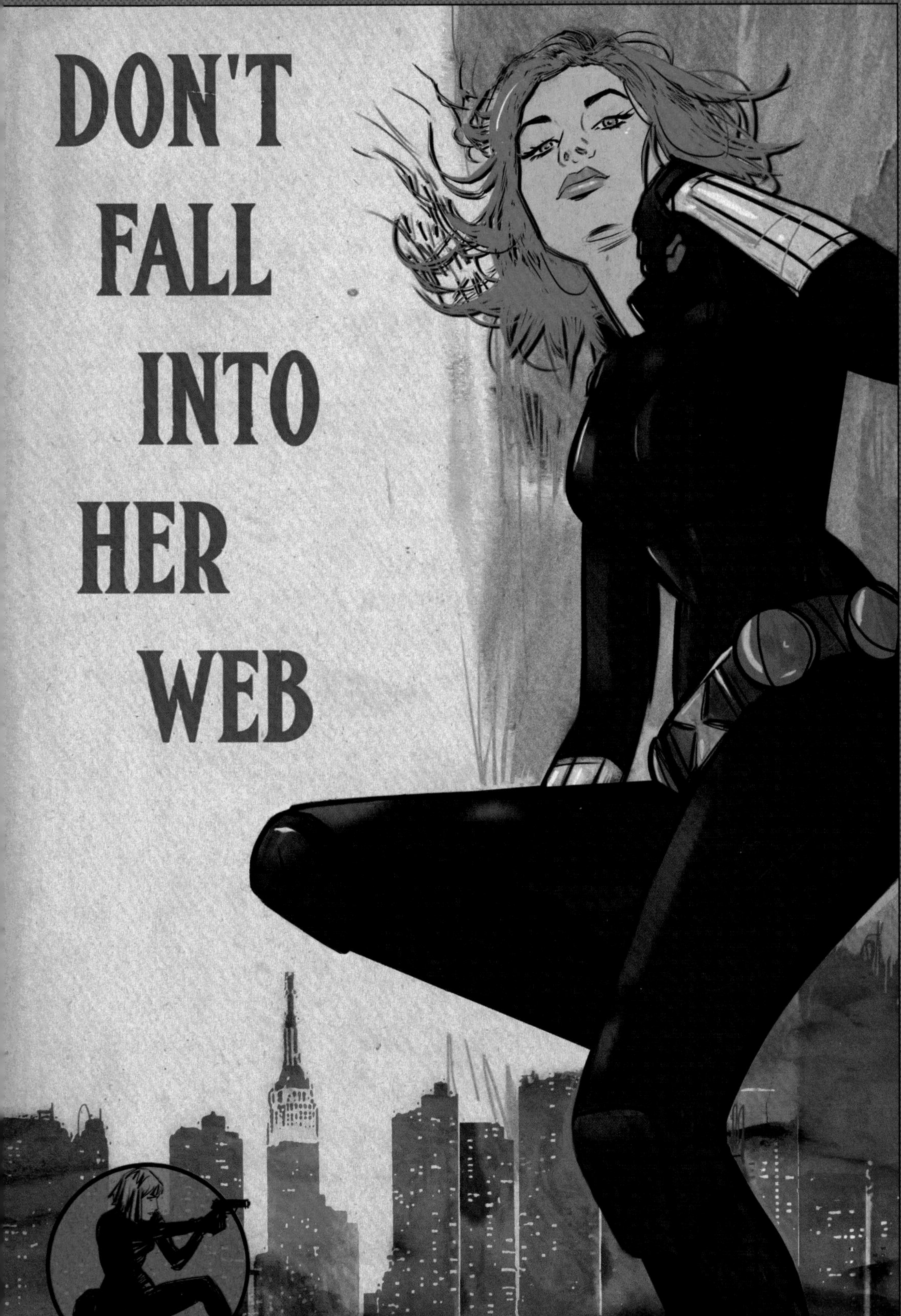
DON'T
FALL
INTO
HER
WEB

TULA LOTAY
NO. 1 VARIANT

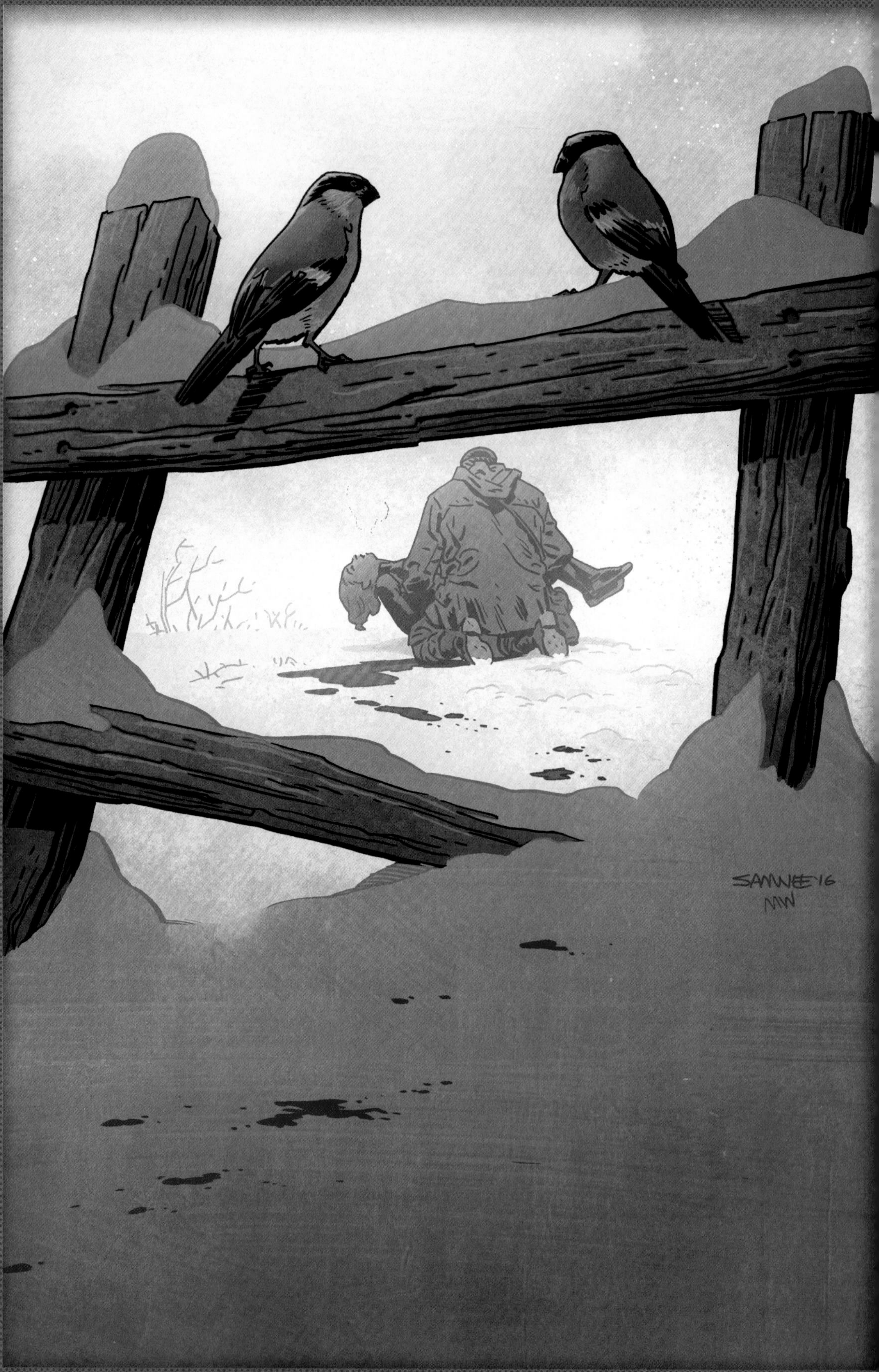
SAMNEE '16
MW

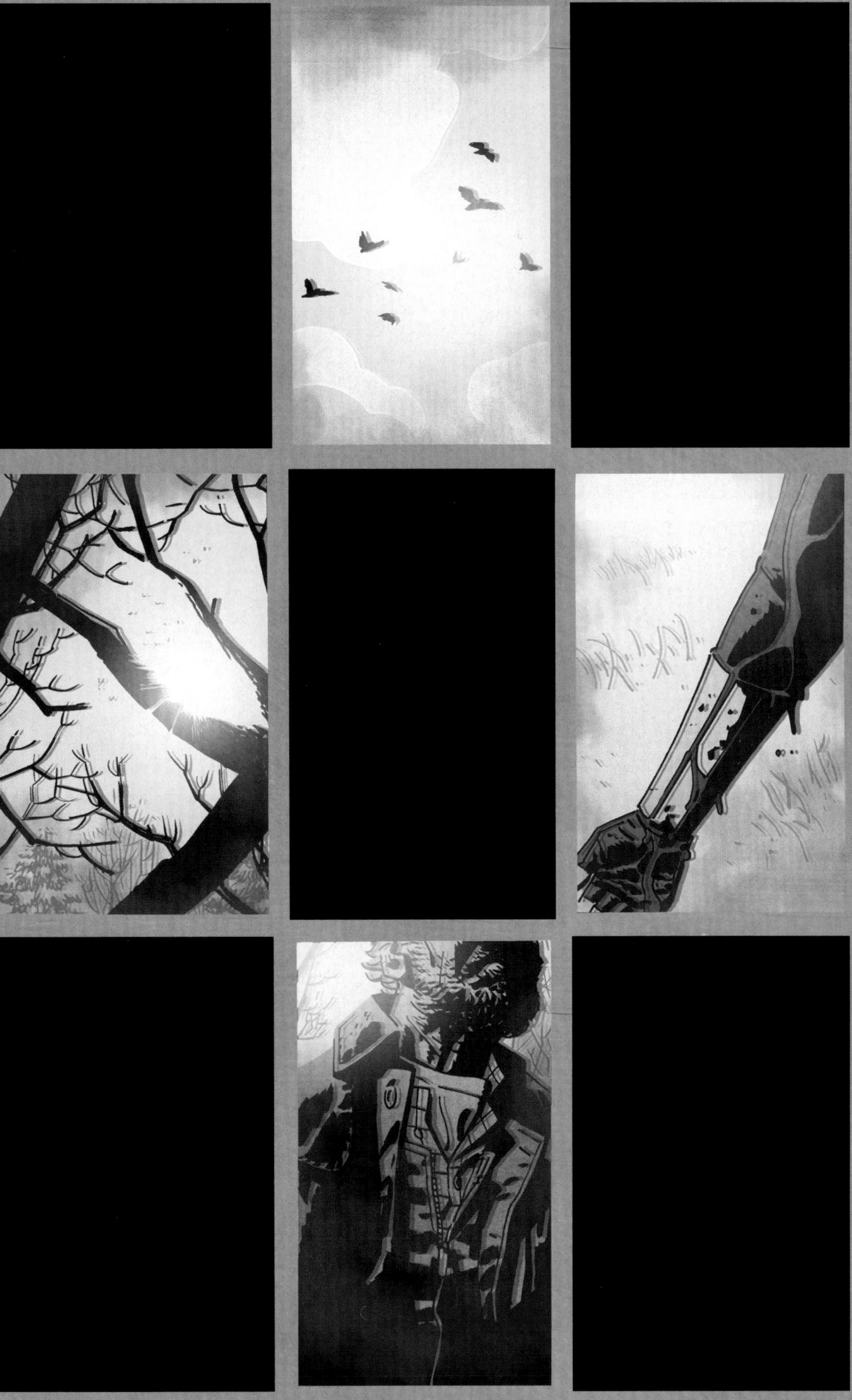

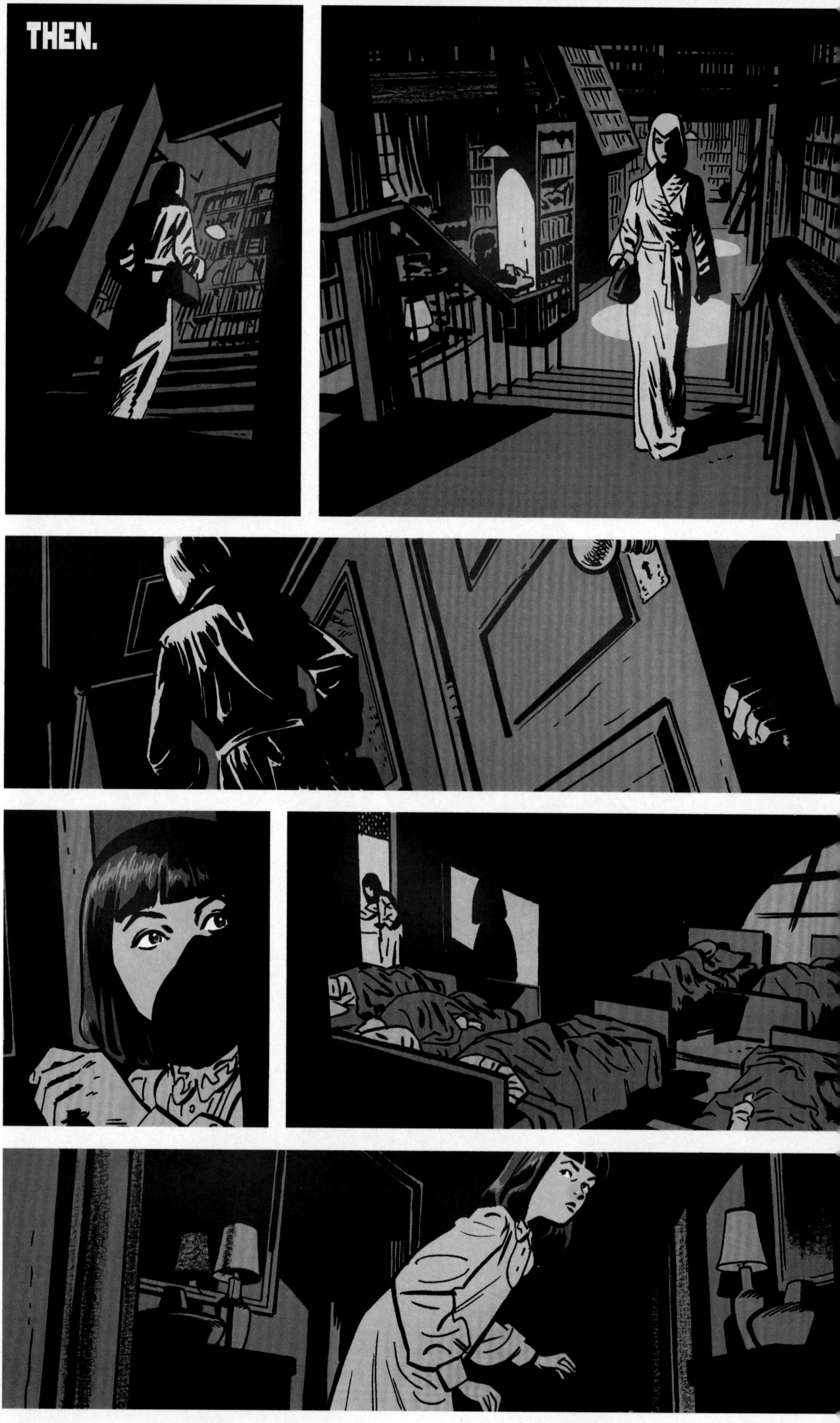
THEN.

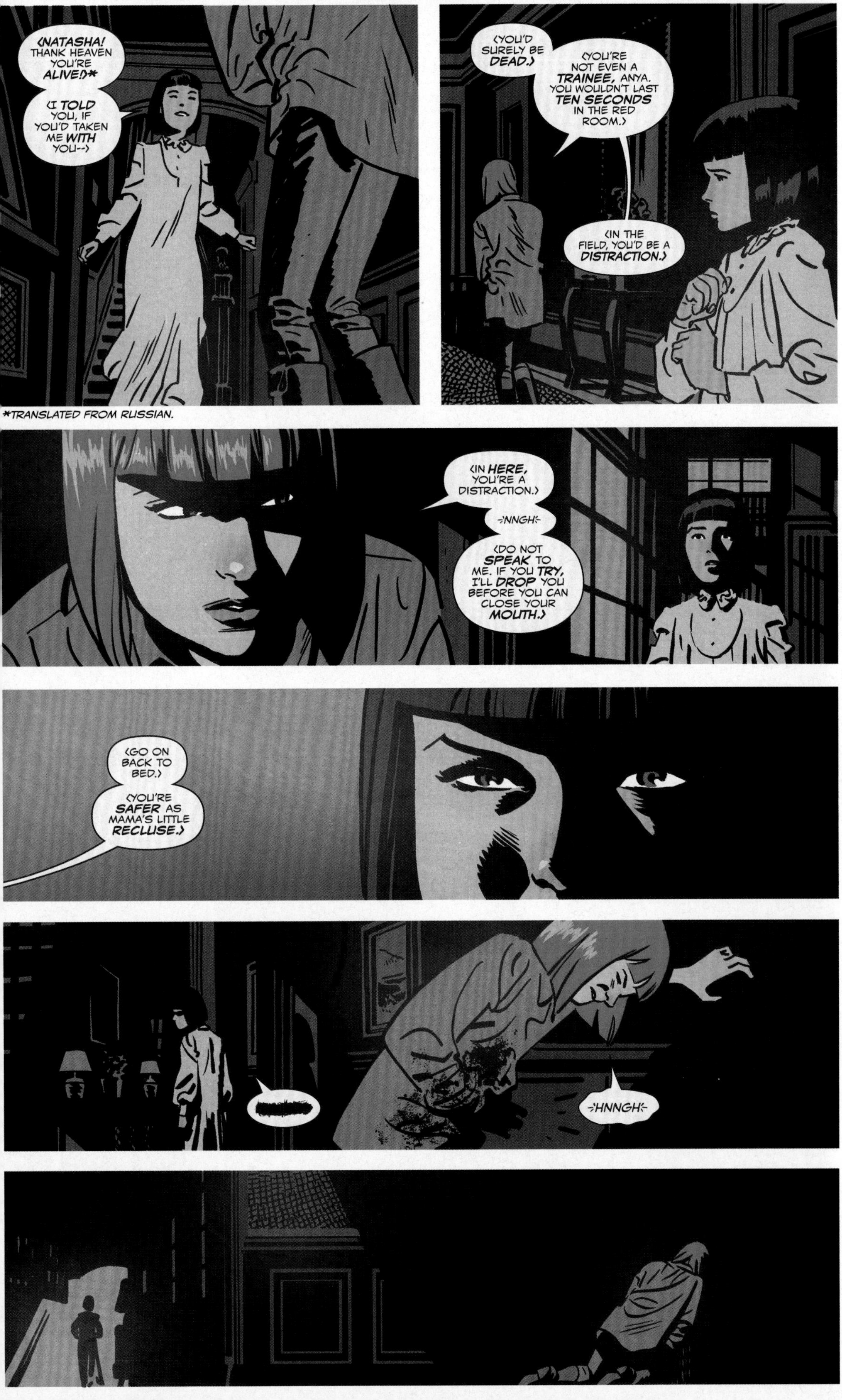
‹NATASHA! THANK HEAVEN YOU'RE ALIVE!›*
‹I TOLD YOU, IF YOU'D TAKEN ME WITH YOU--›
‹YOU'D SURELY BE DEAD.›
‹YOU'RE NOT EVEN A TRAINEE, ANYA. YOU WOULDN'T LAST TEN SECONDS IN THE RED ROOM.›
‹IN THE FIELD, YOU'D BE A DISTRACTION.›
‹IN HERE, YOU'RE A DISTRACTION.›
-NNGH-
‹DO NOT SPEAK TO ME. IF YOU TRY, I'LL DROP YOU BEFORE YOU CAN CLOSE YOUR MOUTH.›
‹GO ON BACK TO BED.›
‹YOU'RE SAFER AS MAMA'S LITTLE RECLUSE.›
-HNNGH-

*TRANSLATED FROM RUSSIAN.

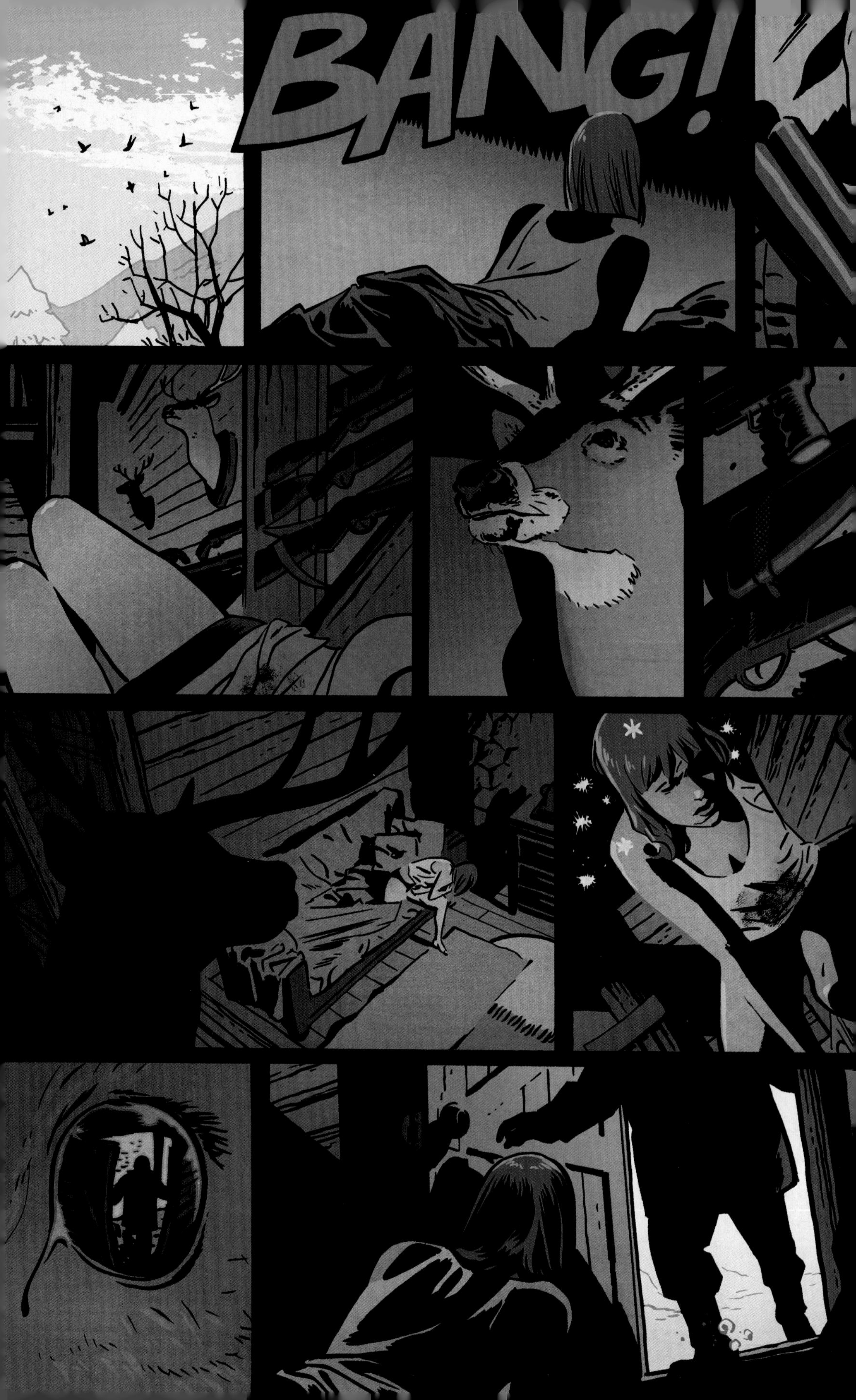
BANG!

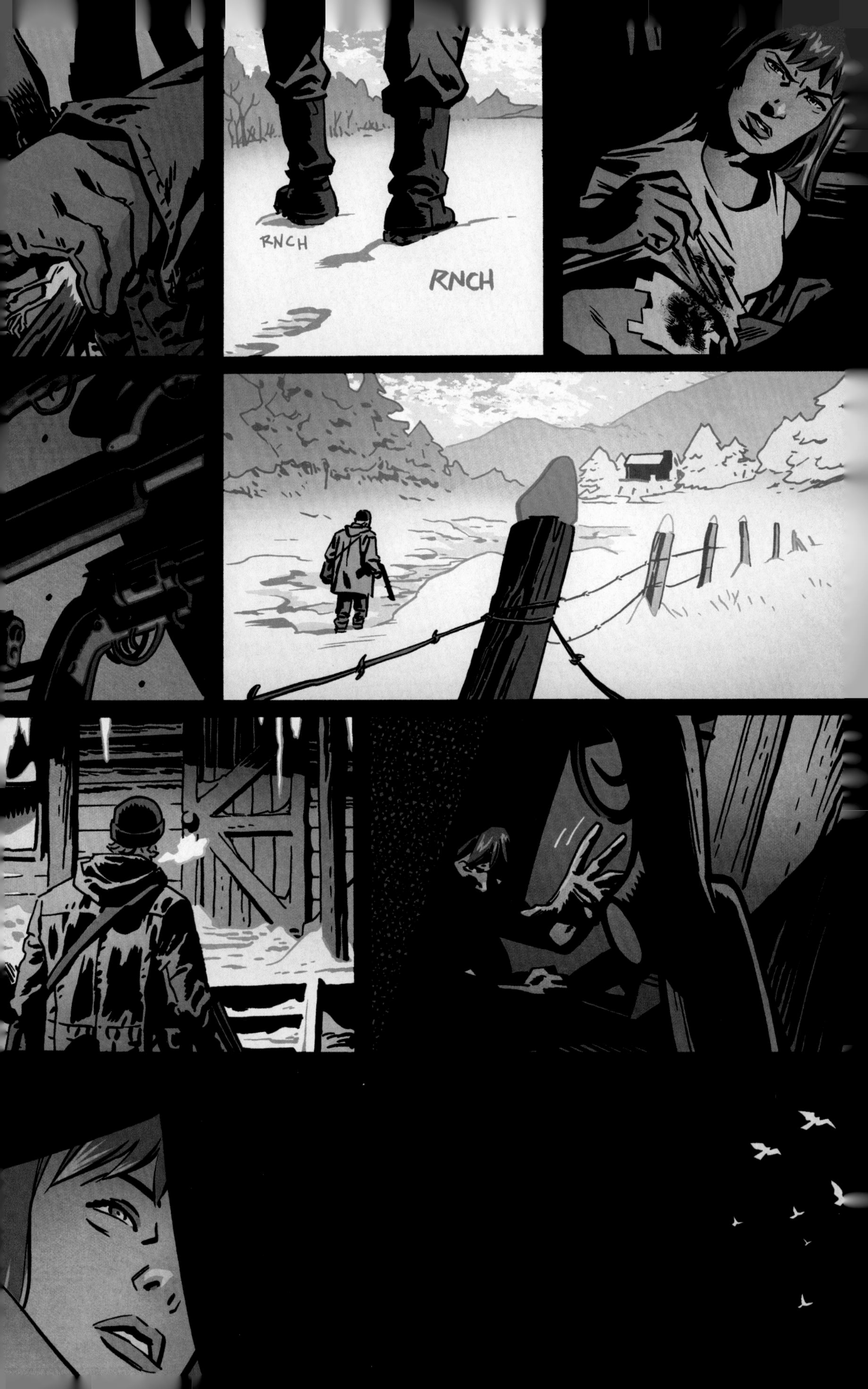
RNCH
RNCH

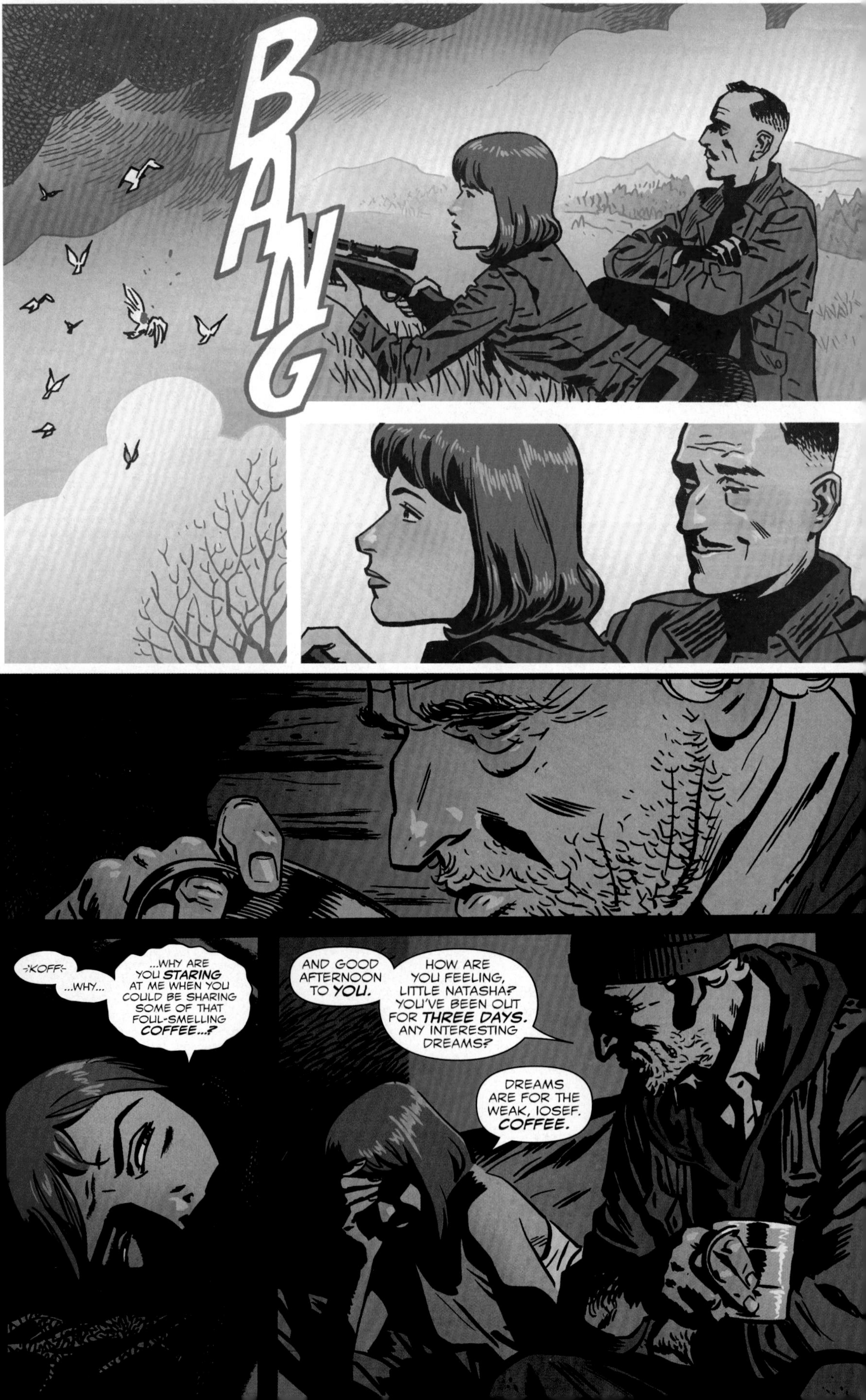
BANG
-KOFF-
...WHY...
...WHY ARE YOU STARING AT ME WHEN YOU COULD BE SHARING SOME OF THAT FOUL-SMELLING COFFEE...?
AND GOOD AFTERNOON TO YOU.
HOW ARE YOU FEELING, LITTLE NATASHA? YOU'VE BEEN OUT FOR THREE DAYS. ANY INTERESTING DREAMS?
DREAMS ARE FOR THE WEAK, IOSEF. COFFEE.

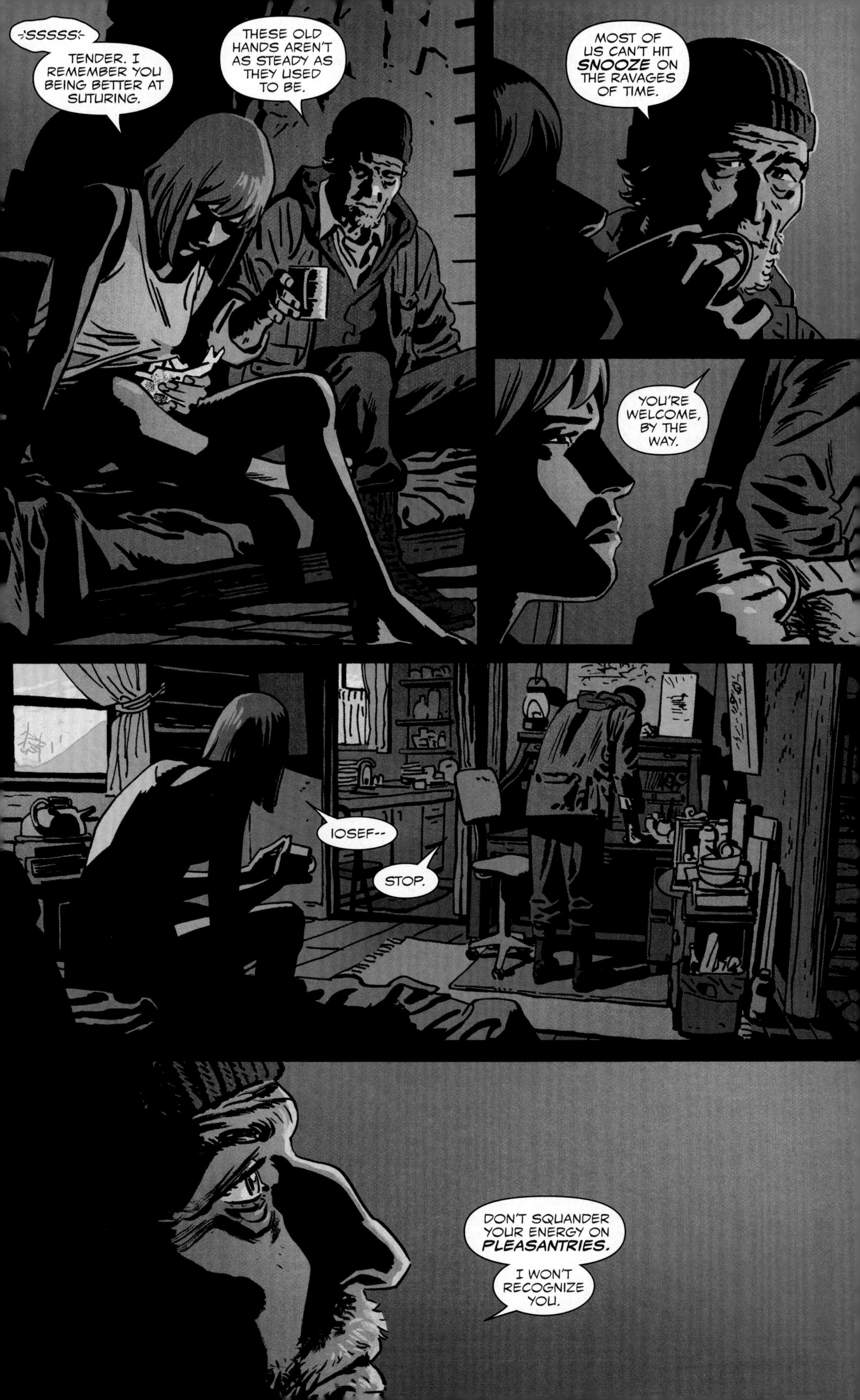
-SSSSS-
TENDER. I REMEMBER YOU BEING BETTER AT SUTURING.
THESE OLD HANDS AREN'T AS STEADY AS THEY USED TO BE.
MOST OF US CAN'T HIT SNOOZE ON THE RAVAGES OF TIME.
YOU'RE WELCOME, BY THE WAY.
IOSEF--
STOP.
DON'T SQUANDER YOUR ENERGY ON PLEASANTRIES.
I WON'T RECOGNIZE YOU.

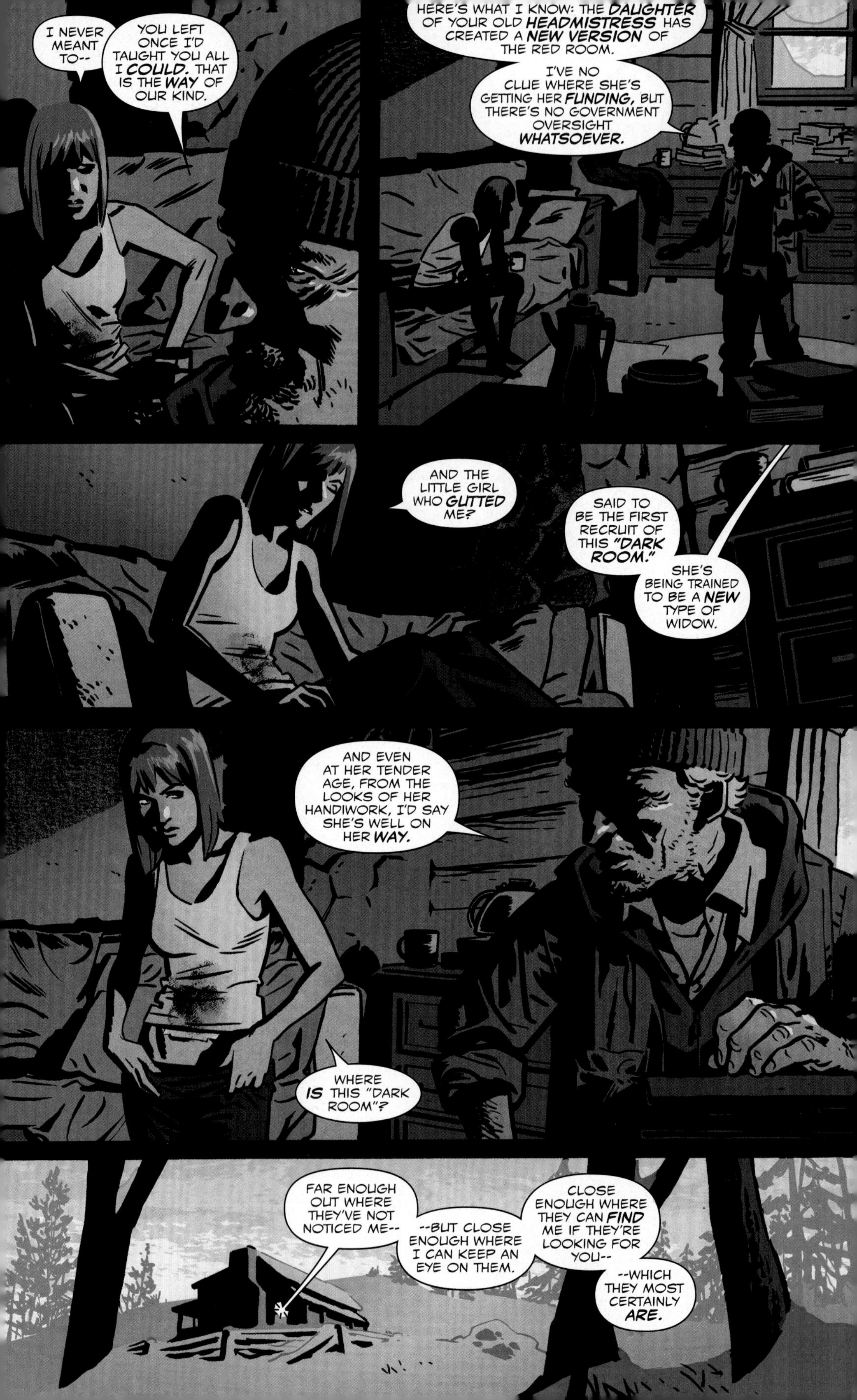
I NEVER MEANT TO--
YOU LEFT ONCE I'D TAUGHT YOU ALL I COULD. THAT IS THE WAY OF OUR KIND.
HERE'S WHAT I KNOW: THE DAUGHTER OF YOUR OLD HEADMISTRESS HAS CREATED A NEW VERSION OF THE RED ROOM.
I'VE NO CLUE WHERE SHE'S GETTING HER FUNDING, BUT THERE'S NO GOVERNMENT OVERSIGHT WHATSOEVER.
AND THE LITTLE GIRL WHO GUTTED ME?
SAID TO BE THE FIRST RECRUIT OF THIS "DARK ROOM."
SHE'S BEING TRAINED TO BE A NEW TYPE OF WIDOW.
AND EVEN AT HER TENDER AGE, FROM THE LOOKS OF HER HANDIWORK, I'D SAY SHE'S WELL ON HER WAY.
WHERE IS THIS "DARK ROOM"?
FAR ENOUGH OUT WHERE THEY'VE NOT NOTICED ME--
--BUT CLOSE ENOUGH WHERE I CAN KEEP AN EYE ON THEM.
CLOSE ENOUGH WHERE THEY CAN FIND ME IF THEY'RE LOOKING FOR YOU--
--WHICH THEY MOST CERTAINLY ARE.

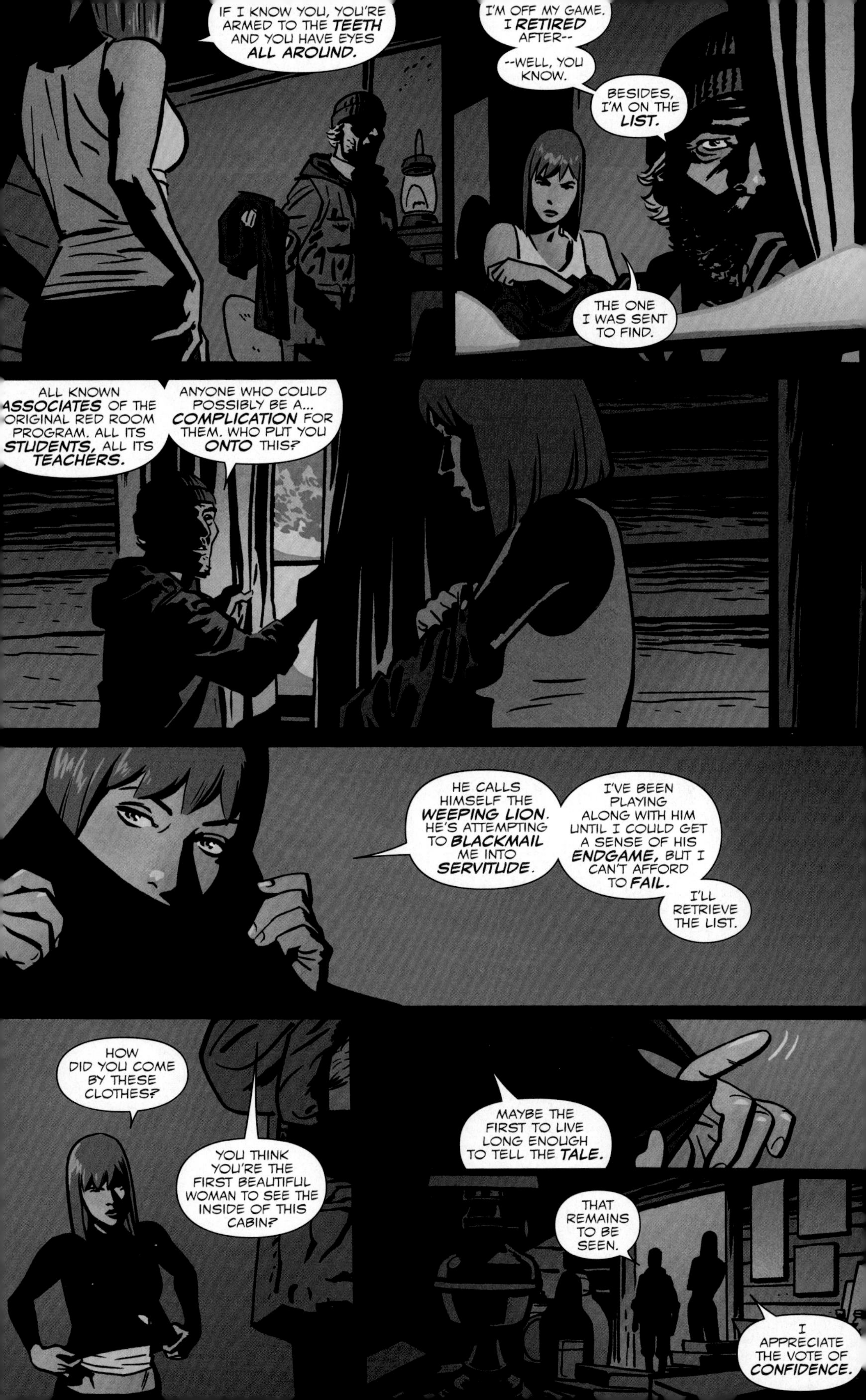
IF I KNOW YOU, YOU'RE ARMED TO THE TEETH AND YOU HAVE EYES ALL AROUND.
I'M OFF MY GAME. I RETIRED AFTER--
--WELL, YOU KNOW.
BESIDES, I'M ON THE LIST.
THE ONE I WAS SENT TO FIND.
ALL KNOWN ASSOCIATES OF THE ORIGINAL RED ROOM PROGRAM. ALL ITS STUDENTS, ALL ITS TEACHERS.
ANYONE WHO COULD POSSIBLY BE A... COMPLICATION FOR THEM. WHO PUT YOU ONTO THIS?
HE CALLS HIMSELF THE WEEPING LION. HE'S ATTEMPTING TO BLACKMAIL ME INTO SERVITUDE.
I'VE BEEN PLAYING ALONG WITH HIM UNTIL I COULD GET A SENSE OF HIS ENDGAME, BUT I CAN'T AFFORD TO FAIL.
I'LL RETRIEVE THE LIST.
HOW DID YOU COME BY THESE CLOTHES?
YOU THINK YOU'RE THE FIRST BEAUTIFUL WOMAN TO SEE THE INSIDE OF THIS CABIN?
MAYBE THE FIRST TO LIVE LONG ENOUGH TO TELL THE TALE.
THAT REMAINS TO BE SEEN.
I APPRECIATE THE VOTE OF CONFIDENCE.

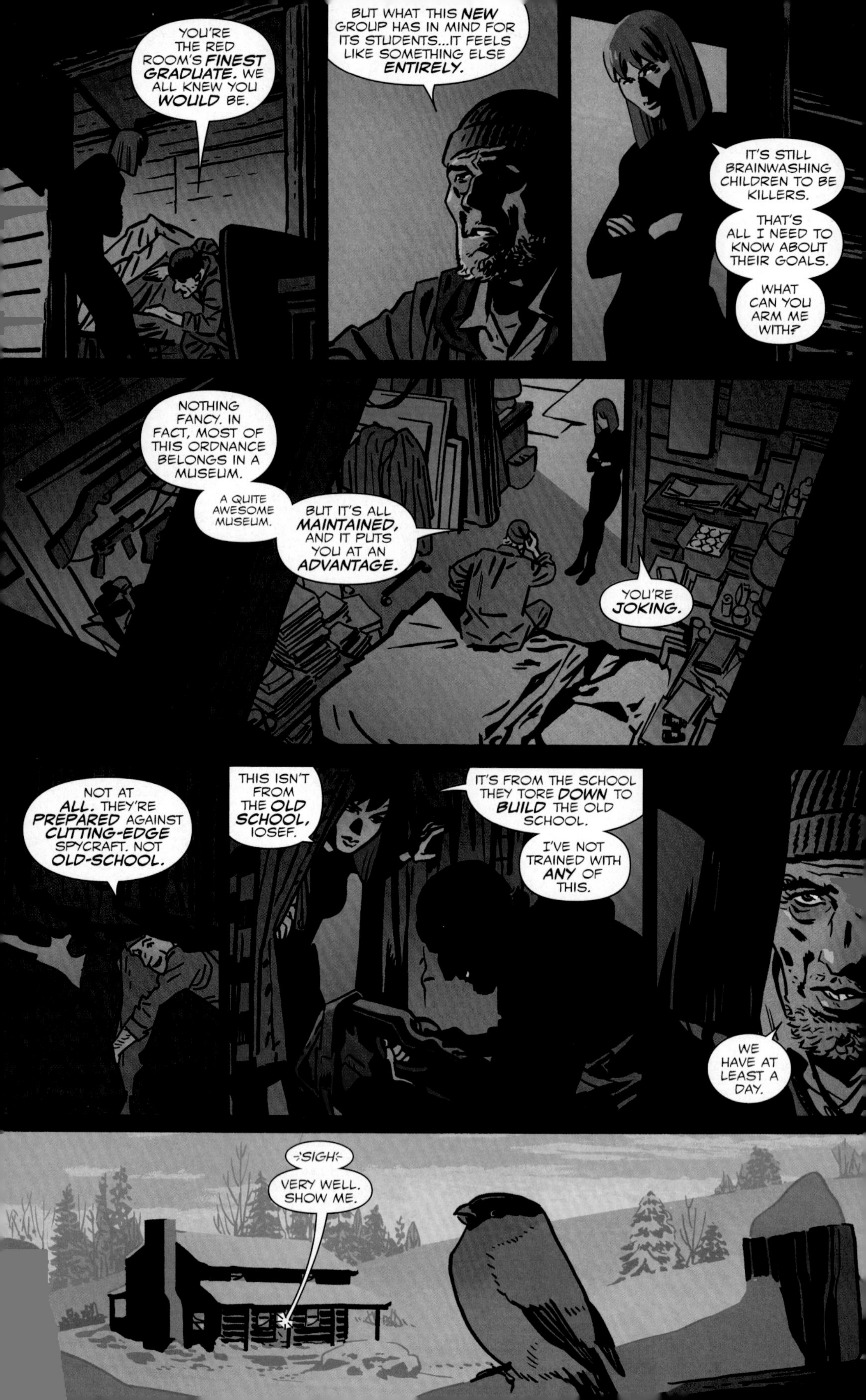
YOU'RE THE RED ROOM'S FINEST GRADUATE. WE ALL KNEW YOU WOULD BE.
BUT WHAT THIS NEW GROUP HAS IN MIND FOR ITS STUDENTS...IT FEELS LIKE SOMETHING ELSE ENTIRELY.
IT'S STILL BRAINWASHING CHILDREN TO BE KILLERS.
THAT'S ALL I NEED TO KNOW ABOUT THEIR GOALS.
WHAT CAN YOU ARM ME WITH?
NOTHING FANCY. IN FACT, MOST OF THIS ORDNANCE BELONGS IN A MUSEUM.
A QUITE AWESOME MUSEUM.
BUT IT'S ALL MAINTAINED, AND IT PUTS YOU AT AN ADVANTAGE.
YOU'RE JOKING.
NOT AT ALL. THEY'RE PREPARED AGAINST CUTTING-EDGE SPYCRAFT. NOT OLD-SCHOOL.
THIS ISN'T FROM THE OLD SCHOOL, IOSEF.
IT'S FROM THE SCHOOL THEY TORE DOWN TO BUILD THE OLD SCHOOL.
I'VE NOT TRAINED WITH ANY OF THIS.
WE HAVE AT LEAST A DAY.
SIGH
VERY WELL. SHOW ME.

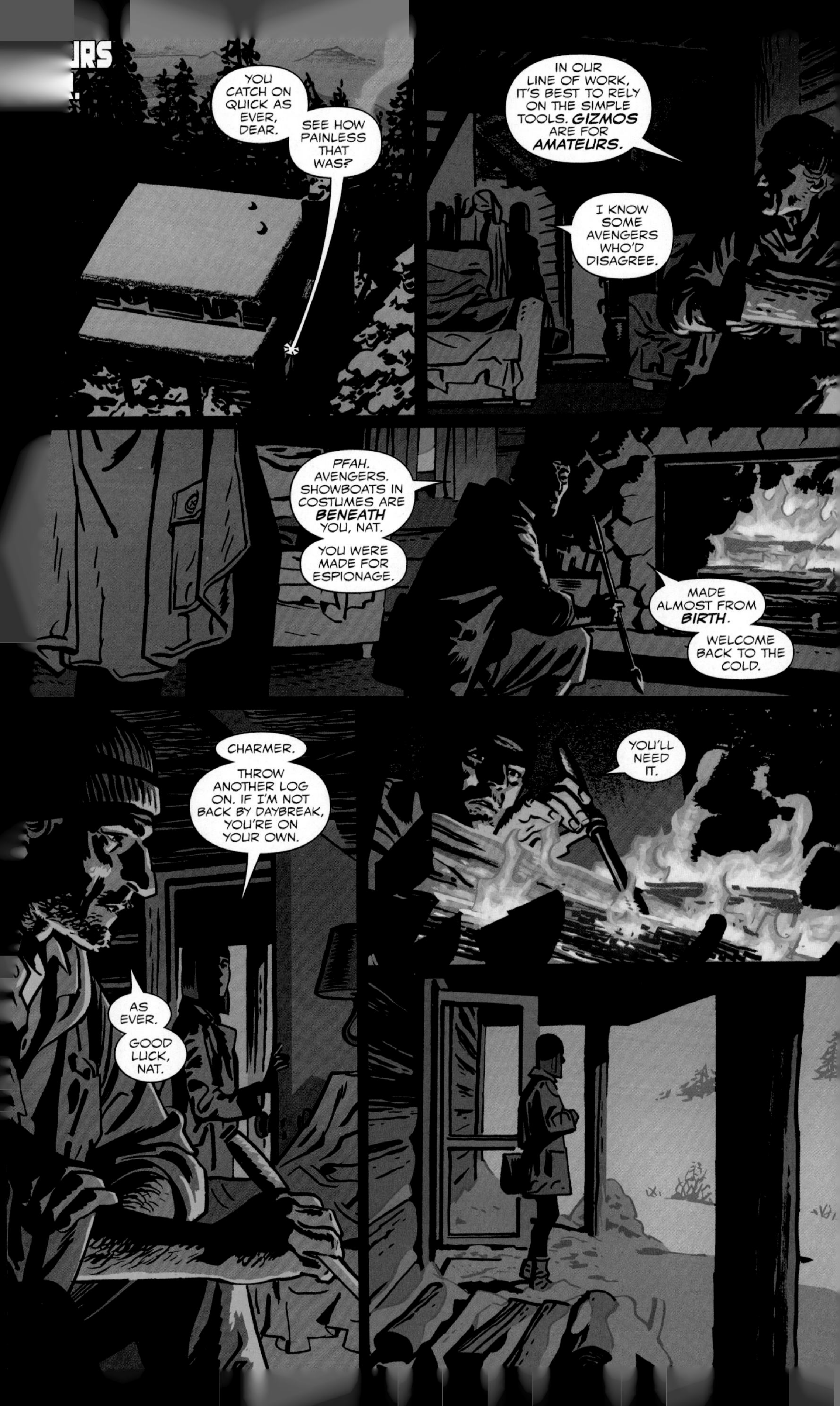
YOU CATCH ON QUICK AS EVER, DEAR.
SEE HOW PAINLESS THAT WAS?
IN OUR LINE OF WORK, IT'S BEST TO RELY ON THE SIMPLE TOOLS. GIZMOS ARE FOR AMATEURS.
I KNOW SOME AVENGERS WHO'D DISAGREE.
PFAH. AVENGERS. SHOWBOATS IN COSTUMES ARE BENEATH YOU, NAT.
YOU WERE MADE FOR ESPIONAGE.
MADE ALMOST FROM BIRTH.
WELCOME BACK TO THE COLD.
CHARMER.
THROW ANOTHER LOG ON. IF I'M NOT BACK BY DAYBREAK, YOU'RE ON YOUR OWN.
AS EVER.
GOOD LUCK, NAT.
YOU'LL NEED IT.

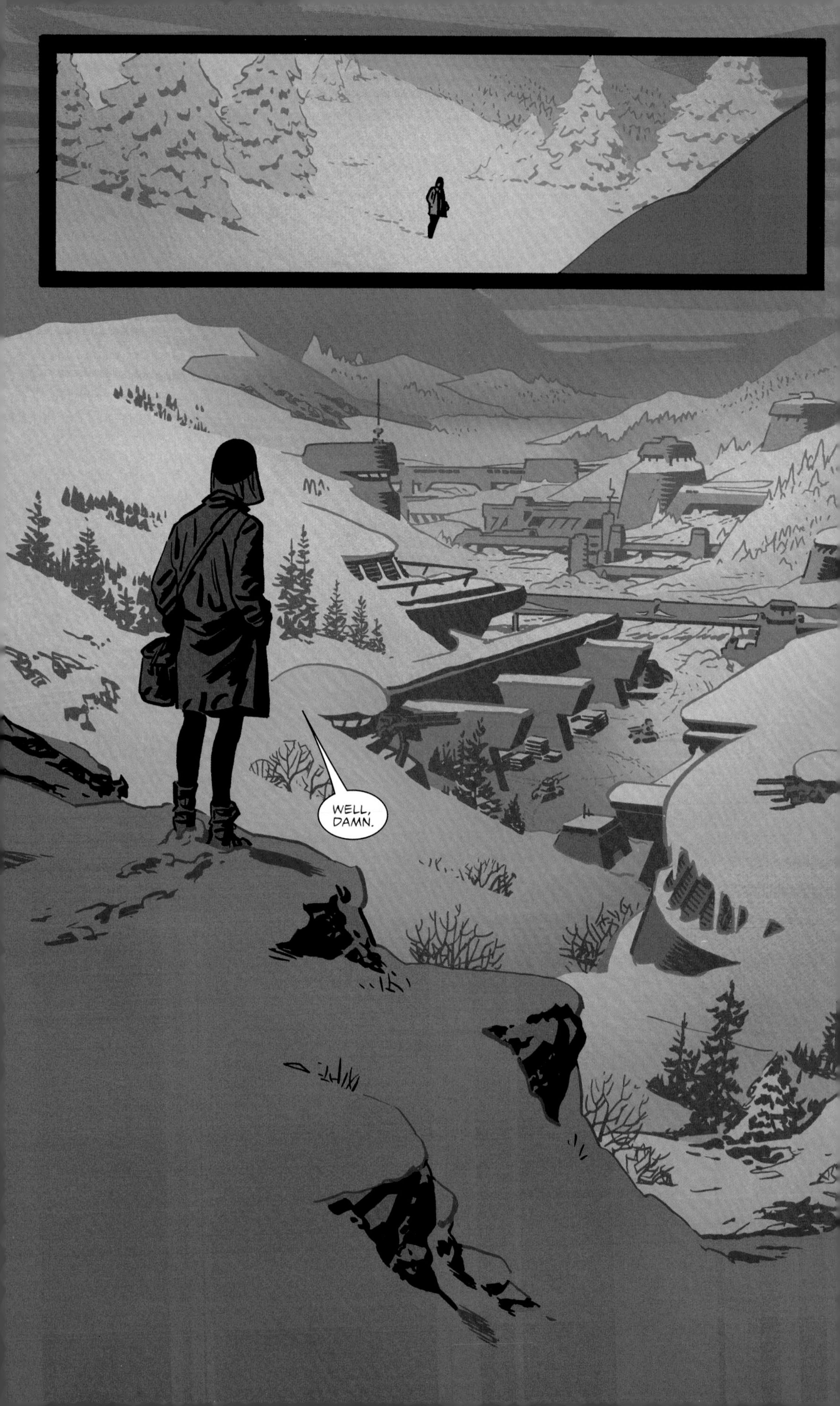
WELL, DAMN.

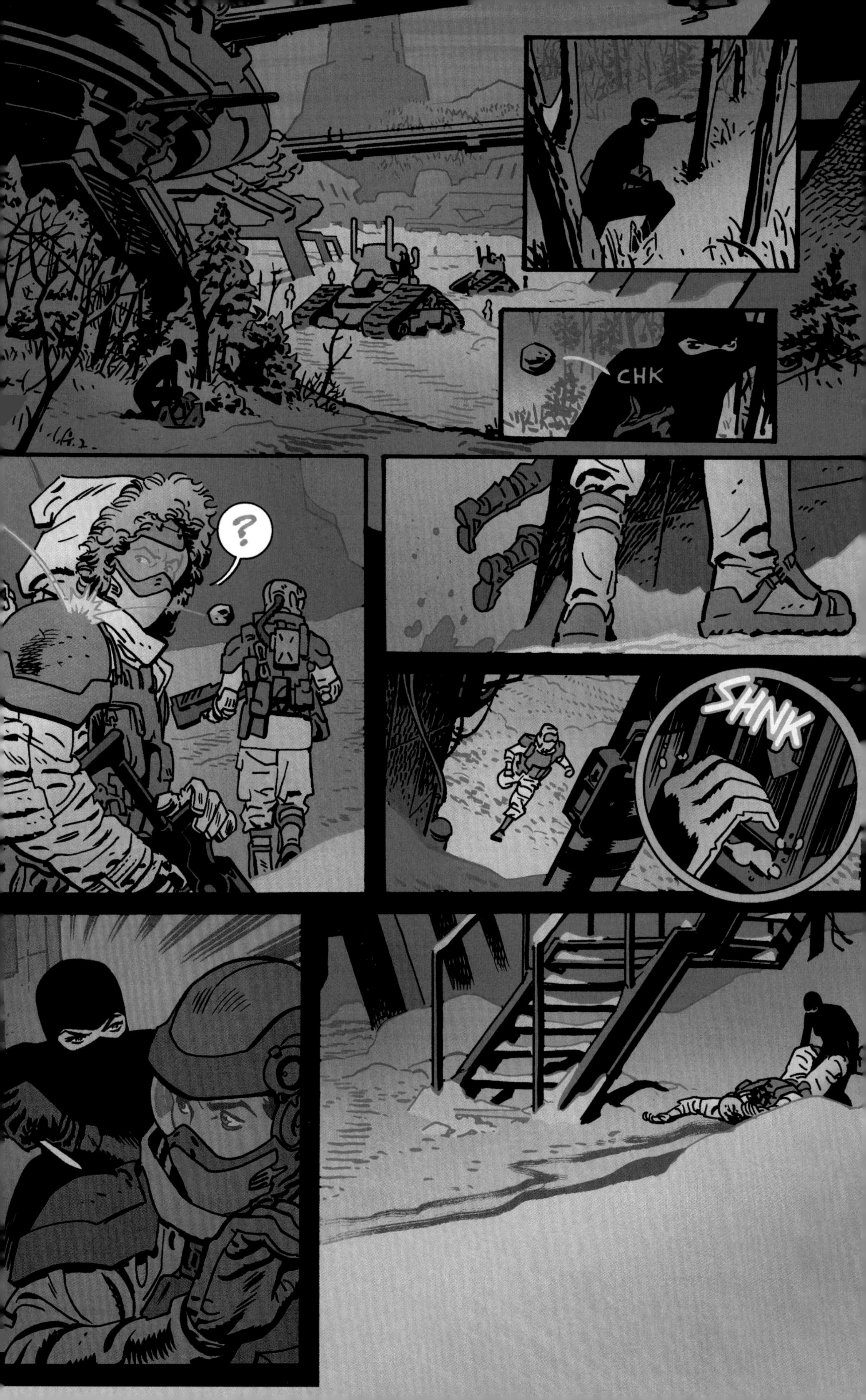
CHK
?
SHNK

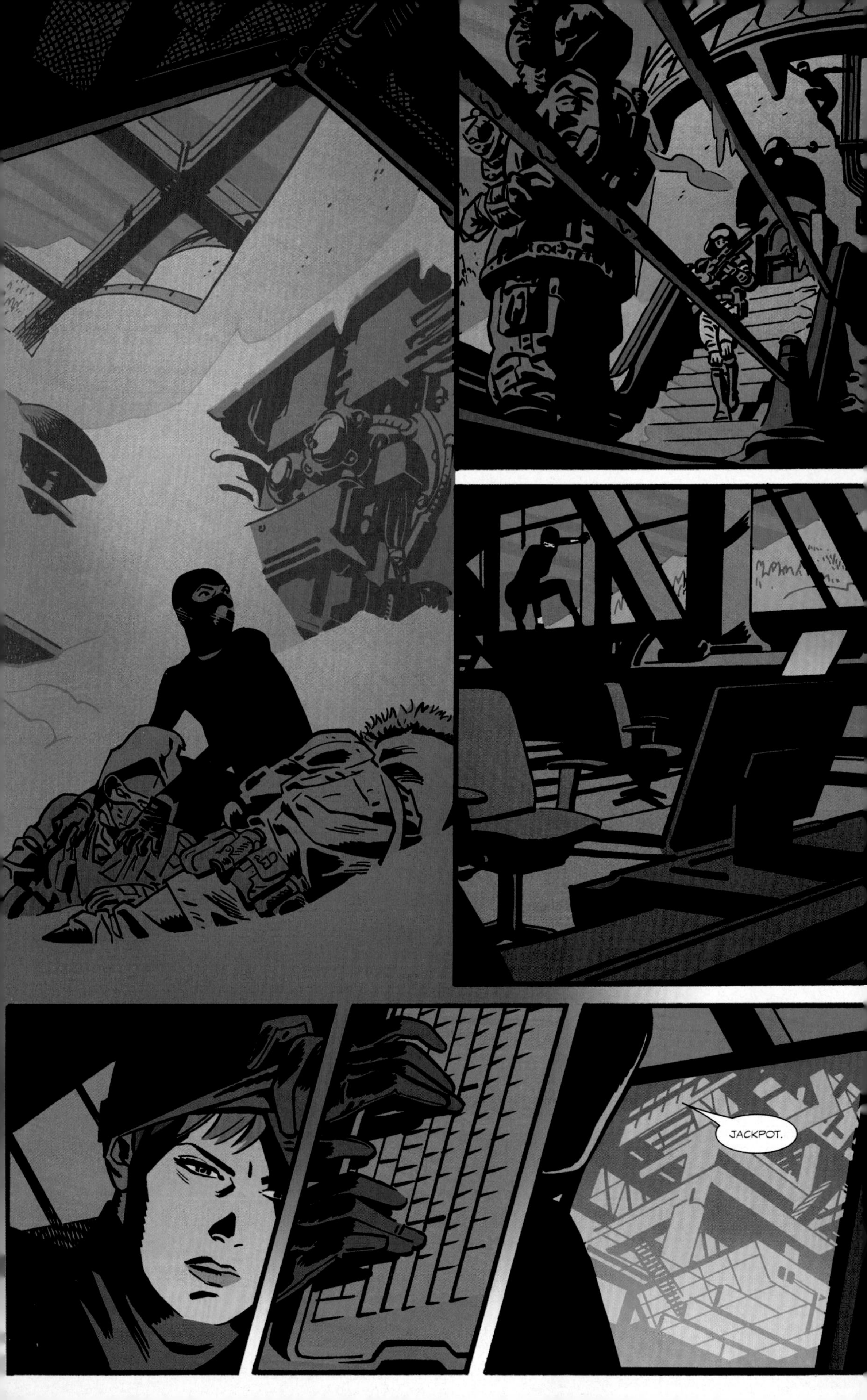
JACKPOT.

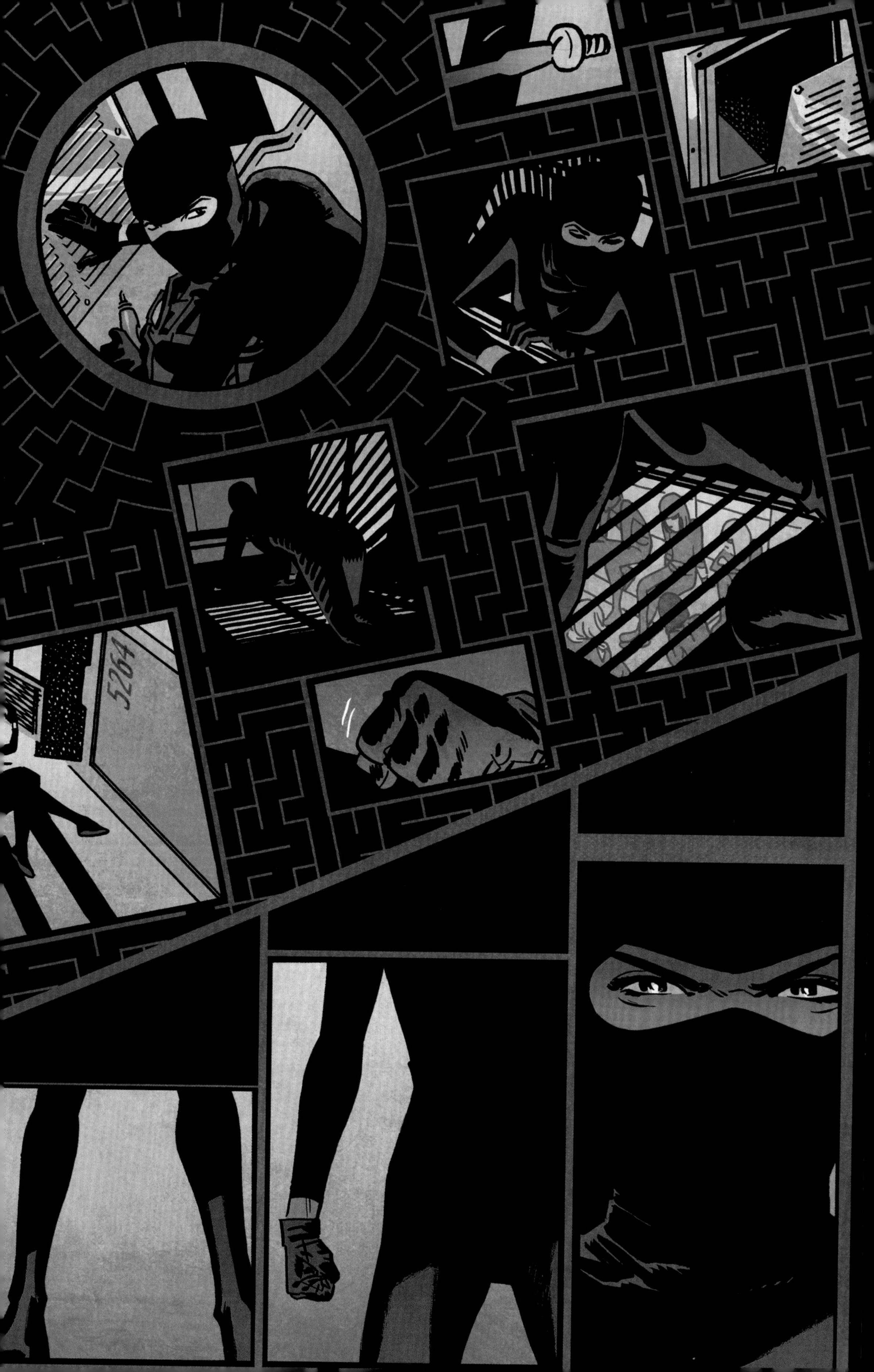
5264

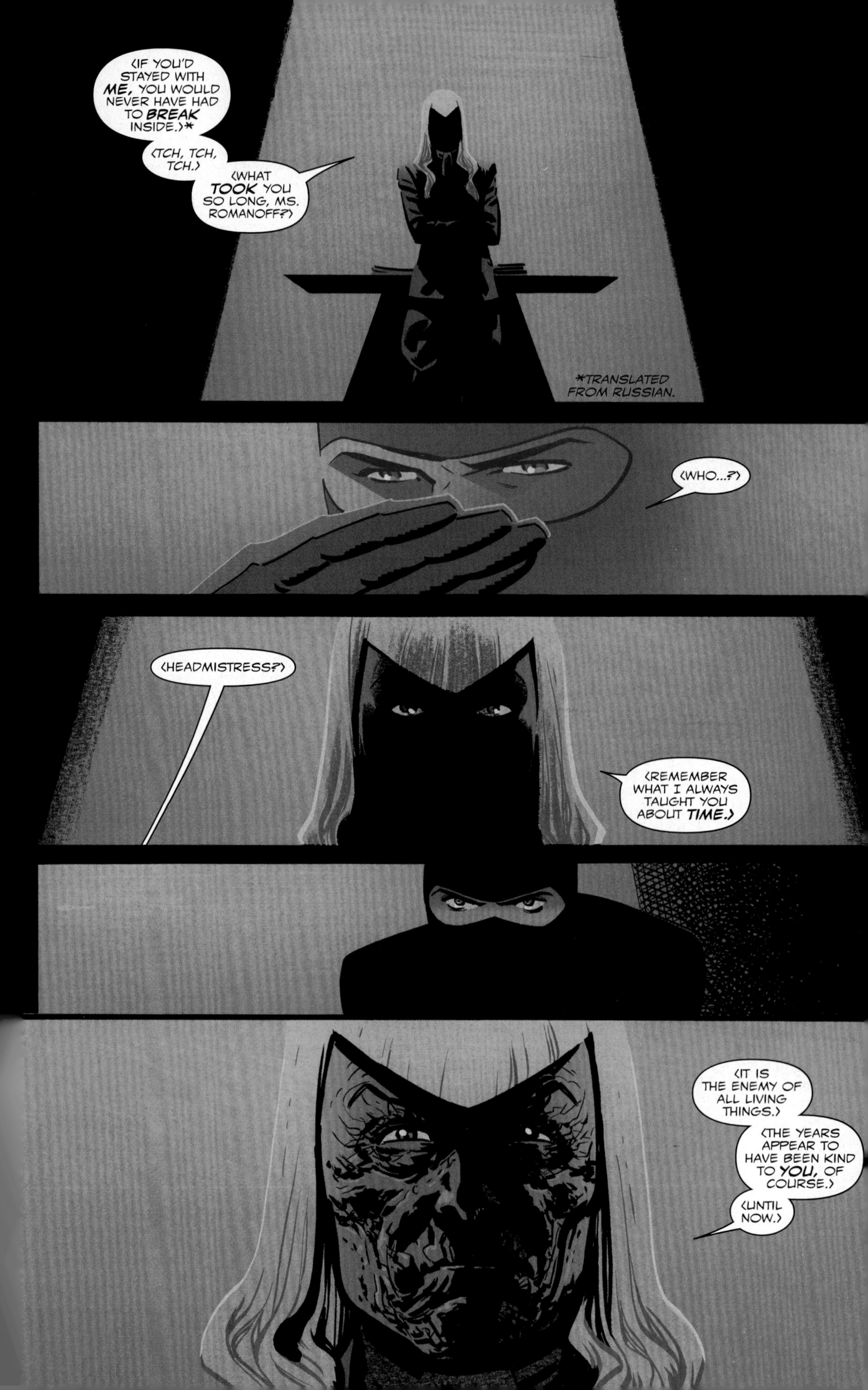

‹IF YOU'D STAYED WITH ME, YOU WOULD NEVER HAVE HAD TO BREAK INSIDE.›*
‹TCH, TCH, TCH.›
‹WHAT TOOK YOU SO LONG, MS. ROMANOFF?›
*TRANSLATED FROM RUSSIAN.
‹WHO...?›
‹HEADMISTRESS?›
‹REMEMBER WHAT I ALWAYS TAUGHT YOU ABOUT TIME.›
‹IT IS THE ENEMY OF ALL LIVING THINGS.›
‹THE YEARS APPEAR TO HAVE BEEN KIND TO YOU, OF COURSE.›
‹UNTIL NOW.›

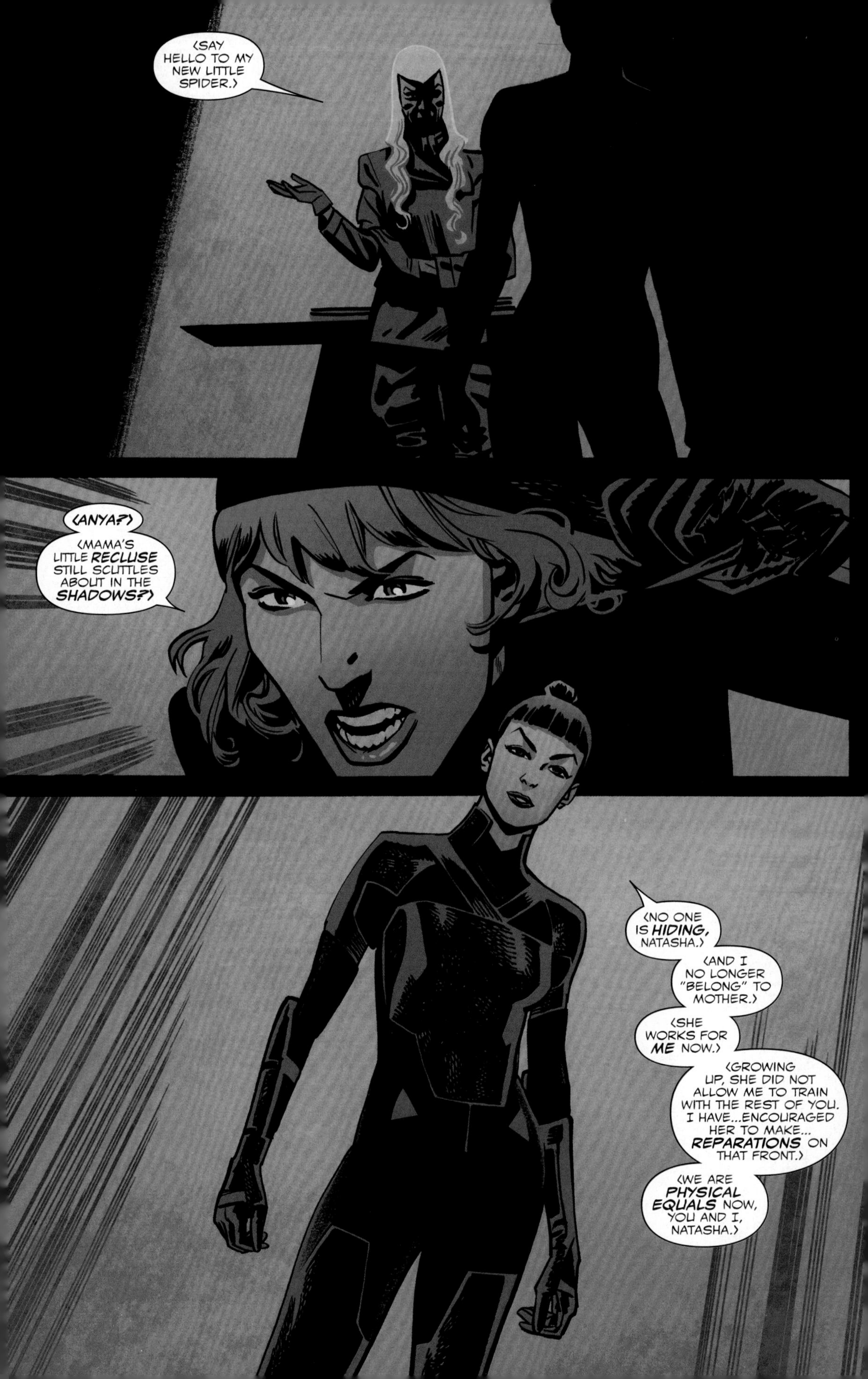
<SAY HELLO TO MY NEW LITTLE SPIDER.>
<ANYA?>
<MAMA'S LITTLE RECLUSE STILL SCUTTLES ABOUT IN THE SHADOWS?>
<NO ONE IS HIDING, NATASHA.>
<AND I NO LONGER "BELONG" TO MOTHER.>
<SHE WORKS FOR ME NOW.>
<GROWING UP, SHE DID NOT ALLOW ME TO TRAIN WITH THE REST OF YOU. I HAVE...ENCOURAGED HER TO MAKE... REPARATIONS ON THAT FRONT.>
<WE ARE PHYSICAL EQUALS NOW, YOU AND I, NATASHA.>

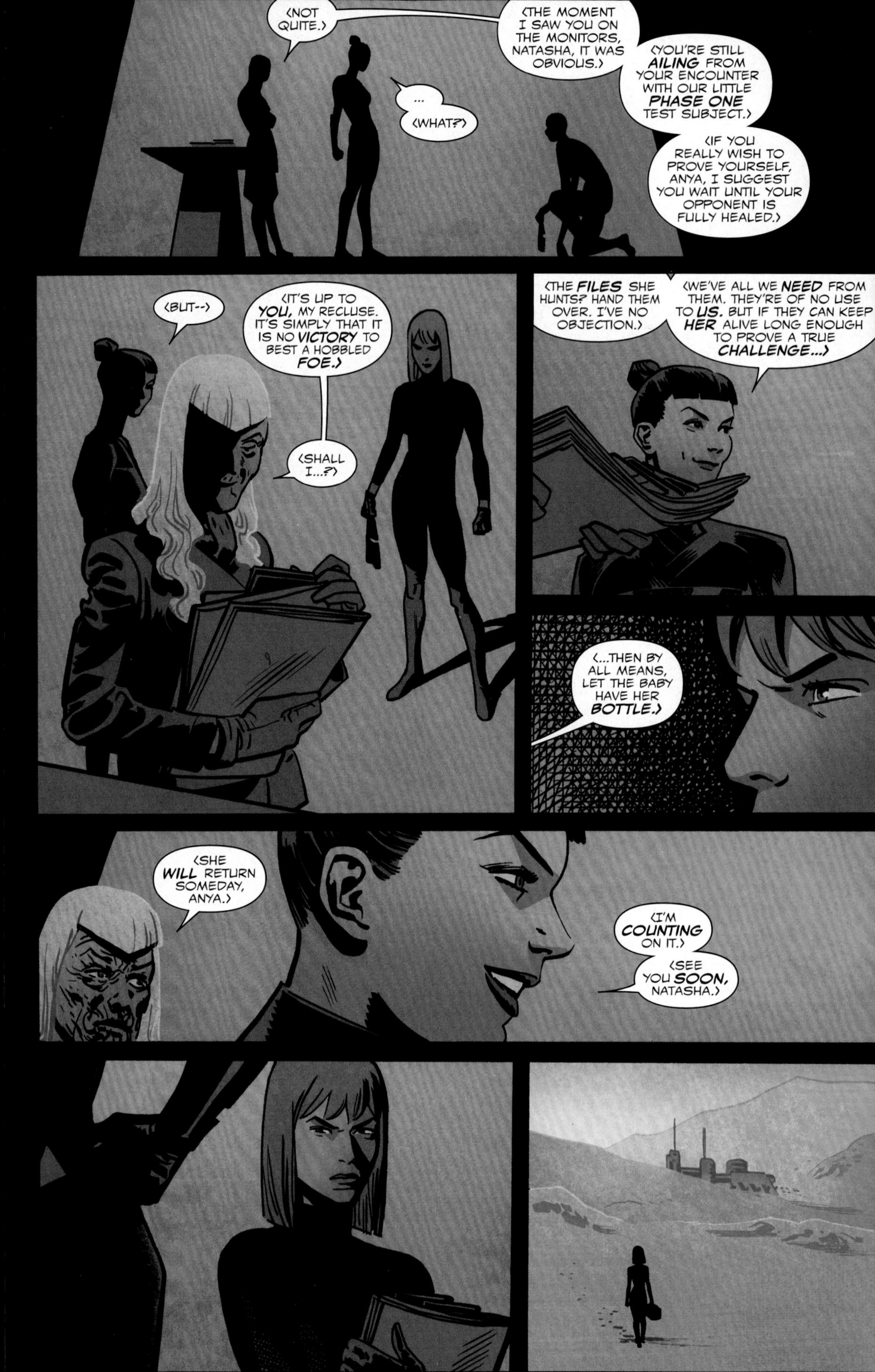

‹NOT QUITE.›
‹THE MOMENT I SAW YOU ON THE MONITORS, NATASHA, IT WAS OBVIOUS.›
... ‹WHAT?›
‹YOU'RE STILL AILING FROM YOUR ENCOUNTER WITH OUR LITTLE PHASE ONE TEST SUBJECT.›
‹IF YOU REALLY WISH TO PROVE YOURSELF, ANYA, I SUGGEST YOU WAIT UNTIL YOUR OPPONENT IS FULLY HEALED.›
‹BUT--›
‹IT'S UP TO YOU, MY RECLUSE. IT'S SIMPLY THAT IT IS NO VICTORY TO BEST A HOBBLED FOE.›
‹SHALL I...?›
‹THE FILES SHE HUNTS? HAND THEM OVER. I'VE NO OBJECTION.›
‹WE'VE ALL WE NEED FROM THEM. THEY'RE OF NO USE TO US. BUT IF THEY CAN KEEP HER ALIVE LONG ENOUGH TO PROVE A TRUE CHALLENGE...›
‹...THEN BY ALL MEANS, LET THE BABY HAVE HER BOTTLE.›
‹SHE WILL RETURN SOMEDAY, ANYA.›
‹I'M COUNTING ON IT.›
‹SEE YOU SOON, NATASHA.›

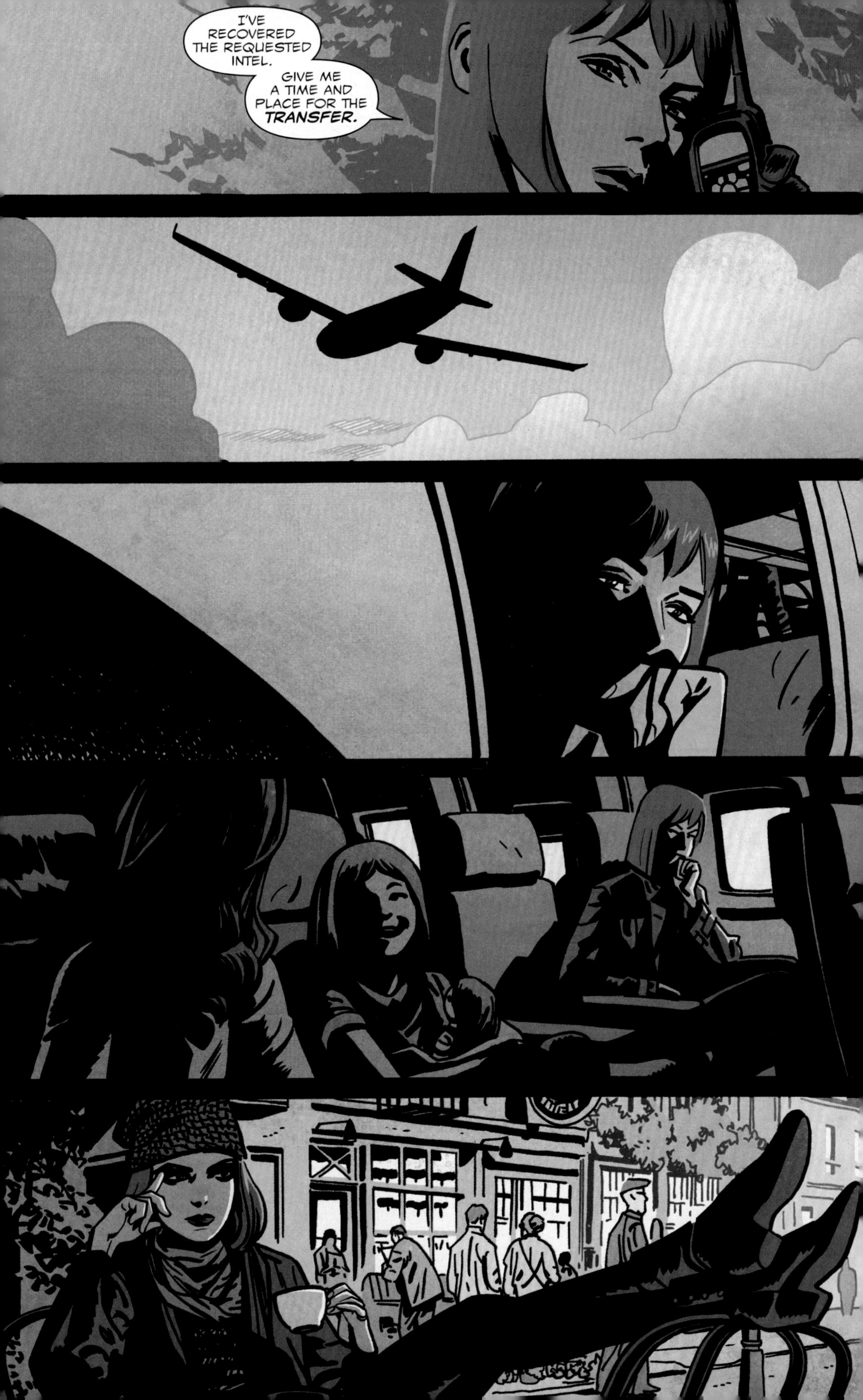
I'VE RECOVERED THE REQUESTED INTEL.
GIVE ME A TIME AND PLACE FOR THE *TRANSFER.*

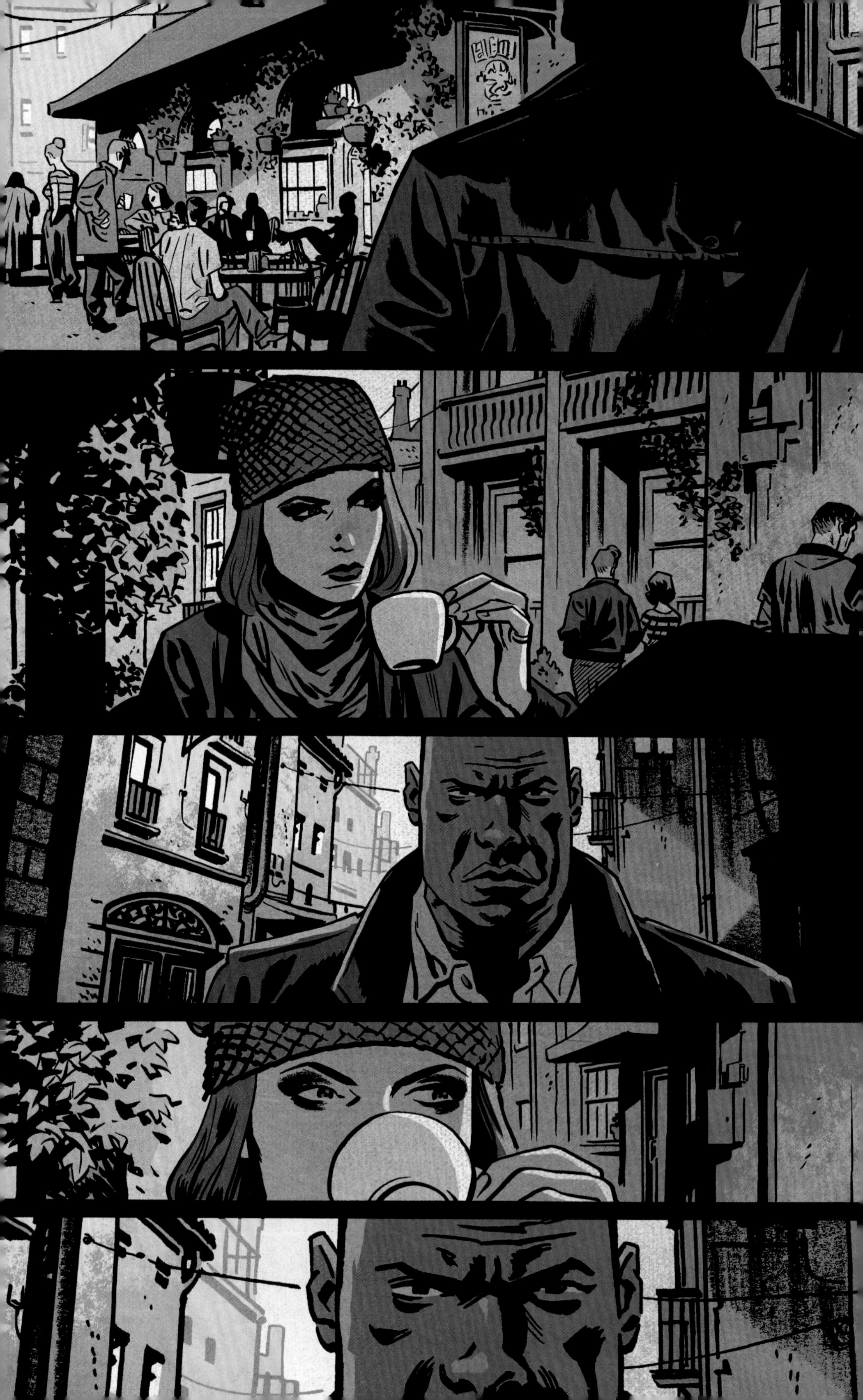

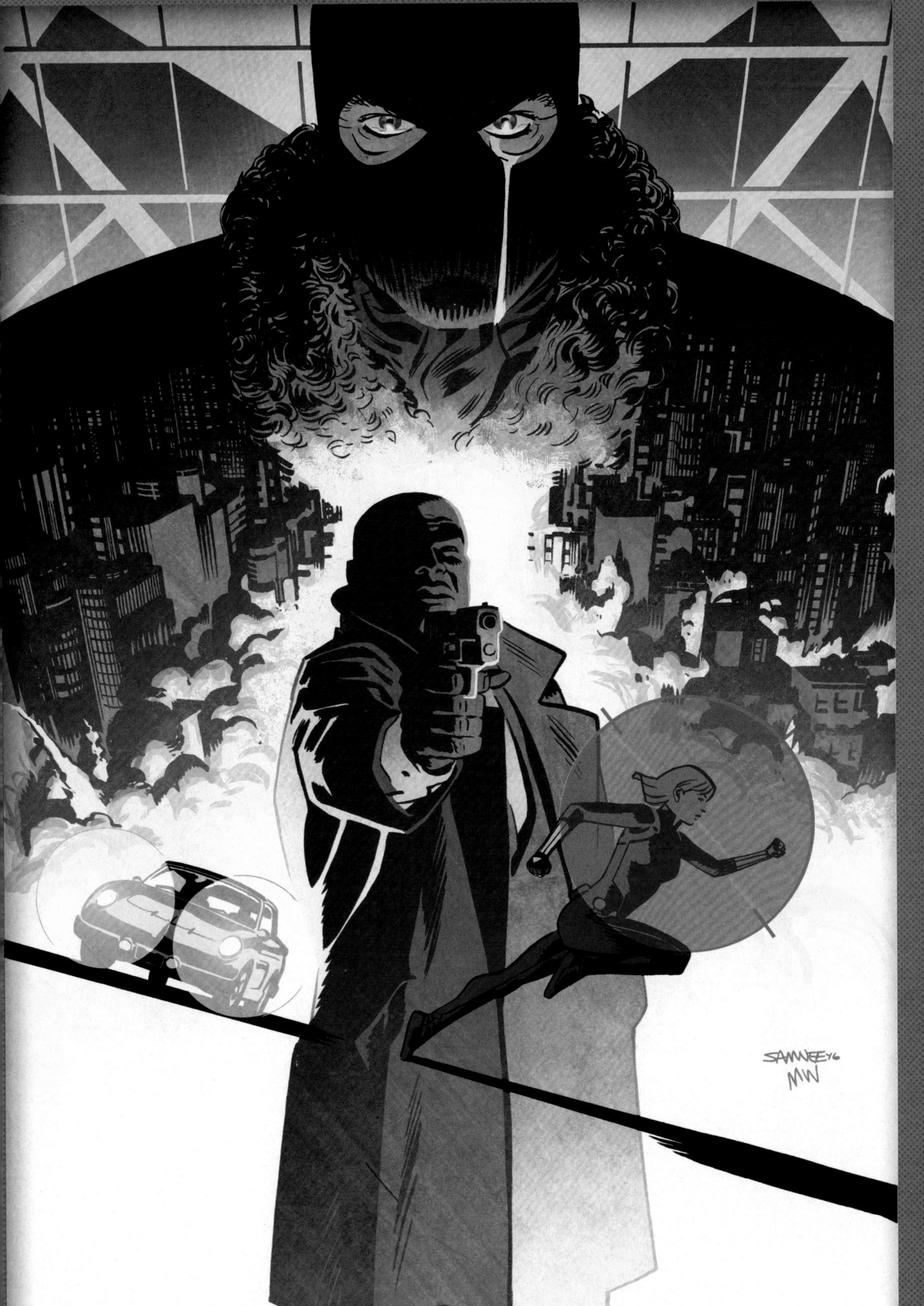
SAMNEE'16
MW

5

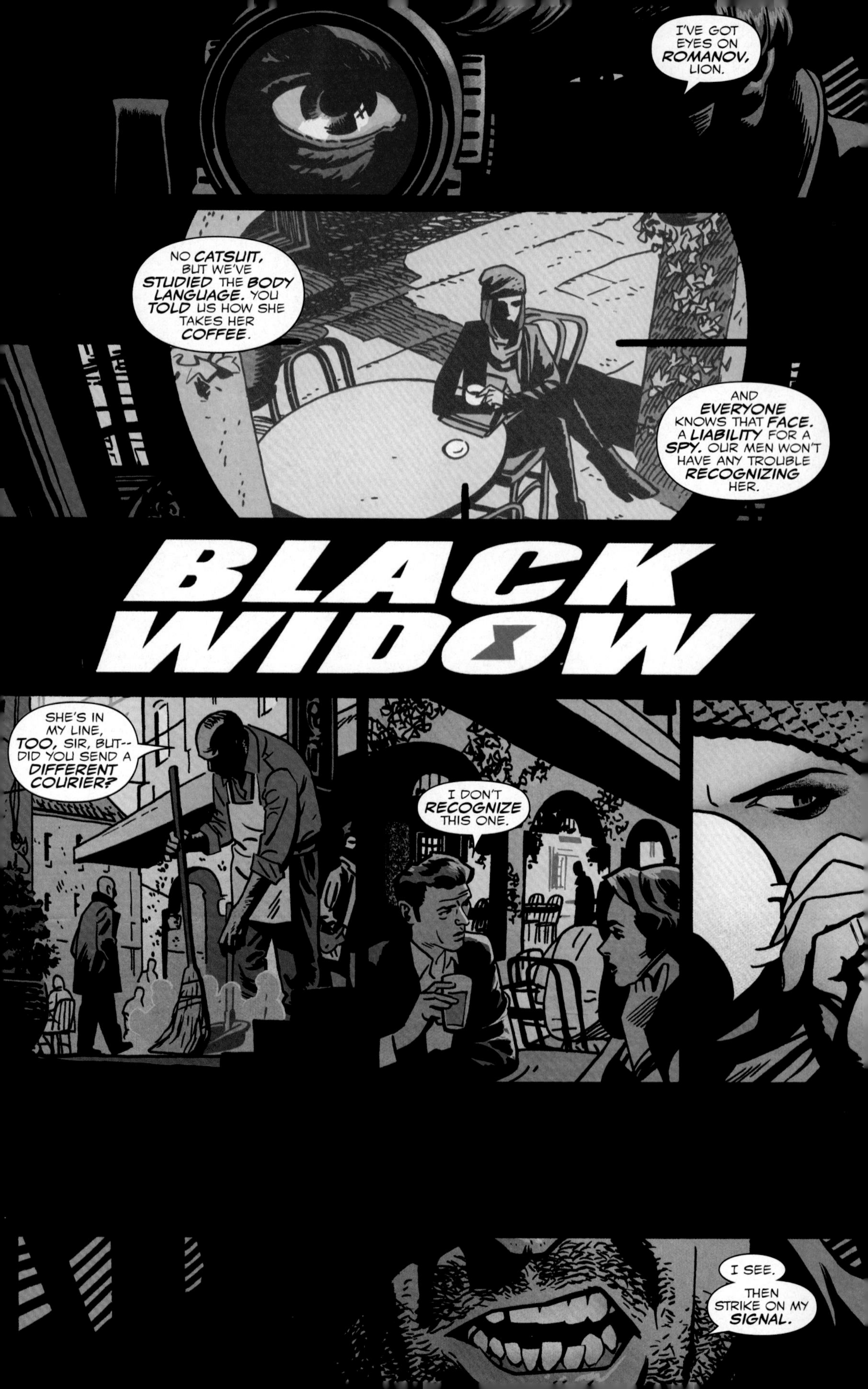
I'VE GOT EYES ON ROMANOV, LION.
NO CATSUIT, BUT WE'VE STUDIED THE BODY LANGUAGE. YOU TOLD US HOW SHE TAKES HER COFFEE.
AND EVERYONE KNOWS THAT FACE. A LIABILITY FOR A SPY. OUR MEN WON'T HAVE ANY TROUBLE RECOGNIZING HER.
BLACK WIDOW
SHE'S IN MY LINE, TOO, SIR, BUT-- DID YOU SEND A DIFFERENT COURIER?
I DON'T RECOGNIZE THIS ONE.
I SEE.
THEN STRIKE ON MY SIGNAL.

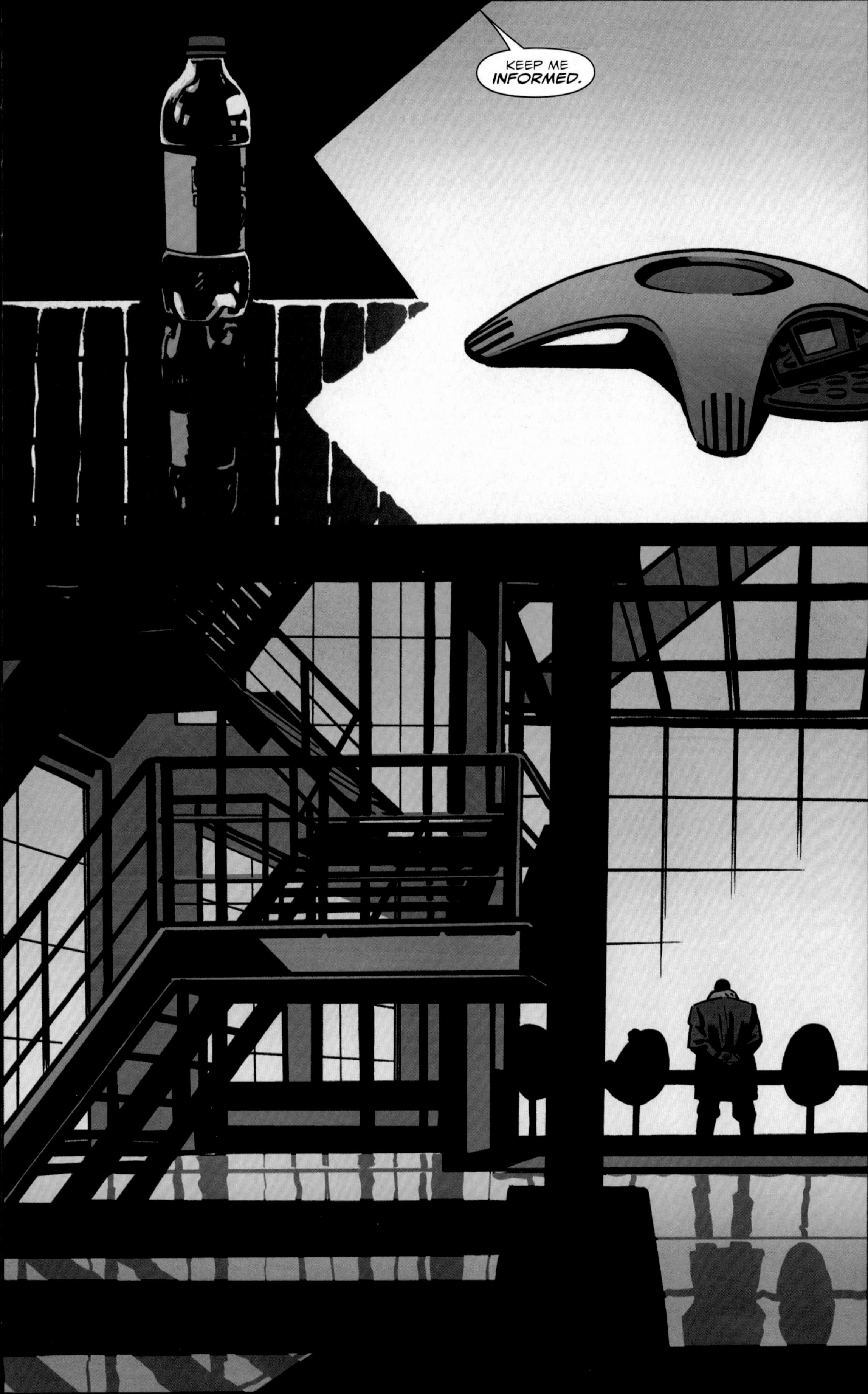
KEEP ME INFORMED.

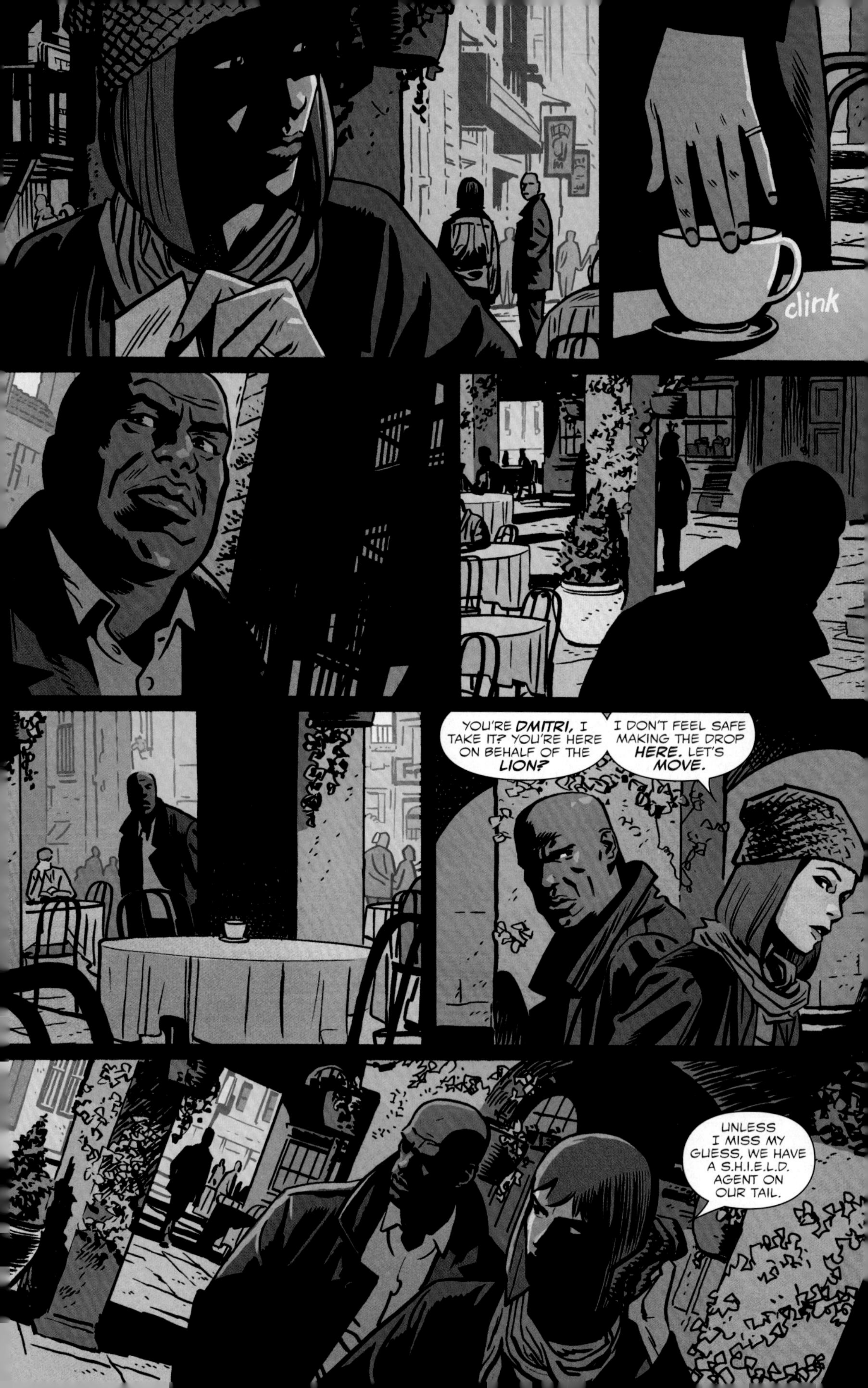

clink
YOU'RE DMITRI, I TAKE IT? YOU'RE HERE ON BEHALF OF THE LION?
I DON'T FEEL SAFE MAKING THE DROP HERE. LET'S MOVE.
UNLESS I MISS MY GUESS, WE HAVE A S.H.I.E.L.D. AGENT ON OUR TAIL.

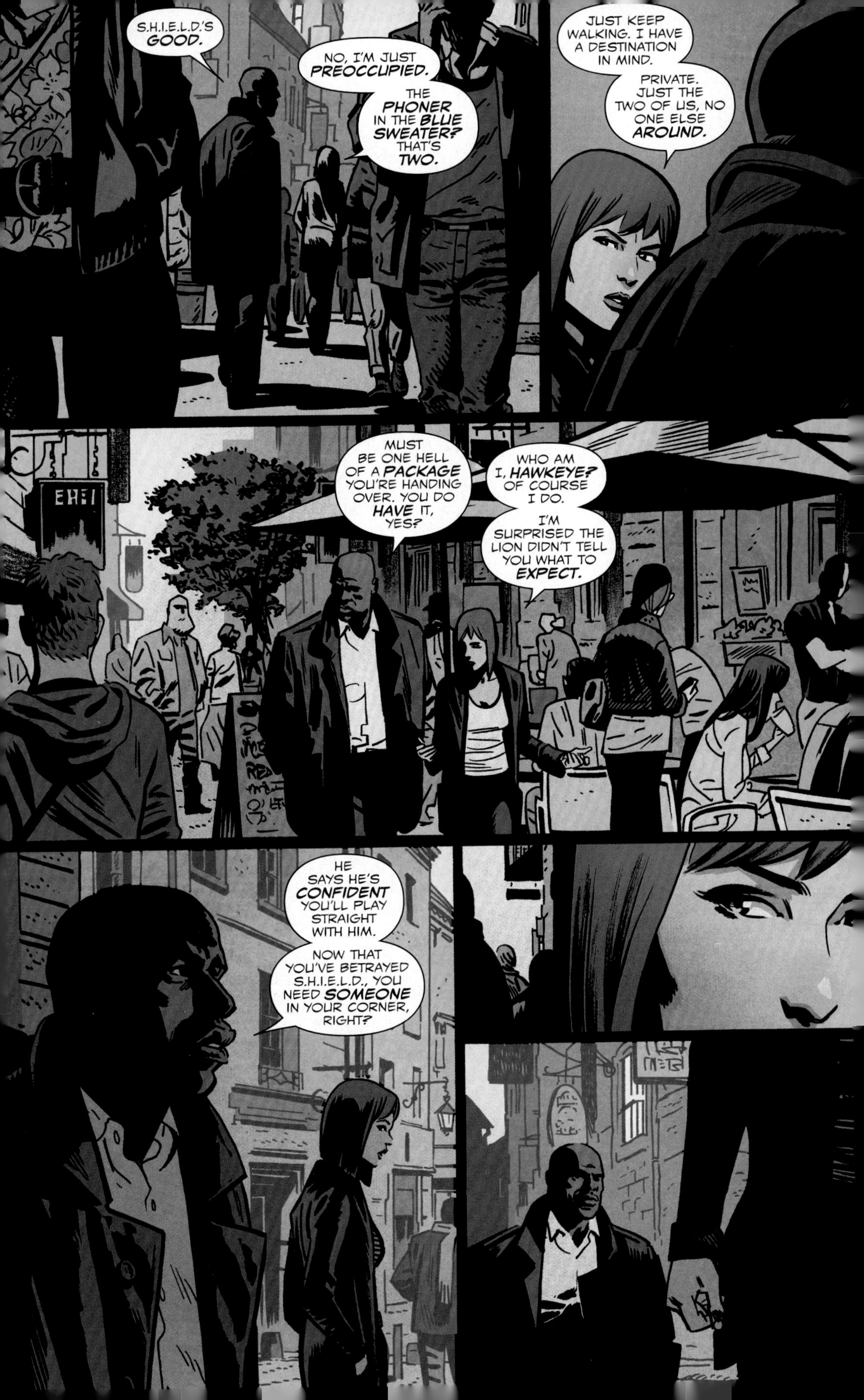
S.H.I.E.L.D.'S GOOD.
NO, I'M JUST PREOCCUPIED.
THE PHONER IN THE BLUE SWEATER? THAT'S TWO.
JUST KEEP WALKING. I HAVE A DESTINATION IN MIND.
PRIVATE. JUST THE TWO OF US, NO ONE ELSE AROUND.
MUST BE ONE HELL OF A PACKAGE YOU'RE HANDING OVER. YOU DO HAVE IT, YES?
WHO AM I, HAWKEYE? OF COURSE I DO.
I'M SURPRISED THE LION DIDN'T TELL YOU WHAT TO EXPECT.
HE SAYS HE'S CONFIDENT YOU'LL PLAY STRAIGHT WITH HIM.
NOW THAT YOU'VE BETRAYED S.H.I.E.L.D., YOU NEED SOMEONE IN YOUR CORNER, RIGHT?

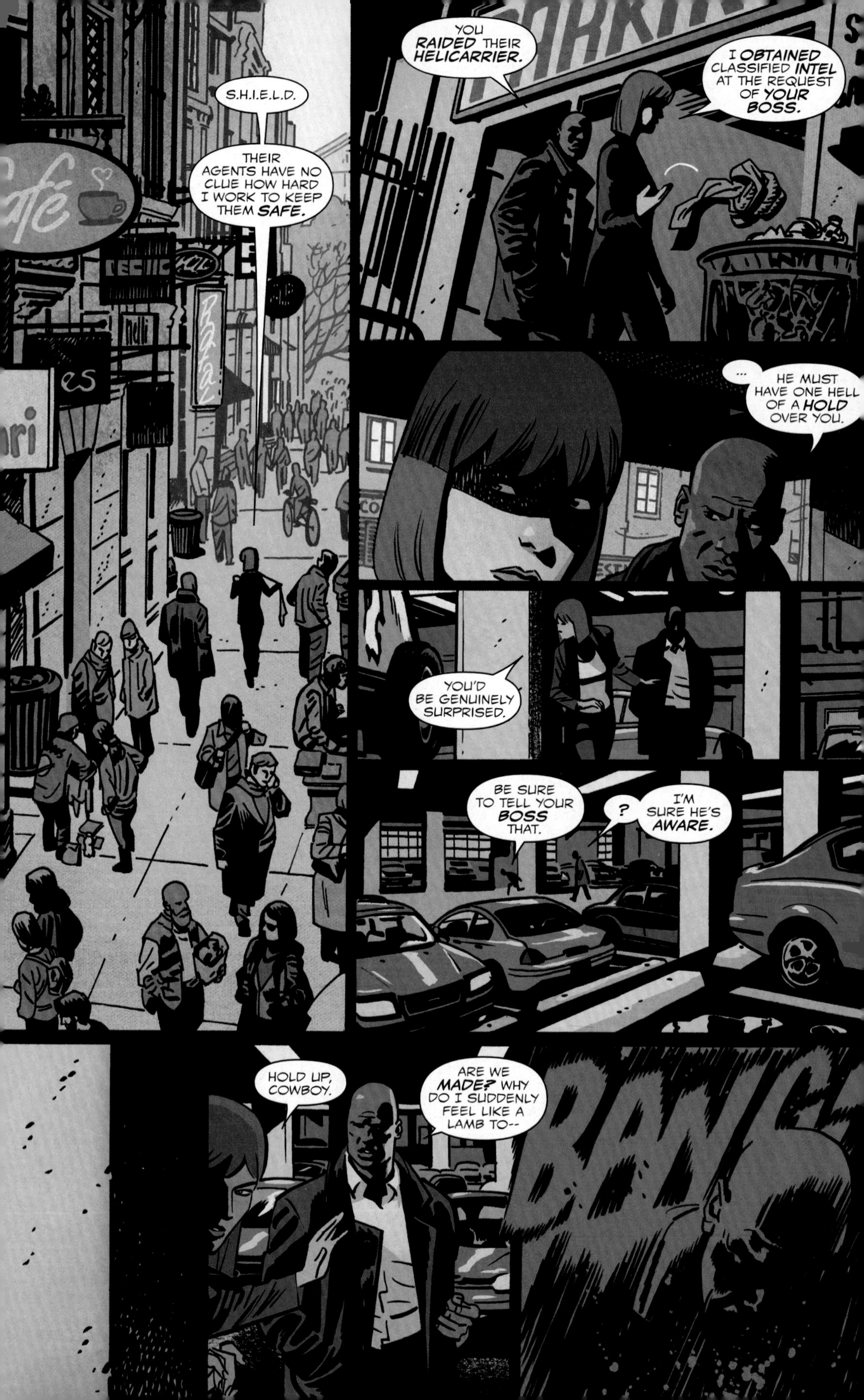
S.H.I.E.L.D.
THEIR AGENTS HAVE NO CLUE HOW HARD I WORK TO KEEP THEM SAFE.
YOU RAIDED THEIR HELICARRIER.
I OBTAINED CLASSIFIED INTEL AT THE REQUEST OF YOUR BOSS.
...
HE MUST HAVE ONE HELL OF A HOLD OVER YOU.
YOU'D BE GENUINELY SURPRISED.
BE SURE TO TELL YOUR BOSS THAT.
?
I'M SURE HE'S AWARE.
HOLD UP, COWBOY.
ARE WE MADE? WHY DO I SUDDENLY FEEL LIKE A LAMB TO--
BANG

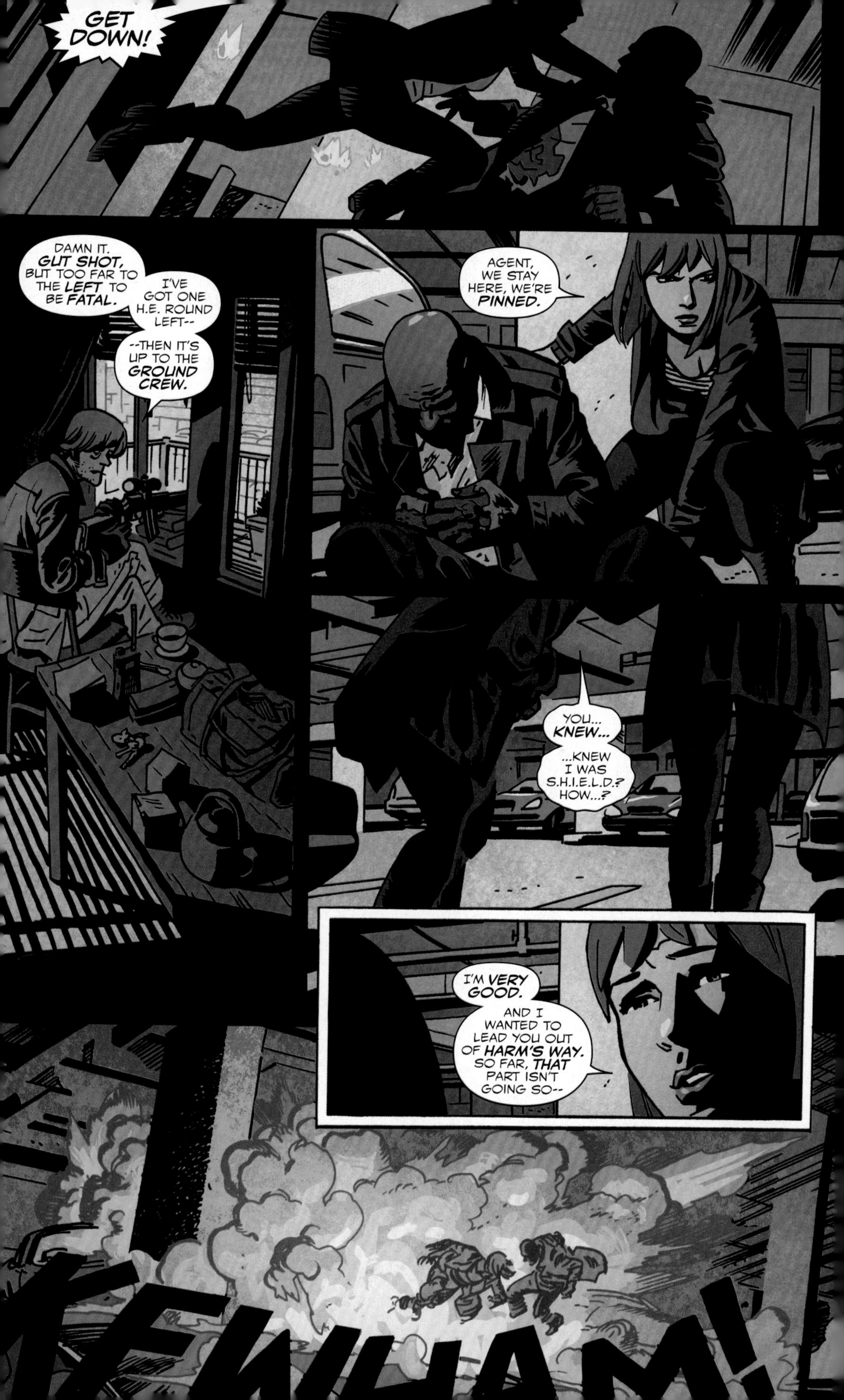
GET DOWN!
DAMN IT. GUT SHOT, BUT TOO FAR TO THE LEFT TO BE FATAL.
I'VE GOT ONE H.E. ROUND LEFT--
--THEN IT'S UP TO THE GROUND CREW.
AGENT, WE STAY HERE, WE'RE PINNED.
YOU... KNEW...
...KNEW I WAS S.H.I.E.L.D.? HOW...?
I'M VERY GOOD.
AND I WANTED TO LEAD YOU OUT OF HARM'S WAY. SO FAR, THAT PART ISN'T GOING SO--
KEWHAM!

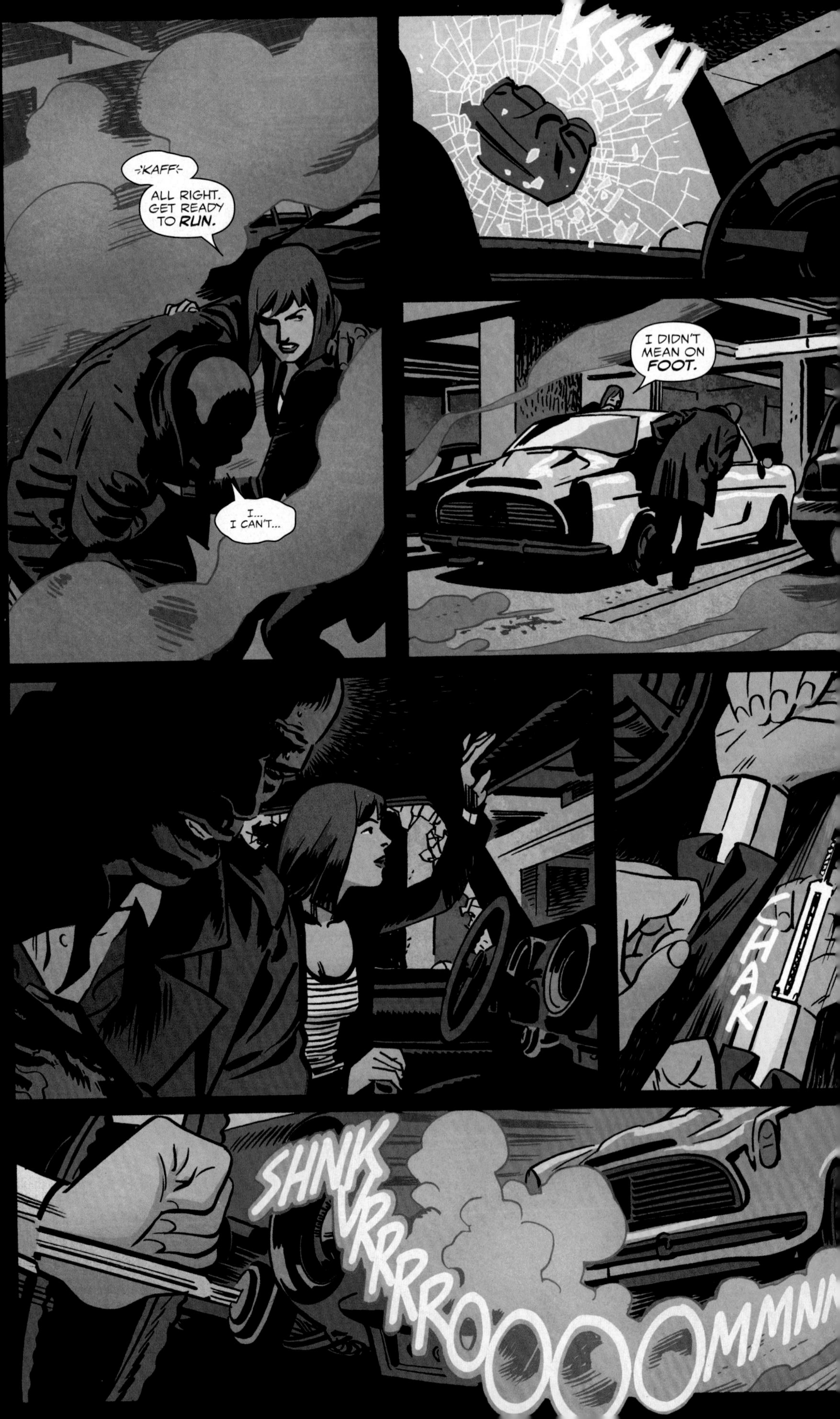

-KAFF-
ALL RIGHT. GET READY TO RUN.
I... I CAN'T...
KSSH
I DIDN'T MEAN ON FOOT.
CHAK
SHNK
URRRROOOOOMMNN

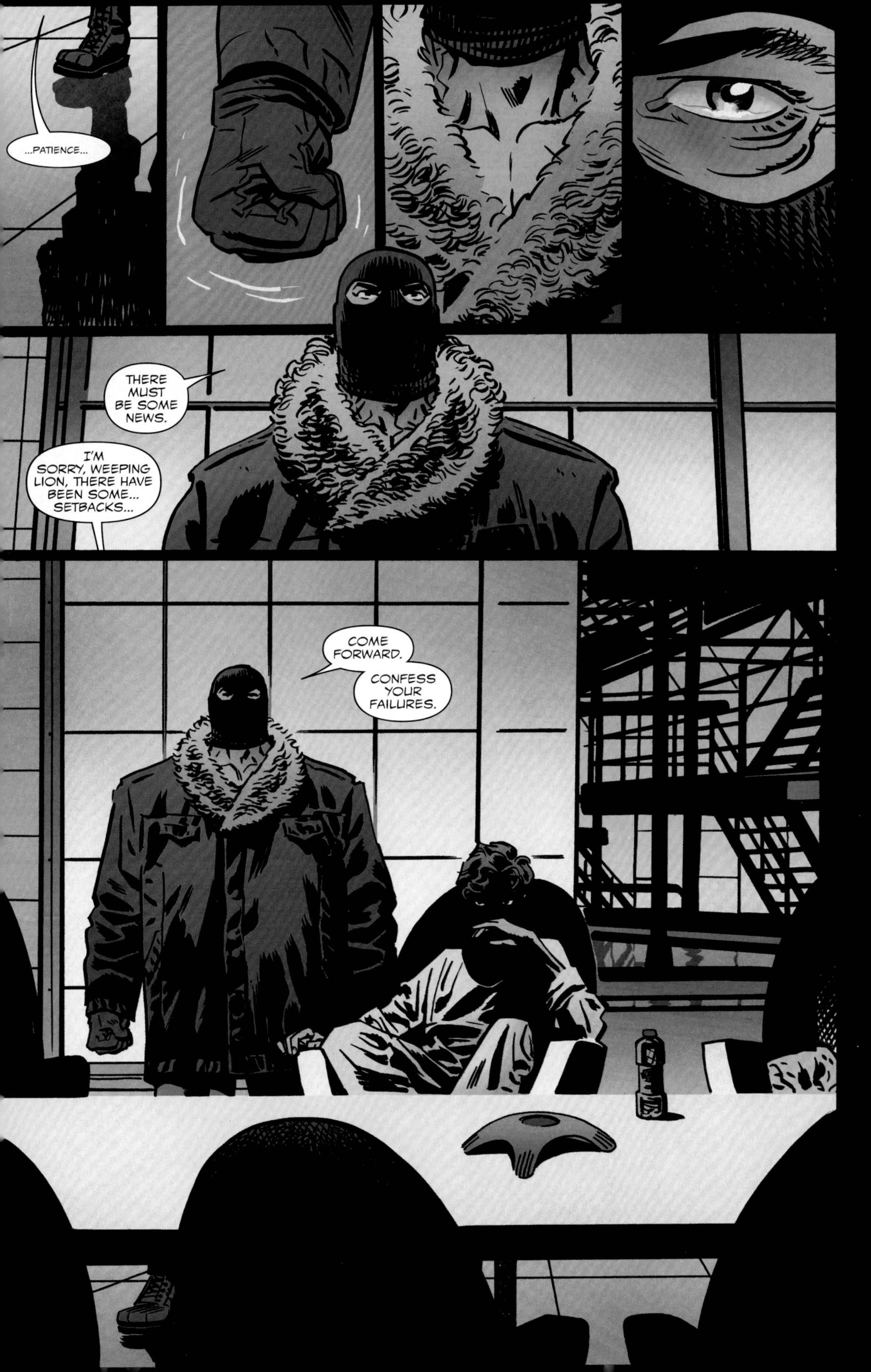
...PATIENCE...
THERE MUST BE SOME NEWS.
I'M SORRY, WEEPING LION, THERE HAVE BEEN SOME... SETBACKS...
COME FORWARD.
CONFESS YOUR FAILURES.

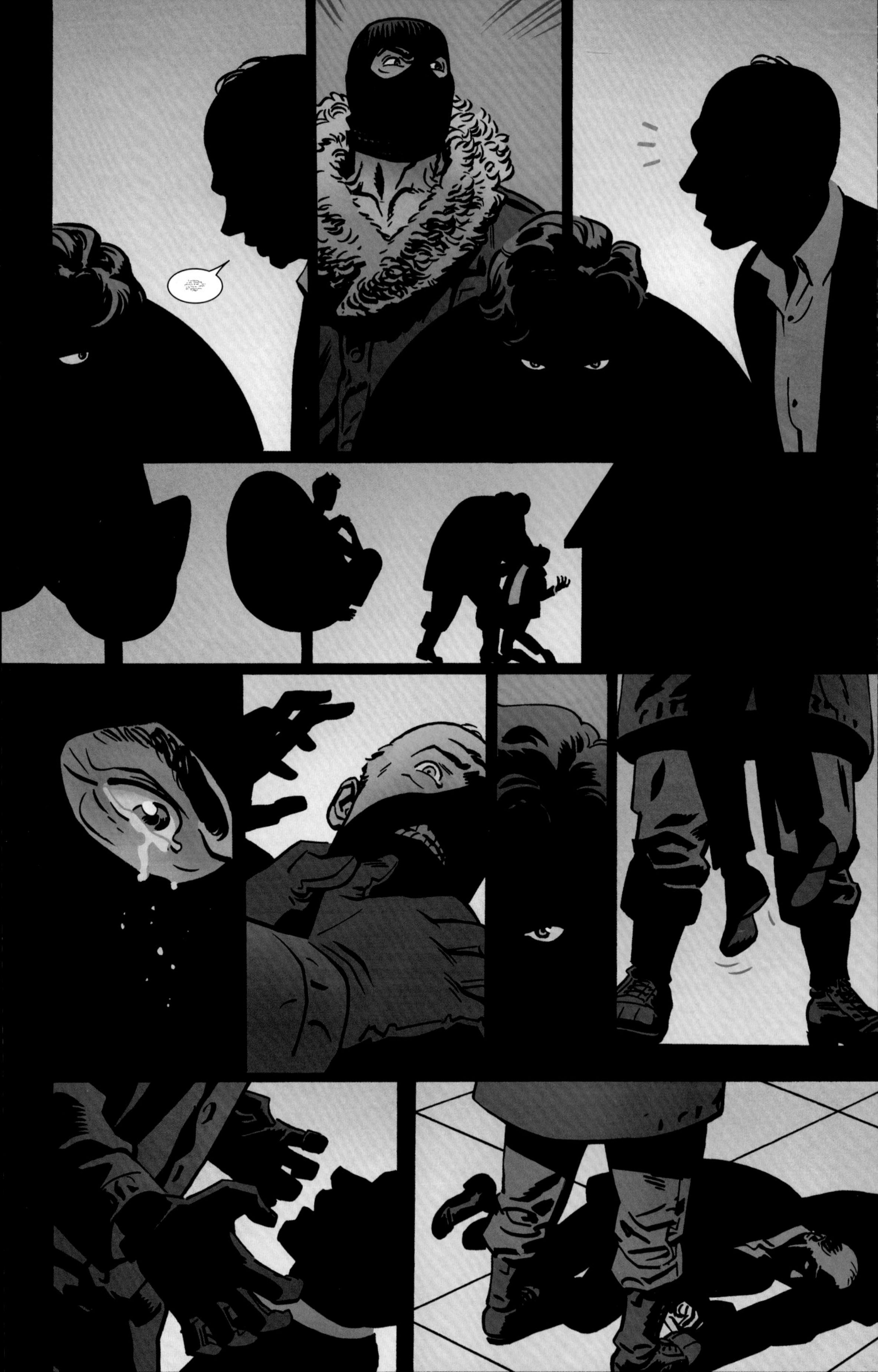

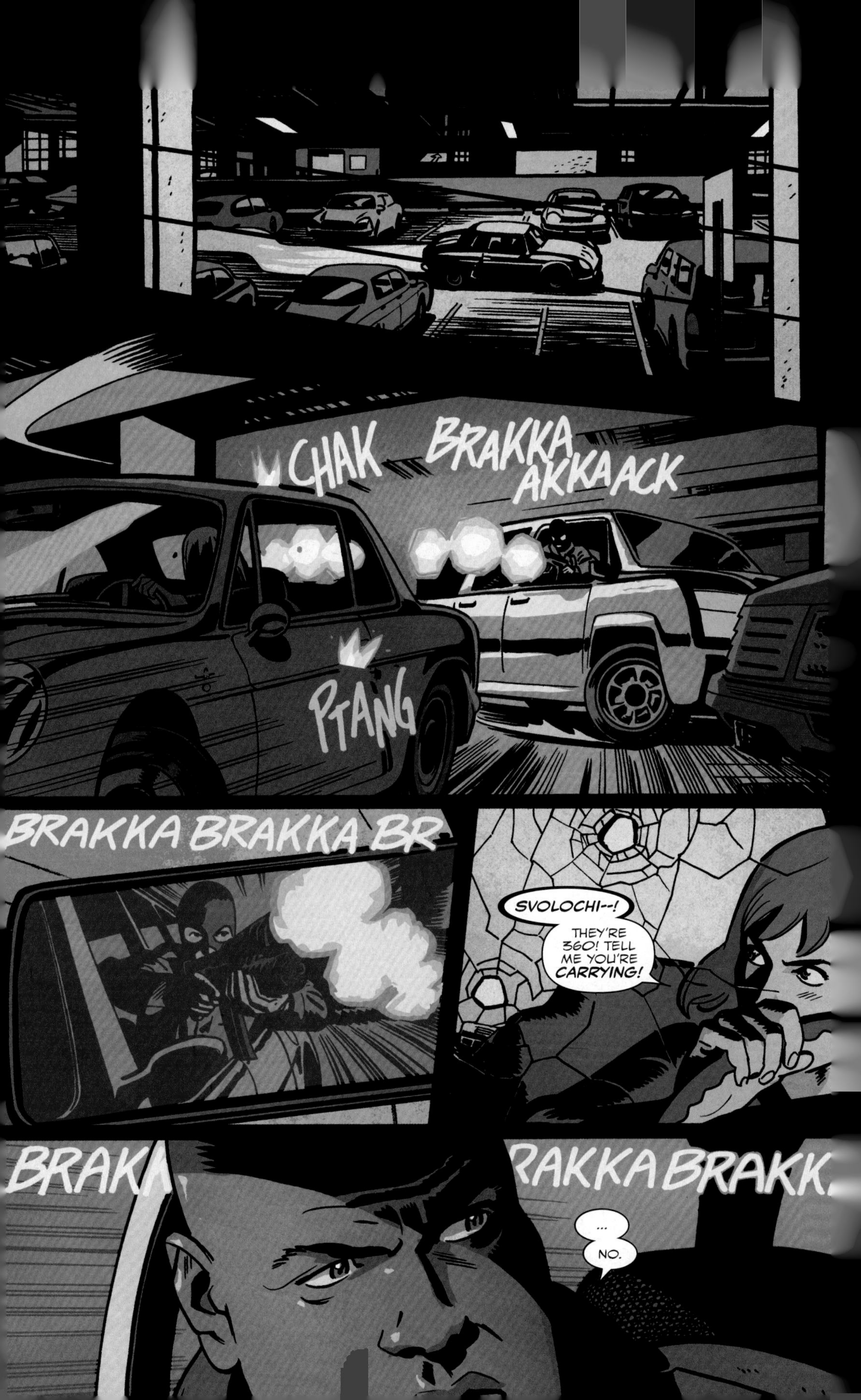

CHAK
BRAKKA AKKAACK
PTANG
BRAKKA BRAKKA BR
SVOLOCHI--!
THEY'RE 360! TELL ME YOU'RE CARRYING!
BRAKKA BRAKKA BRAKK
...
NO.

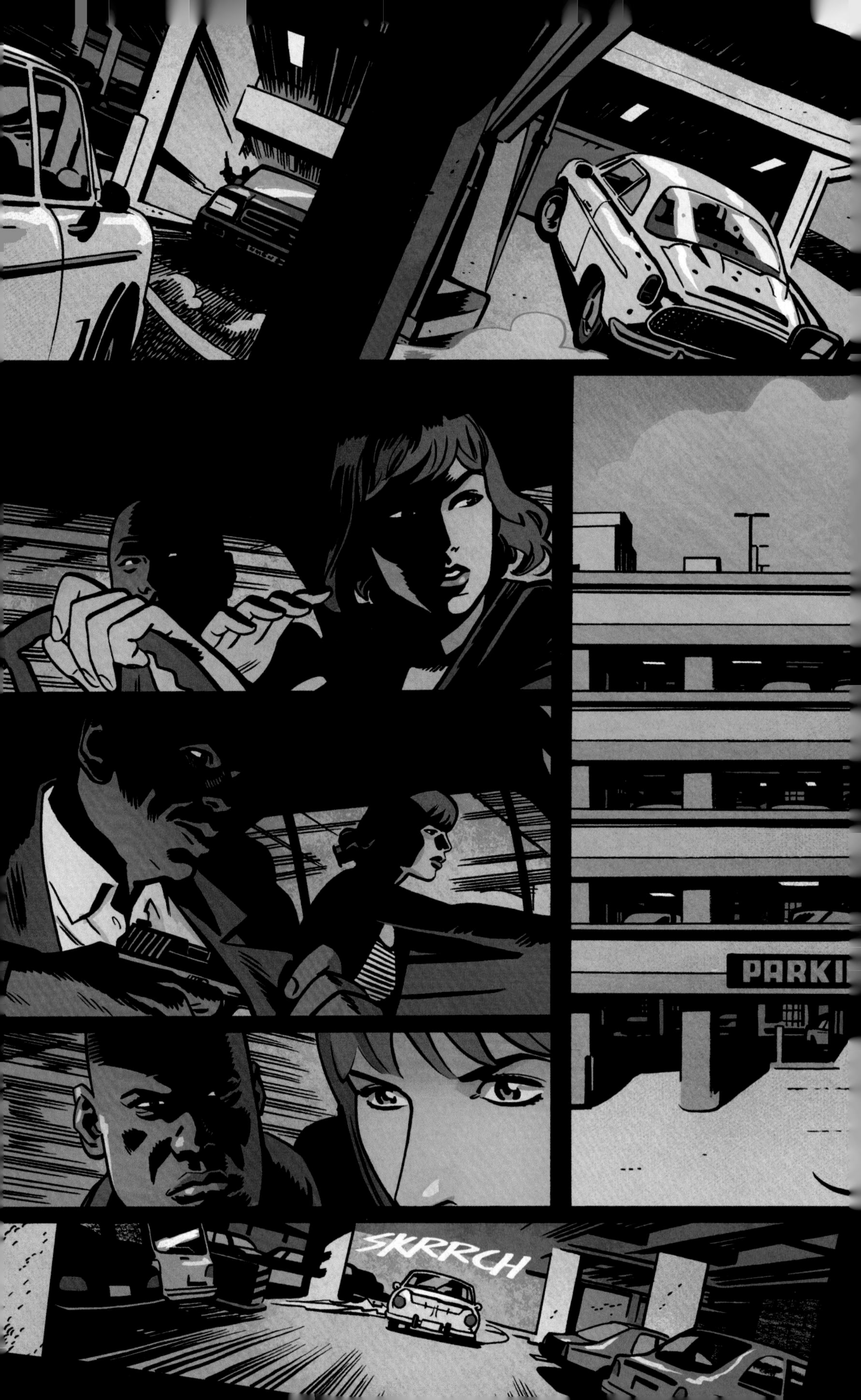
PARKI
SKRRCH

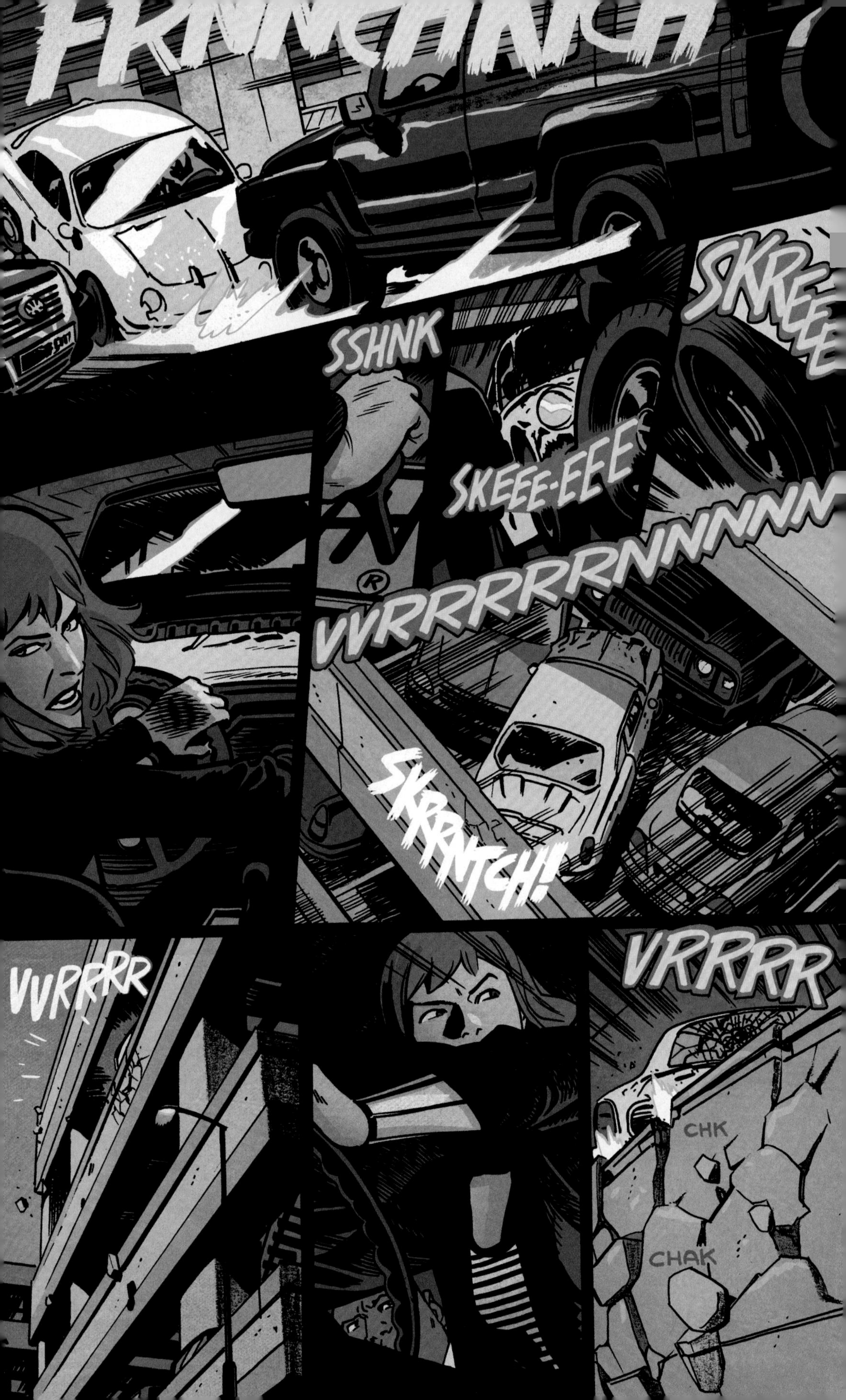
SSHNK
SKREEEE
SKEEE-EEE
VVRRRRRRNNNNNN
SKRRNTCH!
VVURRRR
VRRRRR
CHK
CHAK

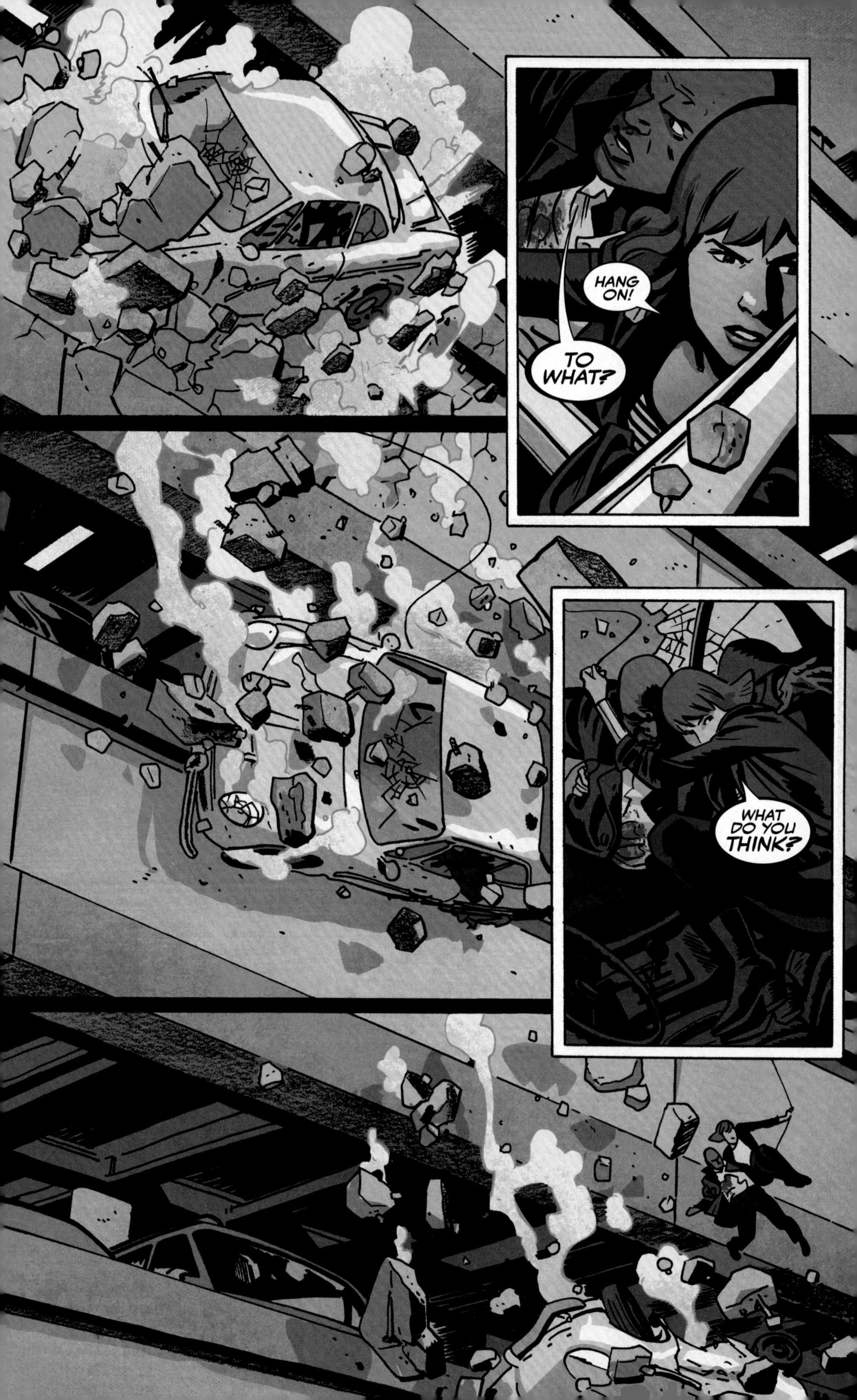
HANG ON!
TO WHAT?
WHAT DO YOU THINK?

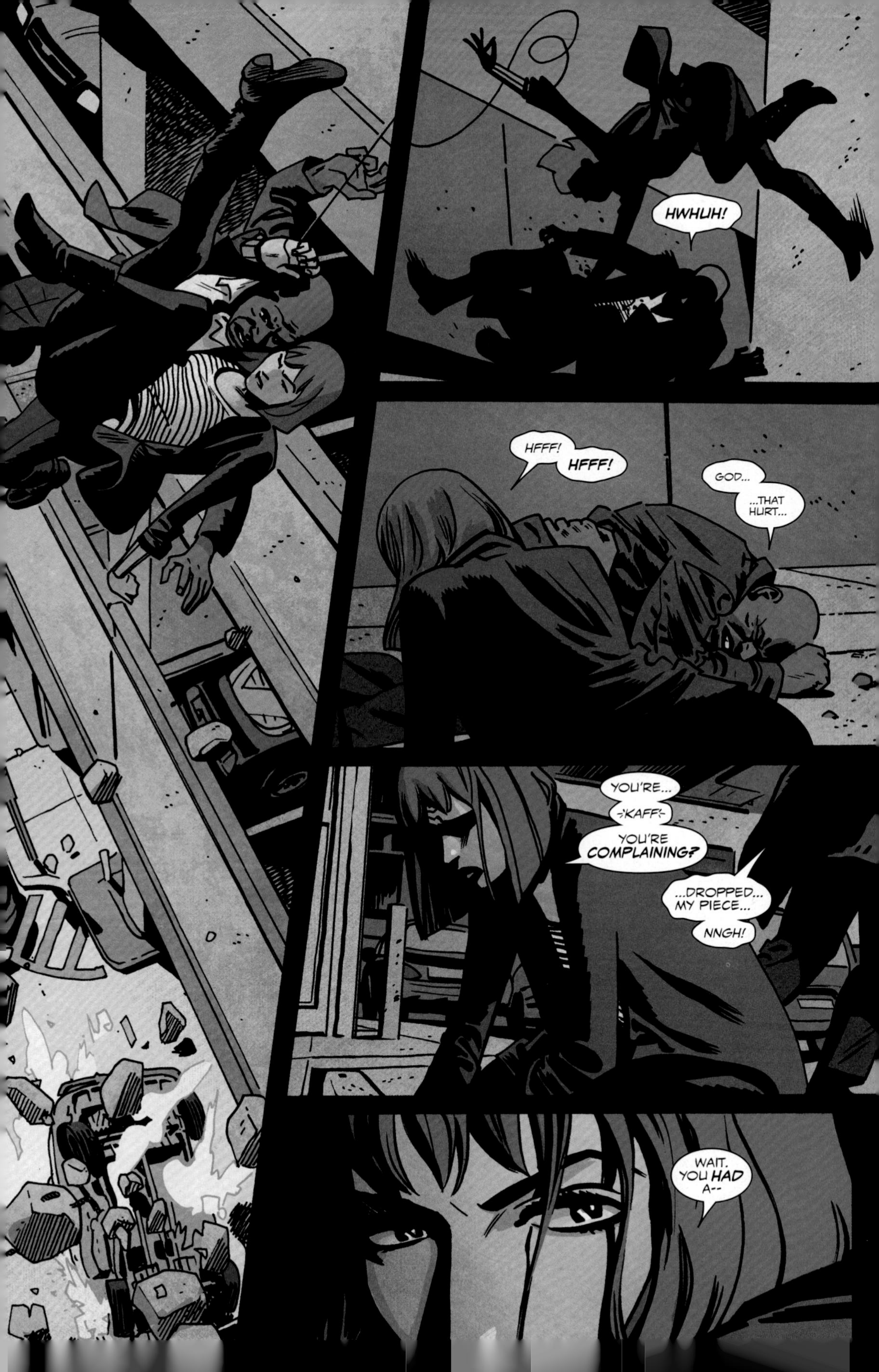
HWHUH!
HFFF! HFFF!
GOD...
...THAT HURT...
YOU'RE...
-KAFF-
YOU'RE COMPLAINING?
...DROPPED... MY PIECE...
NNGH!
WAIT. YOU HAD A--

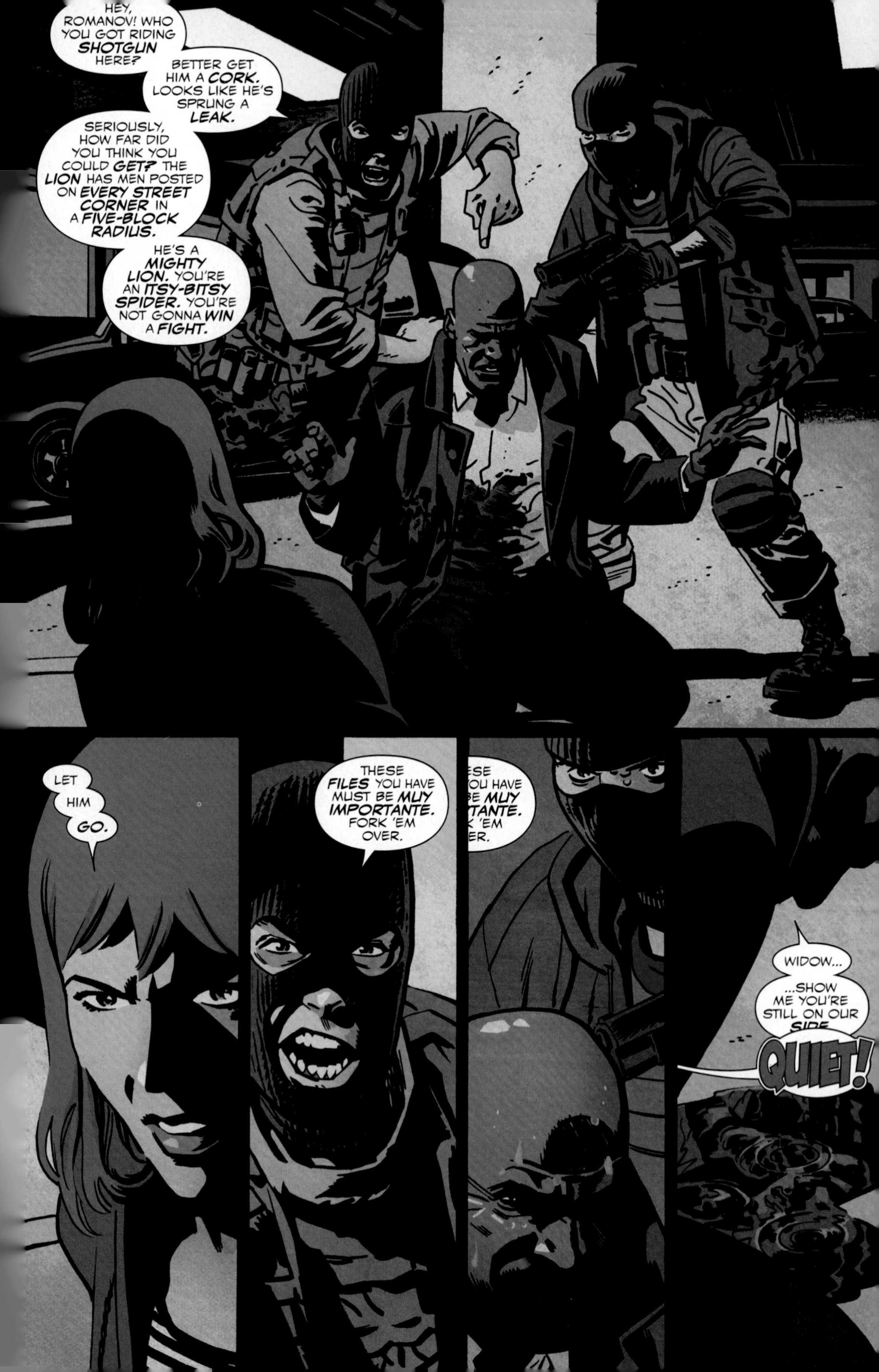

HEY, ROMANOV! WHO YOU GOT RIDING SHOTGUN HERE?
BETTER GET HIM A CORK. LOOKS LIKE HE'S SPRUNG A LEAK.
SERIOUSLY, HOW FAR DID YOU THINK YOU COULD GET? THE LION HAS MEN POSTED ON EVERY STREET CORNER IN A FIVE-BLOCK RADIUS.
HE'S A MIGHTY LION. YOU'RE AN ITSY-BITSY SPIDER. YOU'RE NOT GONNA WIN A FIGHT.
LET HIM GO.
THESE FILES YOU HAVE MUST BE MUY IMPORTANTE. FORK 'EM OVER.
WIDOW...
...SHOW ME YOU'RE STILL ON OUR SIDE
QUIET!

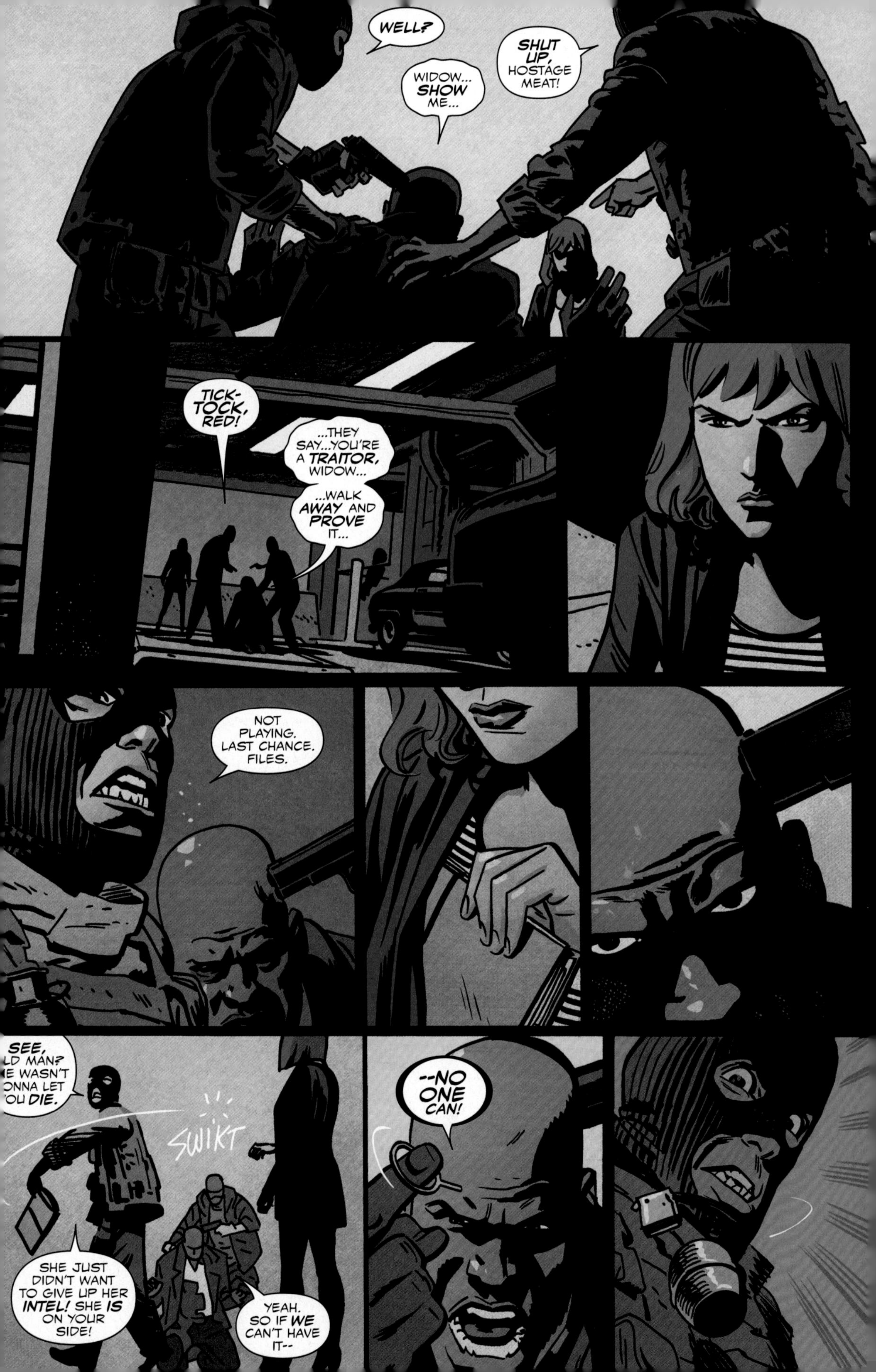
WELL?
WIDOW... SHOW ME...
SHUT UP, HOSTAGE MEAT!
TICK-TOCK, RED!
...THEY SAY...YOU'RE A TRAITOR, WIDOW...
...WALK AWAY AND PROVE IT...
NOT PLAYING. LAST CHANCE. FILES.
SEE, LD MAN? E WASN'T ONNA LET OU DIE.
SWIKT
SHE JUST DIDN'T WANT TO GIVE UP HER INTEL! SHE IS ON YOUR SIDE!
YEAH. SO IF WE CAN'T HAVE IT--
--NO ONE CAN!

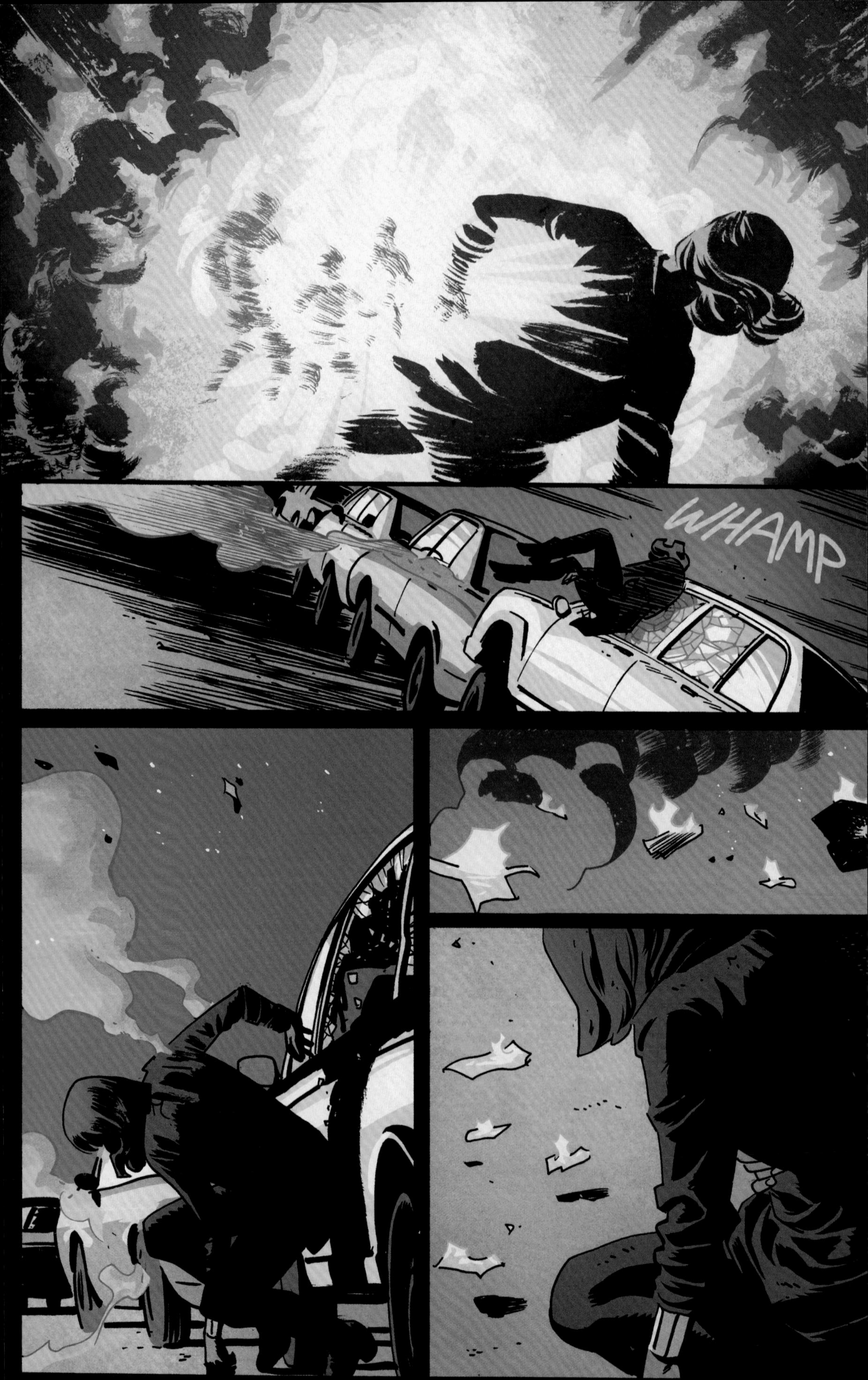
WHAMP

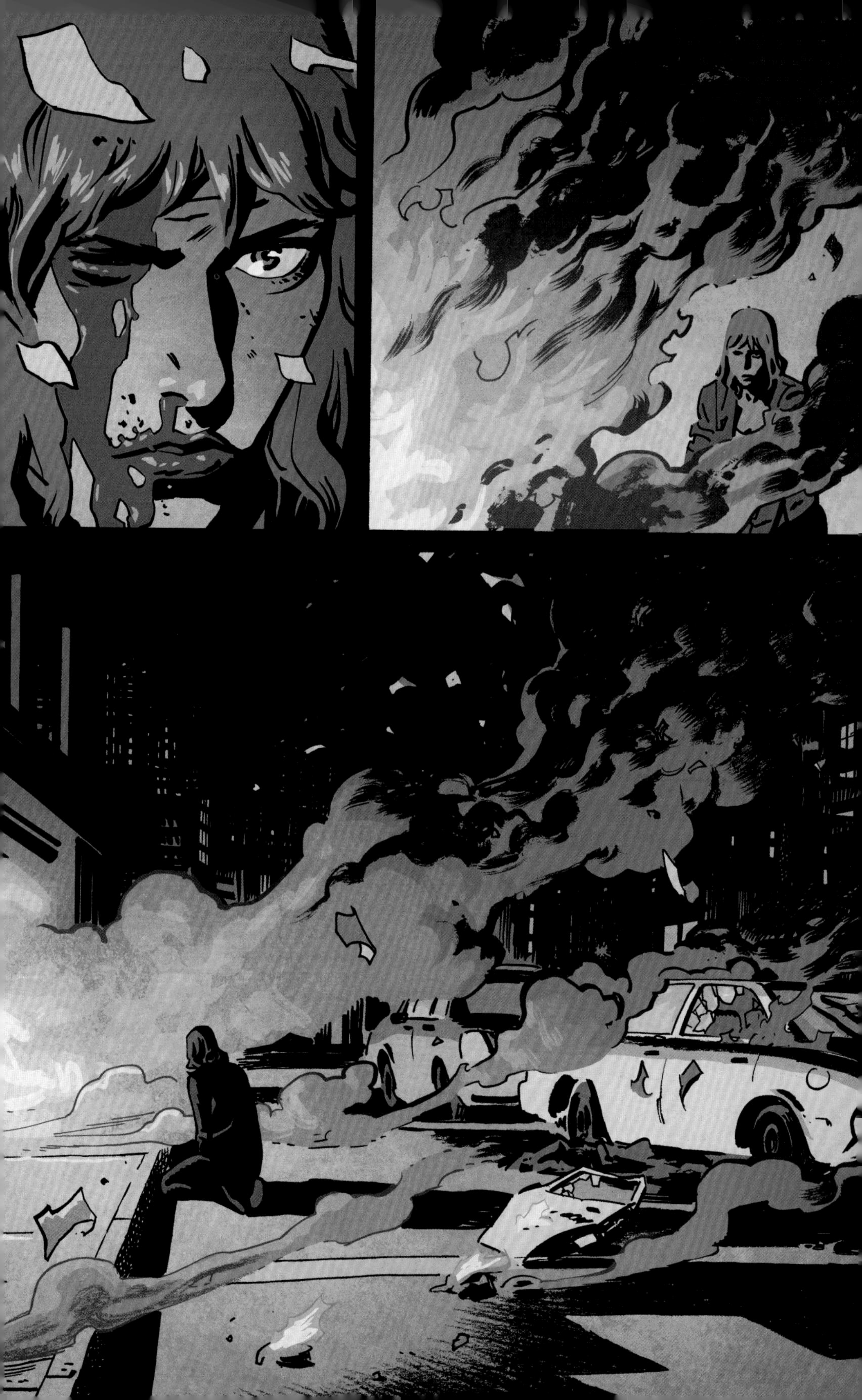

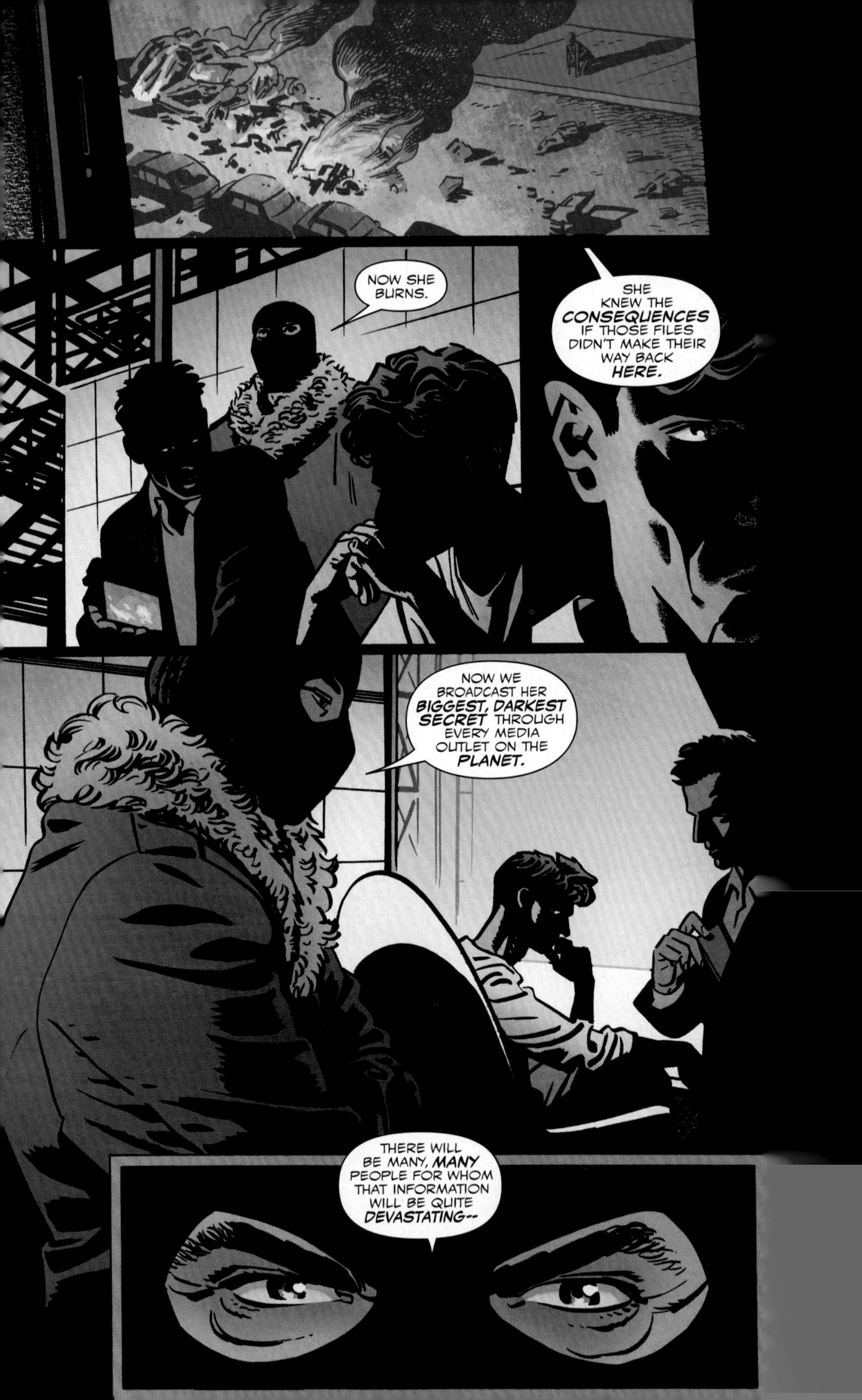
NOW SHE BURNS.
SHE KNEW THE CONSEQUENCES IF THOSE FILES DIDN'T MAKE THEIR WAY BACK HERE.
NOW WE BROADCAST HER BIGGEST, DARKEST SECRET THROUGH EVERY MEDIA OUTLET ON THE PLANET.
THERE WILL BE MANY, MANY PEOPLE FOR WHOM THAT INFORMATION WILL BE QUITE DEVASTATING--

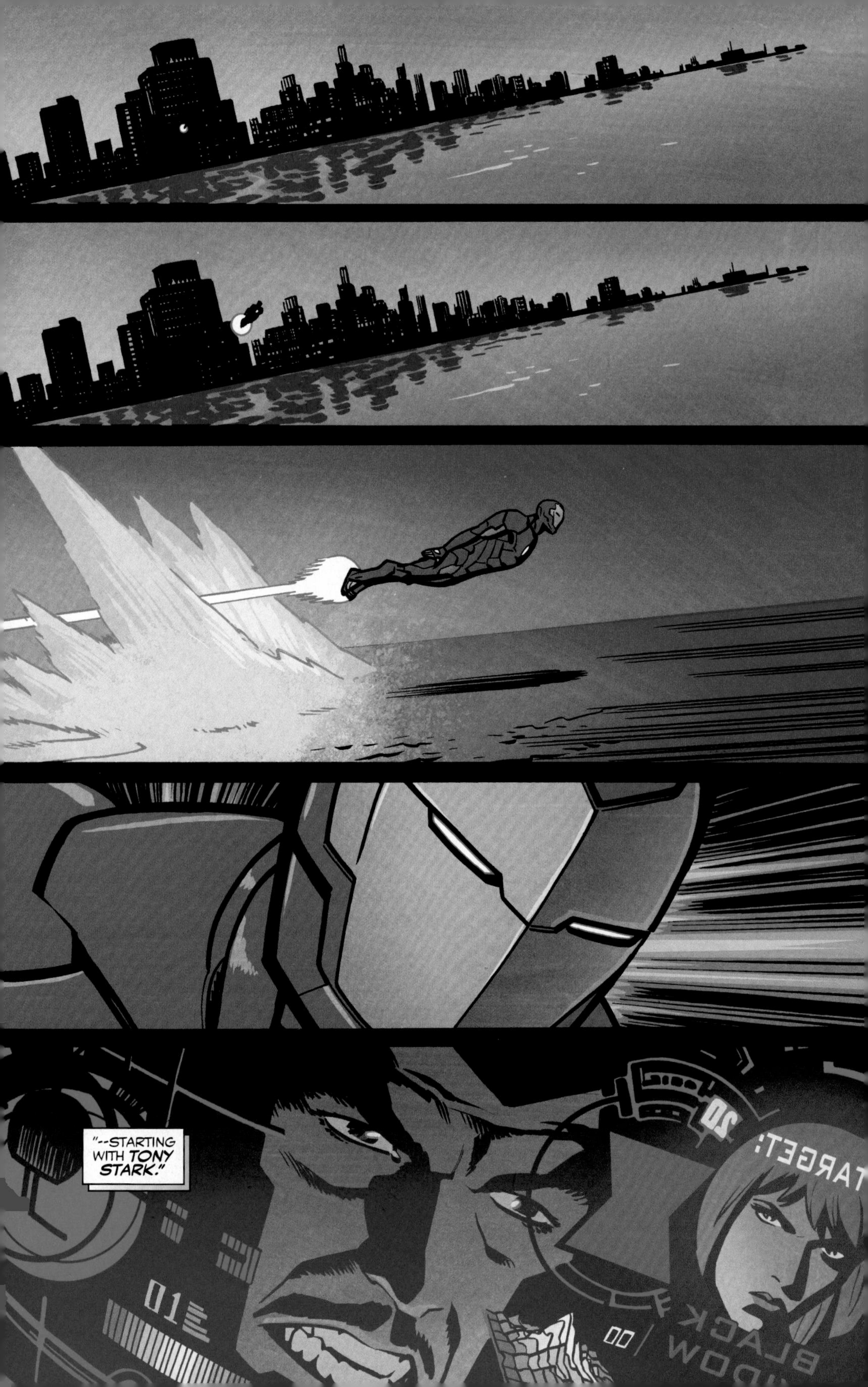
"--STARTING WITH TONY STARK."
20
TARGET:
BLACK WIDOW
01
00

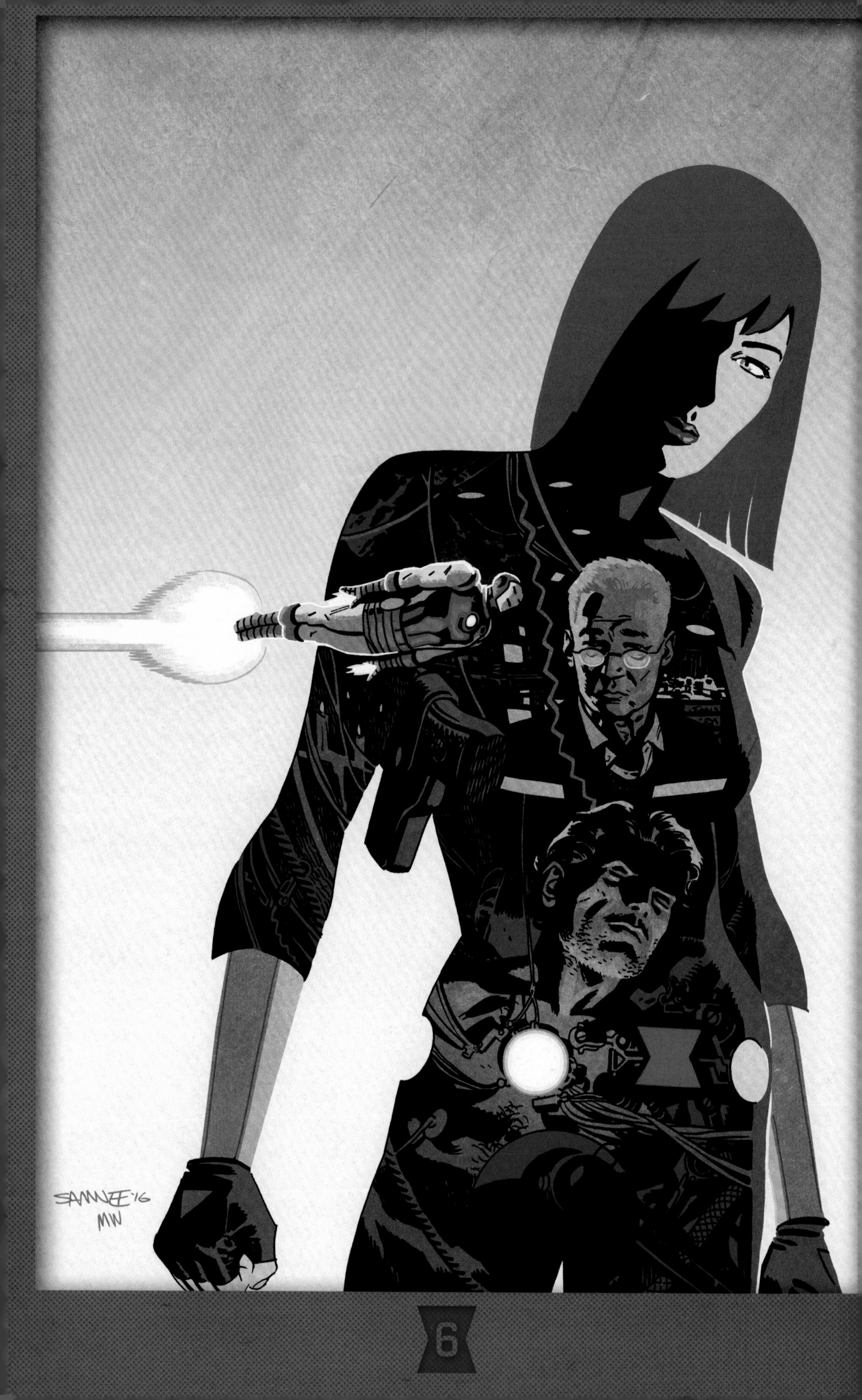
SAMNEE '16
MW
6

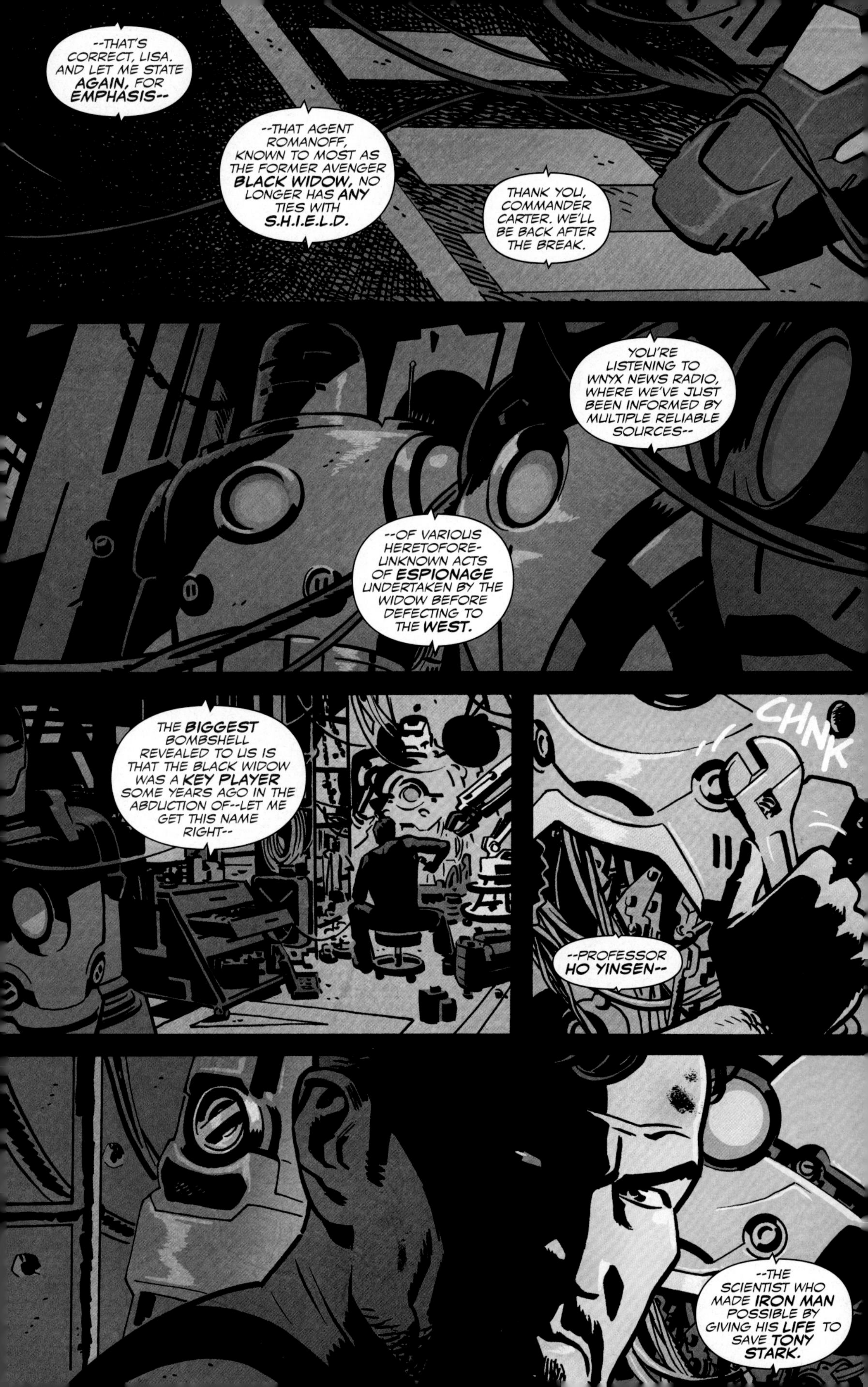
--THAT'S CORRECT, LISA. AND LET ME STATE AGAIN, FOR EMPHASIS--
--THAT AGENT ROMANOFF, KNOWN TO MOST AS THE FORMER AVENGER BLACK WIDOW, NO LONGER HAS ANY TIES WITH S.H.I.E.L.D.
THANK YOU, COMMANDER CARTER. WE'LL BE BACK AFTER THE BREAK.
YOU'RE LISTENING TO WNYX NEWS RADIO, WHERE WE'VE JUST BEEN INFORMED BY MULTIPLE RELIABLE SOURCES--
--OF VARIOUS HERETOFORE-UNKNOWN ACTS OF ESPIONAGE UNDERTAKEN BY THE WIDOW BEFORE DEFECTING TO THE WEST.
THE BIGGEST BOMBSHELL REVEALED TO US IS THAT THE BLACK WIDOW WAS A KEY PLAYER SOME YEARS AGO IN THE ABDUCTION OF--LET ME GET THIS NAME RIGHT--
CHNK
--PROFESSOR HO YINSEN--
--THE SCIENTIST WHO MADE IRON MAN POSSIBLE BY GIVING HIS LIFE TO SAVE TONY STARK.

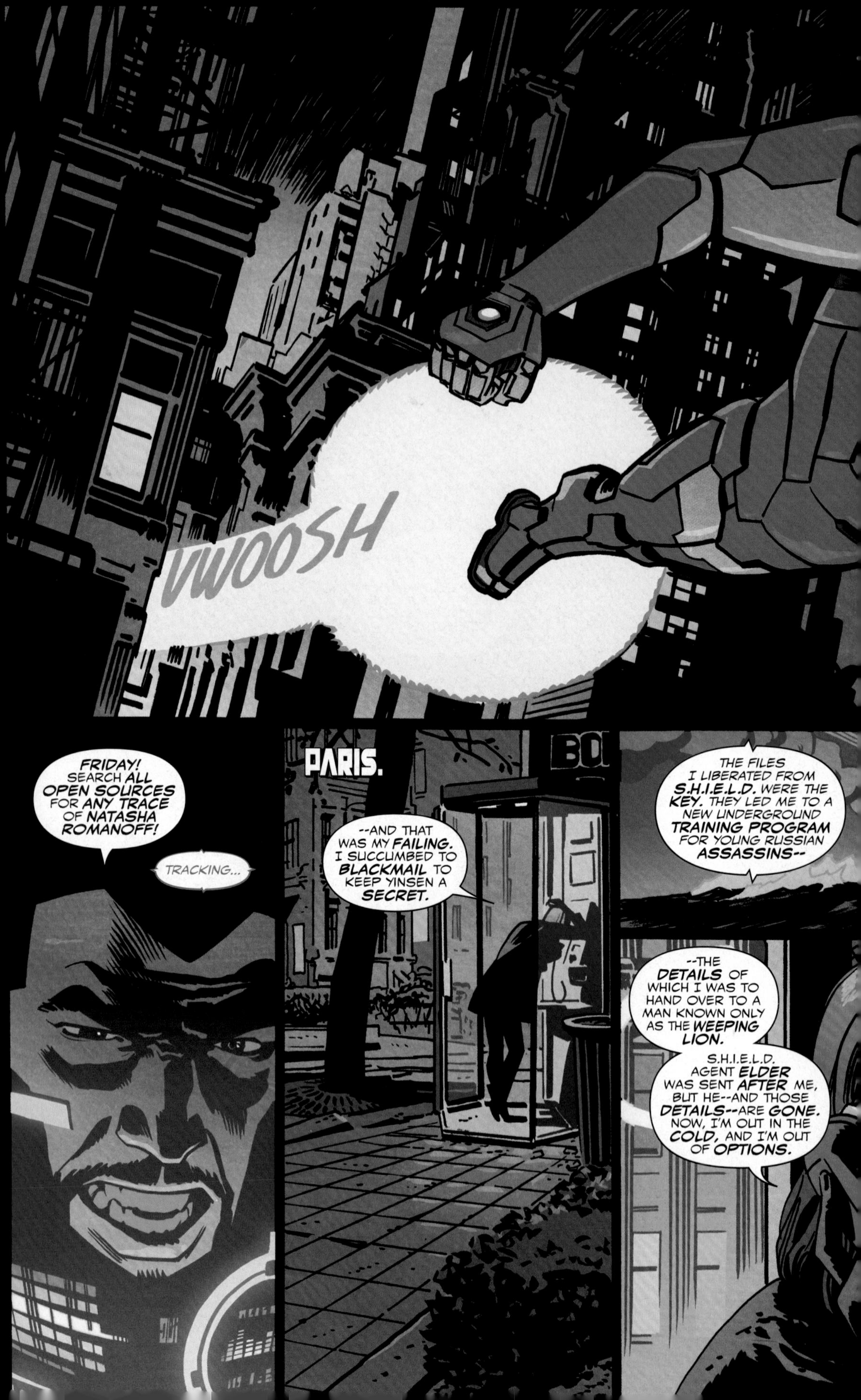
VWOOSH
FRIDAY! SEARCH ALL OPEN SOURCES FOR ANY TRACE OF NATASHA ROMANOFF!
TRACKING...
PARIS.
--AND THAT WAS MY FAILING. I SUCCUMBED TO BLACKMAIL TO KEEP YINSEN A SECRET.
THE FILES I LIBERATED FROM S.H.I.E.L.D. WERE THE KEY. THEY LED ME TO A NEW UNDERGROUND TRAINING PROGRAM FOR YOUNG RUSSIAN ASSASSINS--
--THE DETAILS OF WHICH I WAS TO HAND OVER TO A MAN KNOWN ONLY AS THE WEEPING LION.
S.H.I.E.L.D. AGENT ELDER WAS SENT AFTER ME, BUT HE--AND THOSE DETAILS--ARE GONE. NOW, I'M OUT IN THE COLD, AND I'M OUT OF OPTIONS.

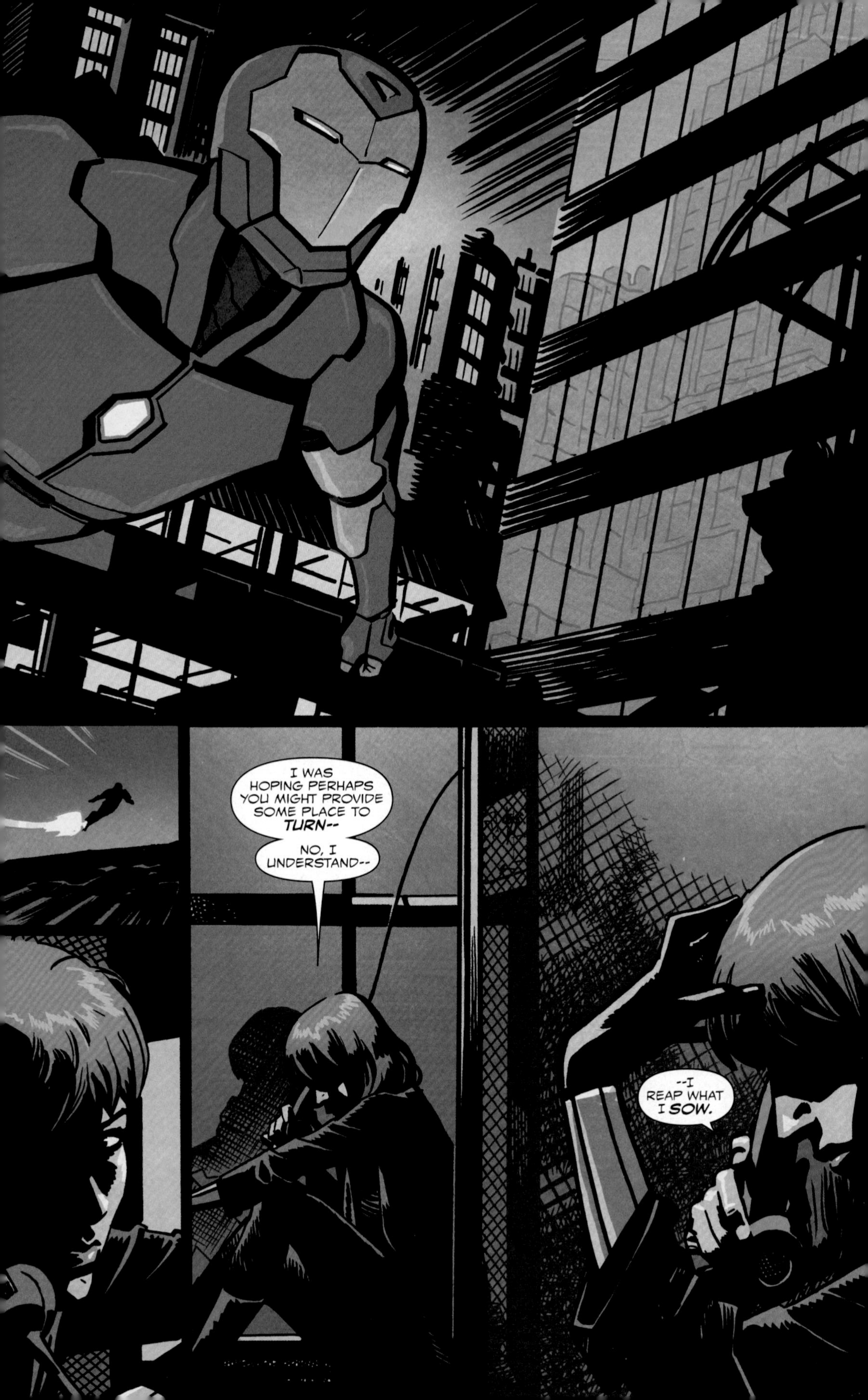
I WAS HOPING PERHAPS YOU MIGHT PROVIDE SOME PLACE TO TURN--
NO, I UNDERSTAND--
--I REAP WHAT I SOW.

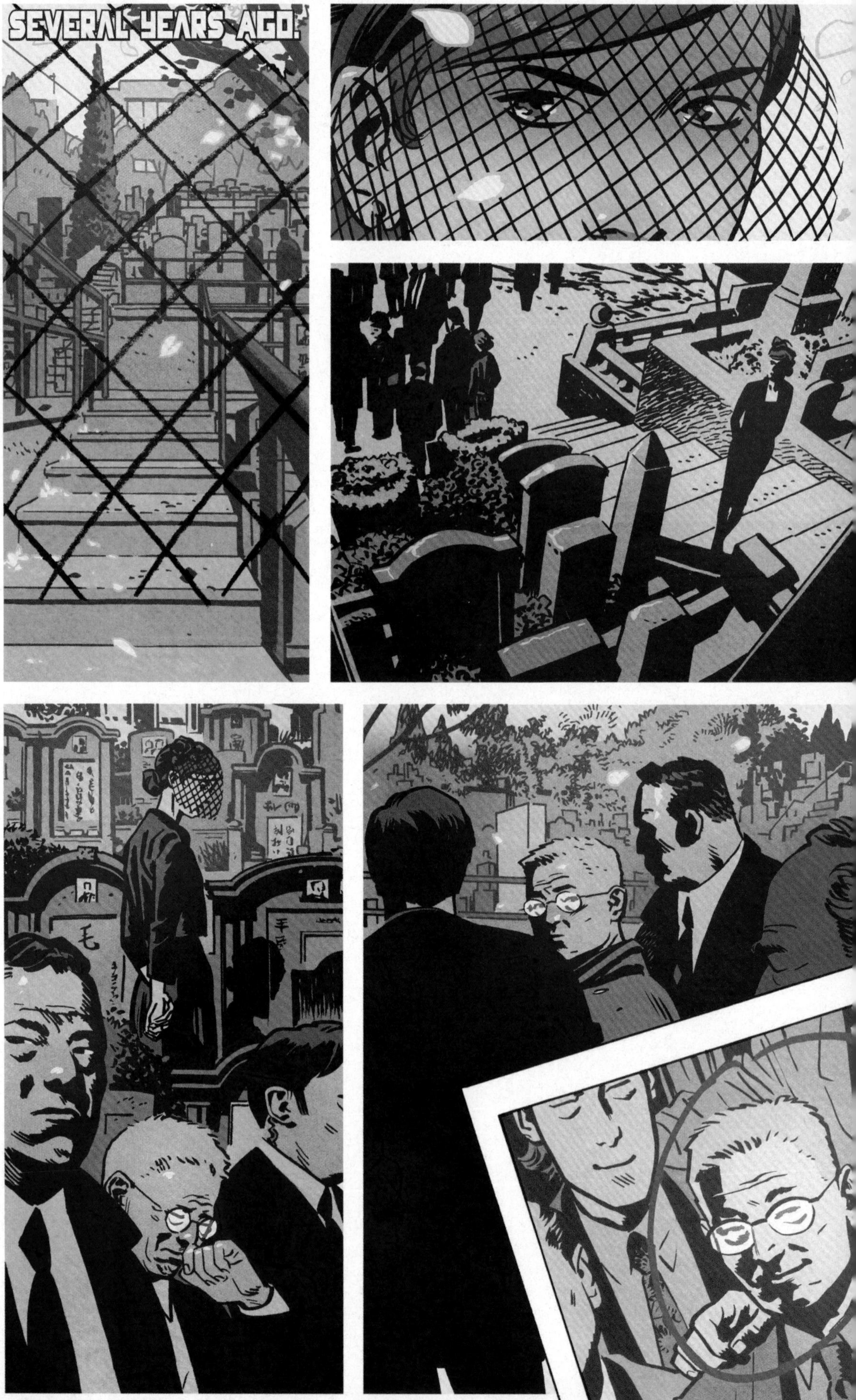
SEVERAL YEARS AGO.

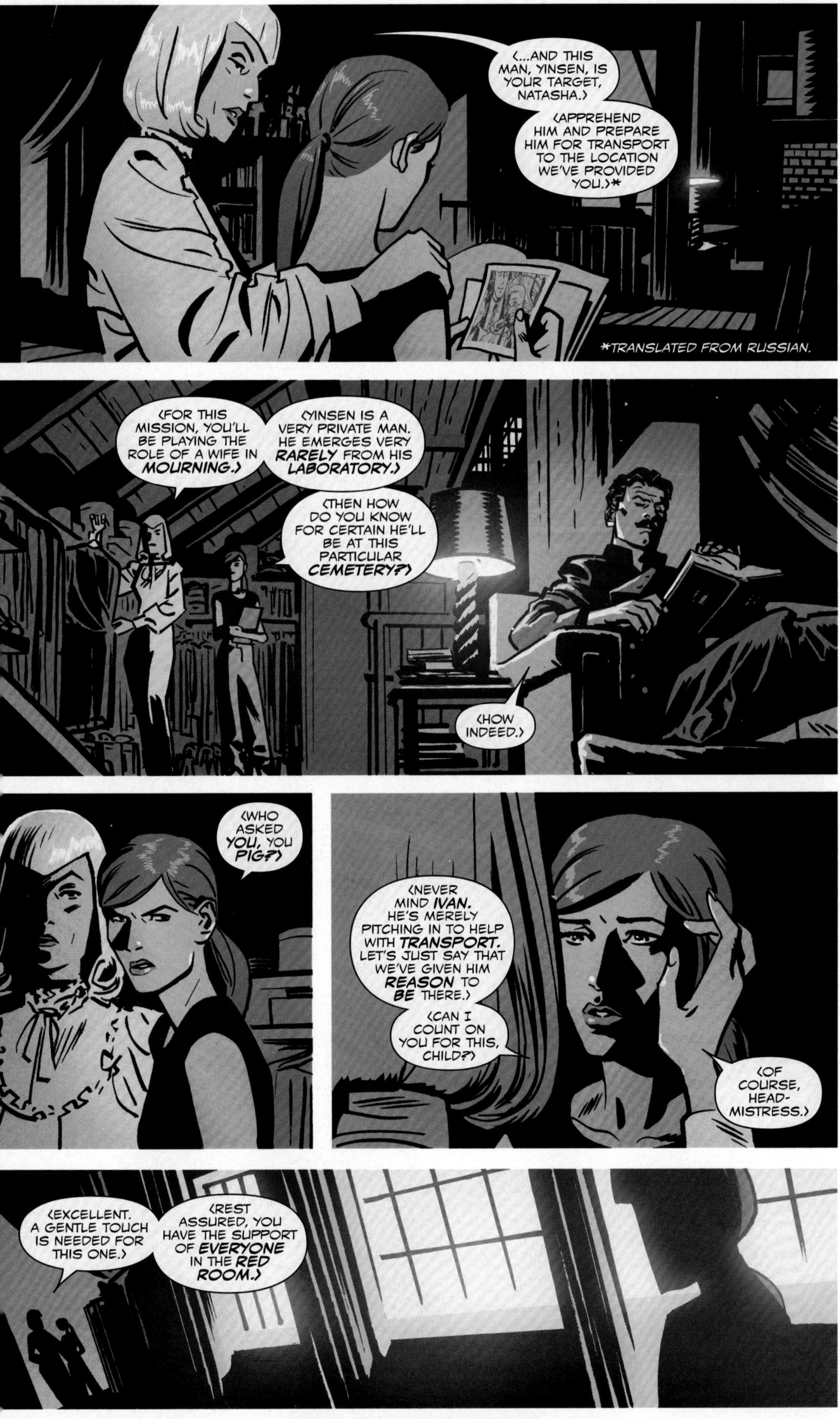
‹...AND THIS MAN, YINSEN, IS YOUR TARGET, NATASHA.›
‹APPREHEND HIM AND PREPARE HIM FOR TRANSPORT TO THE LOCATION WE'VE PROVIDED YOU.›*
*TRANSLATED FROM RUSSIAN.
‹FOR THIS MISSION, YOU'LL BE PLAYING THE ROLE OF A WIFE IN MOURNING.›
‹YINSEN IS A VERY PRIVATE MAN. HE EMERGES VERY RARELY FROM HIS LABORATORY.›
‹THEN HOW DO YOU KNOW FOR CERTAIN HE'LL BE AT THIS PARTICULAR CEMETERY?›
‹HOW INDEED.›
‹WHO ASKED YOU, YOU PIG?›
‹NEVER MIND IVAN. HE'S MERELY PITCHING IN TO HELP WITH TRANSPORT. LET'S JUST SAY THAT WE'VE GIVEN HIM REASON TO BE THERE.›
‹CAN I COUNT ON YOU FOR THIS, CHILD?›
‹OF COURSE, HEAD-MISTRESS.›
‹EXCELLENT. A GENTLE TOUCH IS NEEDED FOR THIS ONE.›
‹REST ASSURED, YOU HAVE THE SUPPORT OF EVERYONE IN THE RED ROOM.›

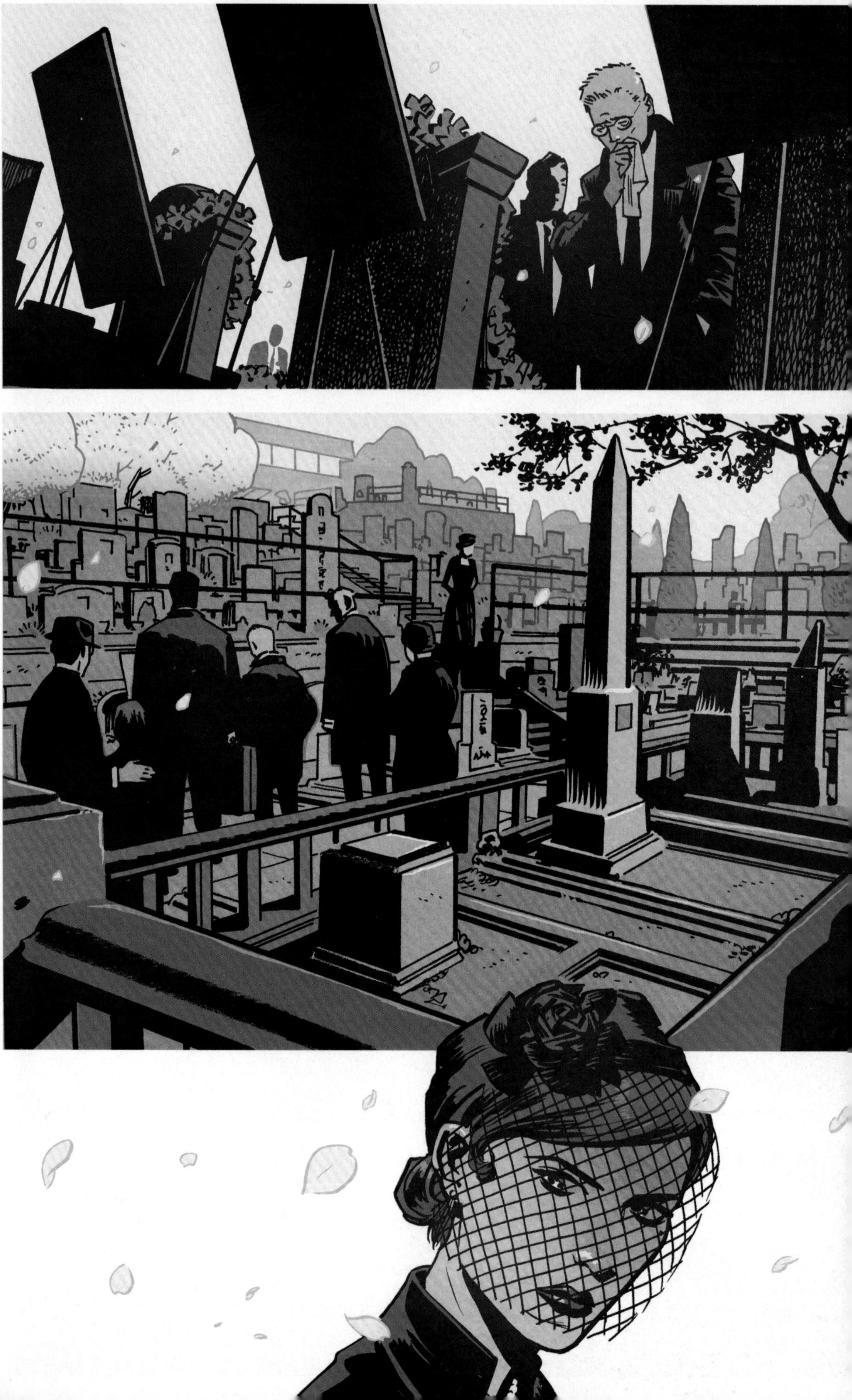

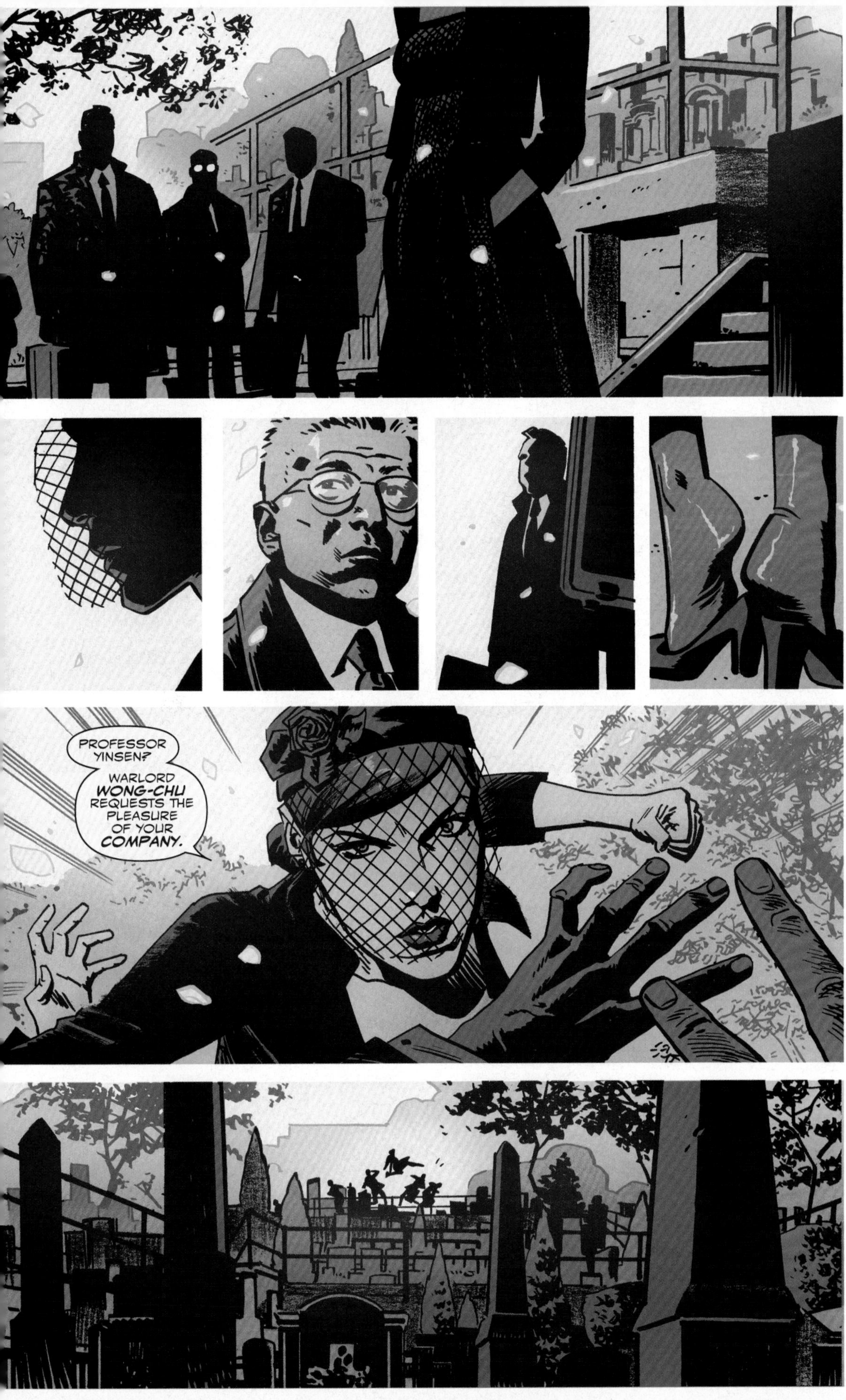
PROFESSOR YINSEN?
WARLORD **WONG-CHU** REQUESTS THE PLEASURE OF YOUR **COMPANY.**

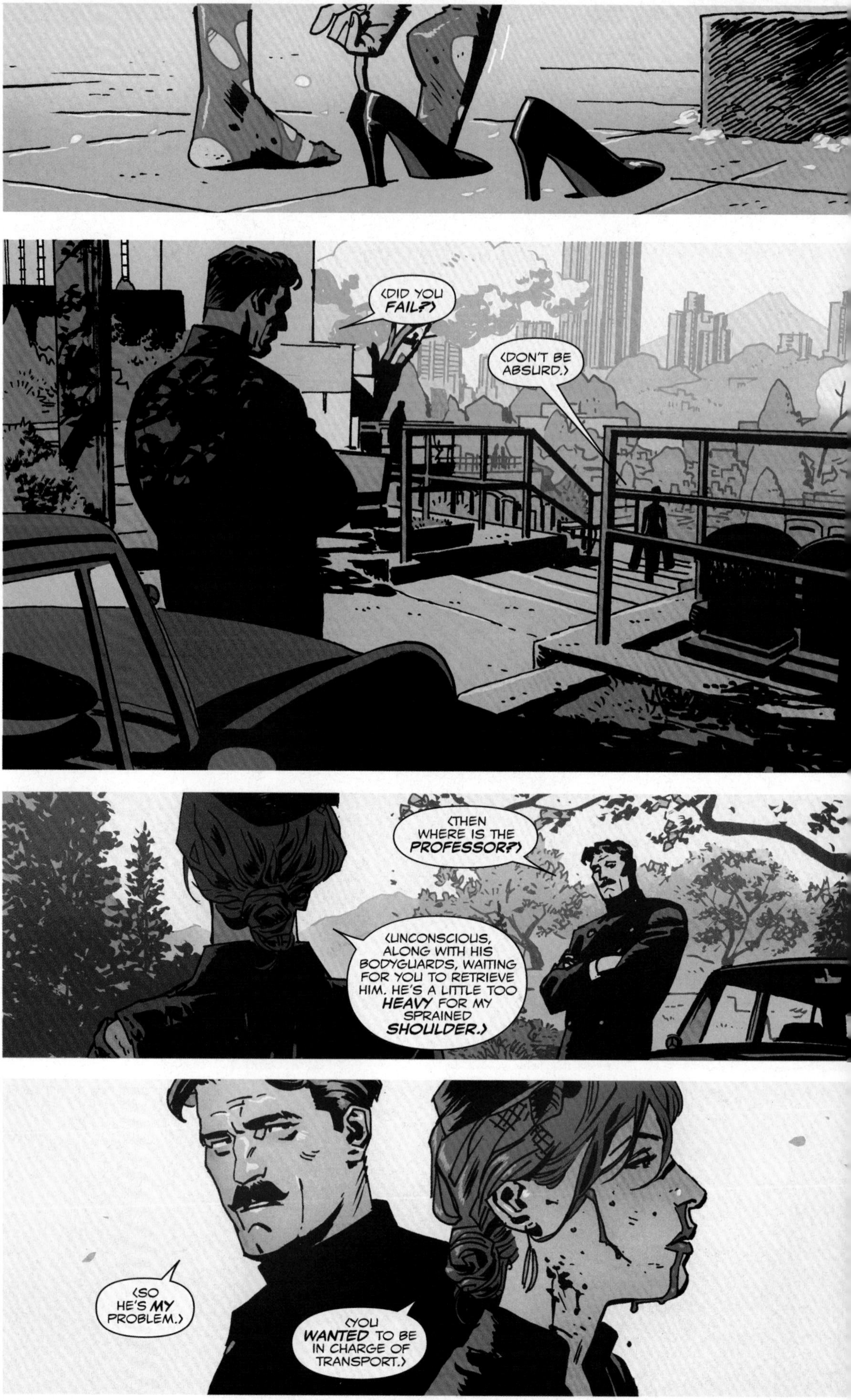
<DID YOU FAIL?>
<DON'T BE ABSURD.>
<THEN WHERE IS THE PROFESSOR?>
<UNCONSCIOUS, ALONG WITH HIS BODYGUARDS, WAITING FOR YOU TO RETRIEVE HIM. HE'S A LITTLE TOO HEAVY FOR MY SPRAINED SHOULDER.>
<SO HE'S MY PROBLEM.>
<YOU WANTED TO BE IN CHARGE OF TRANSPORT.>

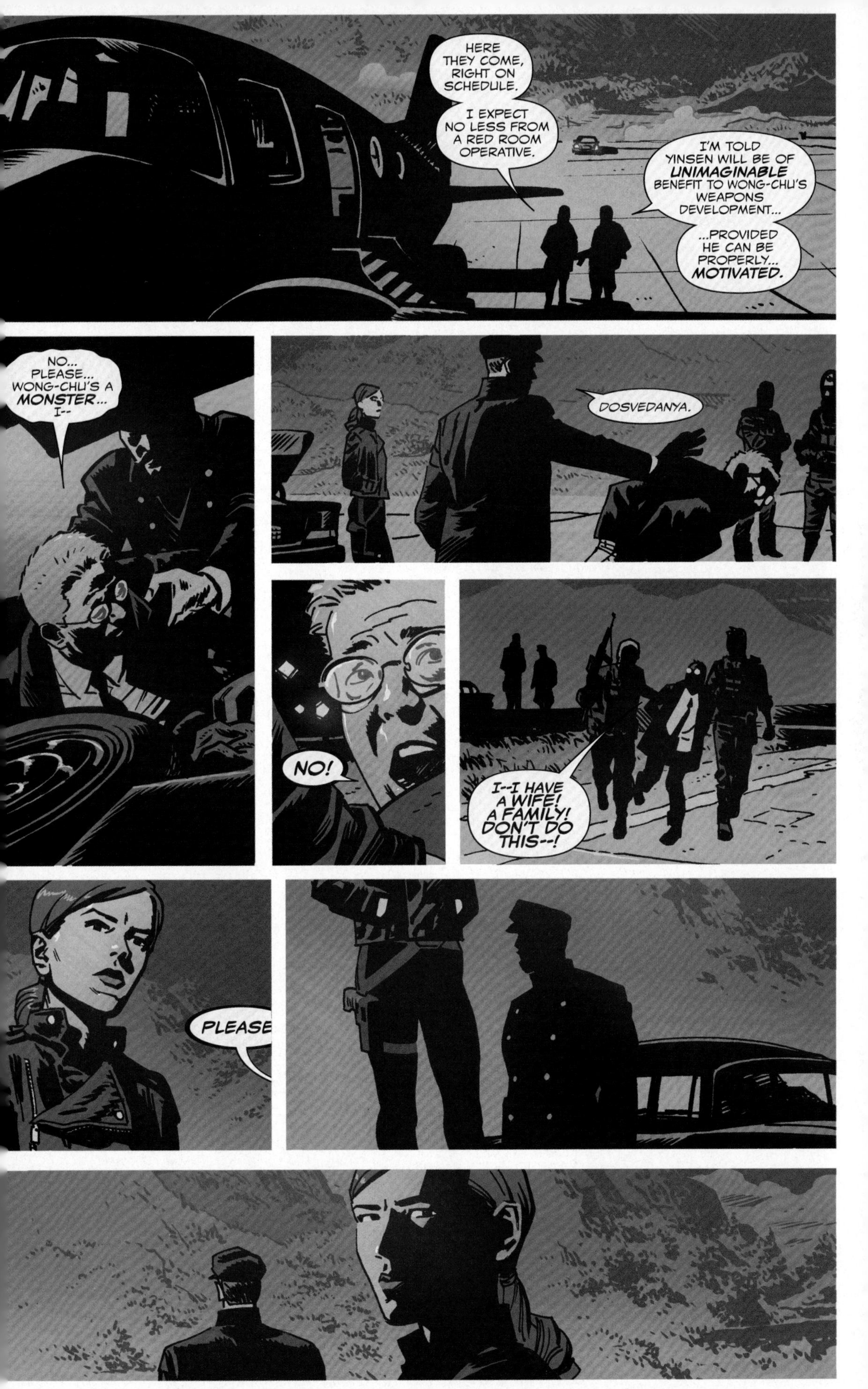
HERE THEY COME, RIGHT ON SCHEDULE.
I EXPECT NO LESS FROM A RED ROOM OPERATIVE.
I'M TOLD YINSEN WILL BE OF UNIMAGINABLE BENEFIT TO WONG-CHU'S WEAPONS DEVELOPMENT...
...PROVIDED HE CAN BE PROPERLY... MOTIVATED.
NO... PLEASE... WONG-CHU'S A MONSTER... I--
DOSVEDANYA.
NO!
I--I HAVE A WIFE! A FAMILY! DON'T DO THIS--!
PLEASE

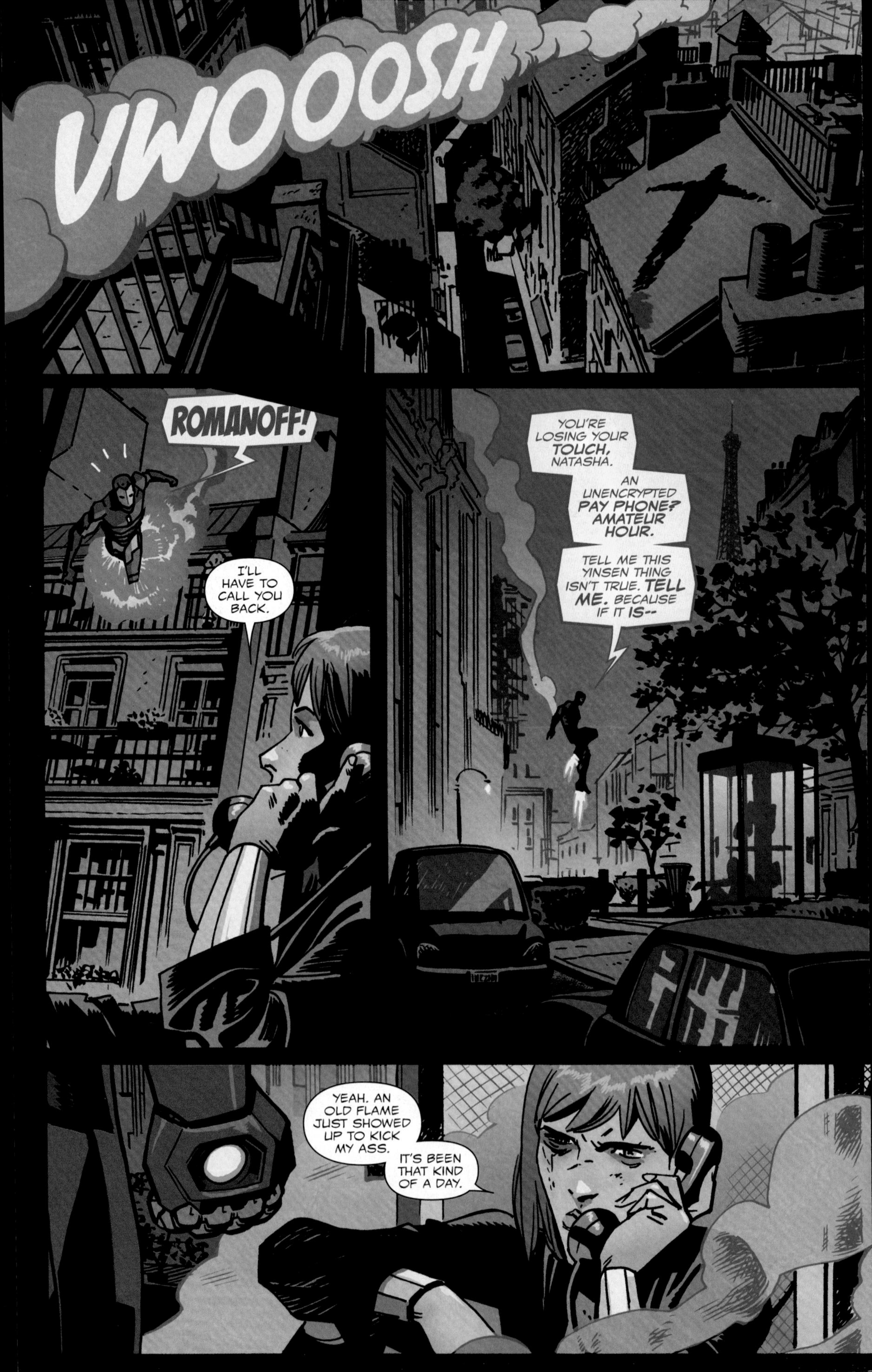
VWOOOSH
ROMANOFF!
I'LL HAVE TO CALL YOU BACK.
YOU'RE LOSING YOUR TOUCH, NATASHA.
AN UNENCRYPTED PAY PHONE? AMATEUR HOUR.
TELL ME THIS YINSEN THING ISN'T TRUE. TELL ME. BECAUSE IF IT IS--
YEAH. AN OLD FLAME JUST SHOWED UP TO KICK MY ASS.
IT'S BEEN THAT KIND OF A DAY.

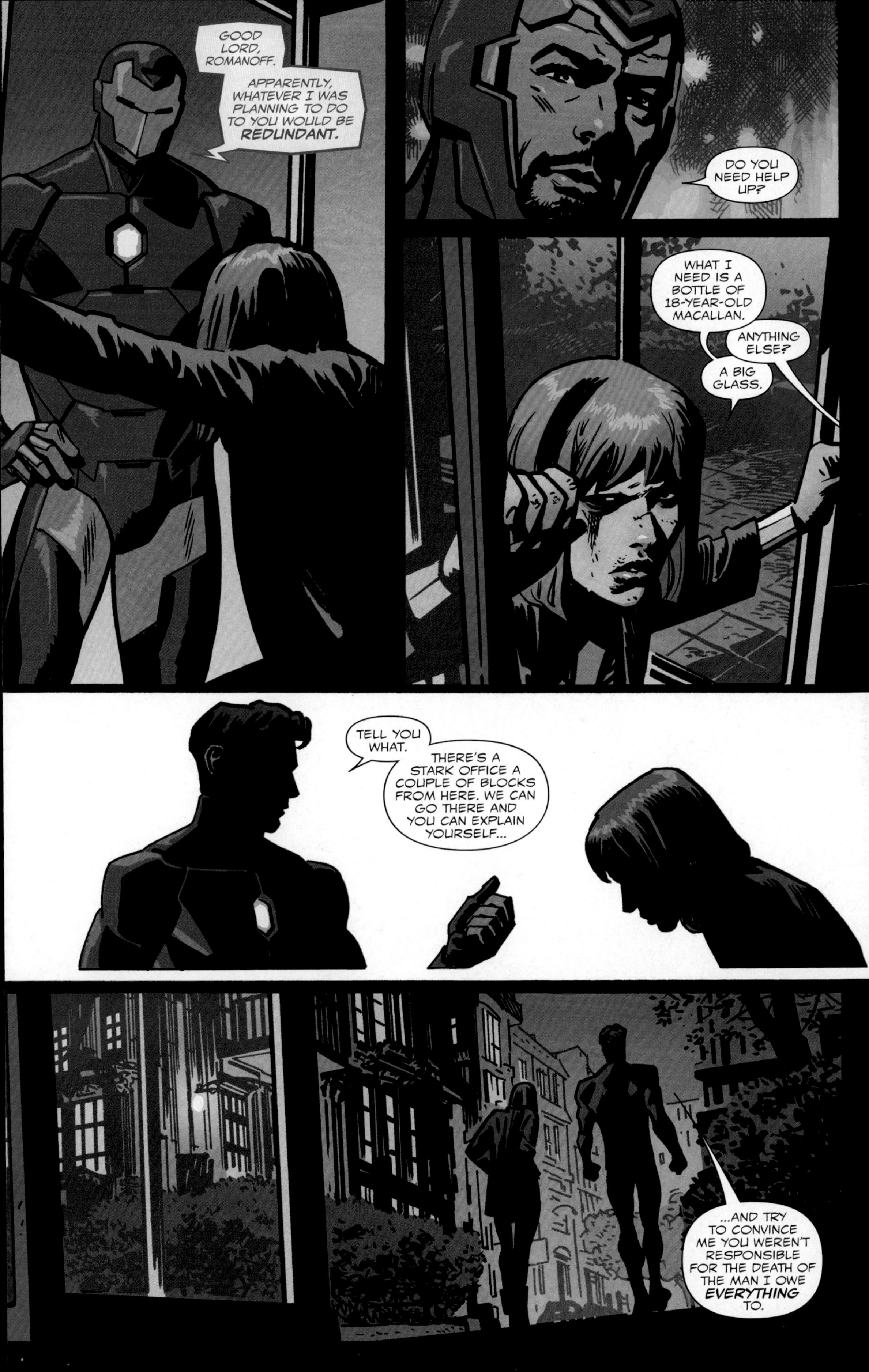
GOOD LORD, ROMANOFF.
APPARENTLY, WHATEVER I WAS PLANNING TO DO TO YOU WOULD BE **REDUNDANT.**
DO YOU NEED HELP UP?
WHAT I NEED IS A BOTTLE OF 18-YEAR-OLD MACALLAN.
ANYTHING ELSE?
A BIG GLASS.
TELL YOU WHAT.
THERE'S A STARK OFFICE A COUPLE OF BLOCKS FROM HERE. WE CAN GO THERE AND YOU CAN EXPLAIN YOURSELF...
...AND TRY TO CONVINCE ME YOU WEREN'T RESPONSIBLE FOR THE DEATH OF THE MAN I OWE ***EVERYTHING*** TO.

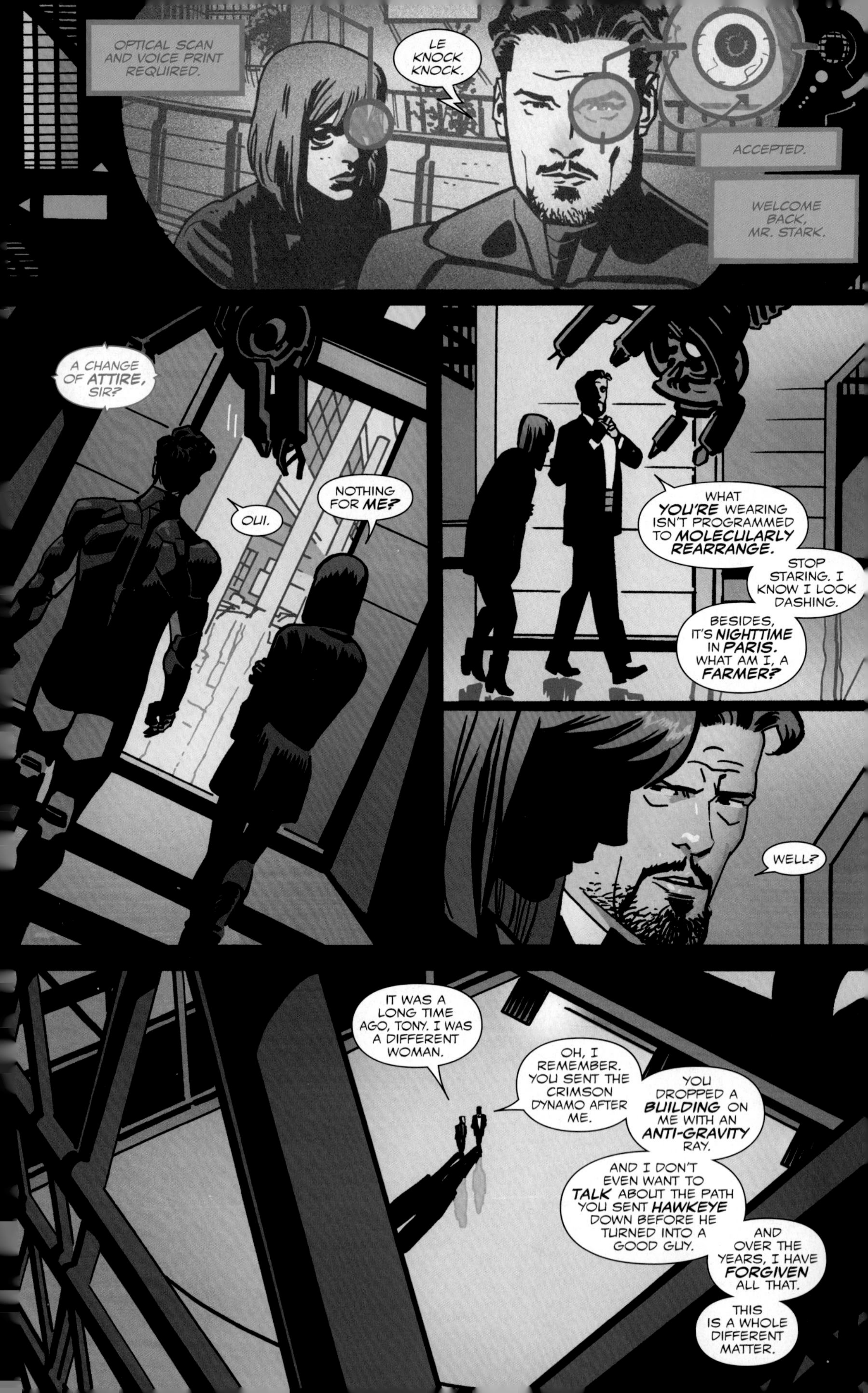
OPTICAL SCAN AND VOICE PRINT REQUIRED.
LE KNOCK KNOCK.
ACCEPTED.
WELCOME BACK, MR. STARK.
A CHANGE OF ATTIRE, SIR?
OUI.
NOTHING FOR ME?
WHAT YOU'RE WEARING ISN'T PROGRAMMED TO MOLECULARLY REARRANGE.
STOP STARING. I KNOW I LOOK DASHING.
BESIDES, IT'S NIGHTTIME IN PARIS. WHAT AM I, A FARMER?
WELL?
IT WAS A LONG TIME AGO, TONY. I WAS A DIFFERENT WOMAN.
OH, I REMEMBER. YOU SENT THE CRIMSON DYNAMO AFTER ME.
YOU DROPPED A BUILDING ON ME WITH AN ANTI-GRAVITY RAY.
AND I DON'T EVEN WANT TO TALK ABOUT THE PATH YOU SENT HAWKEYE DOWN BEFORE HE TURNED INTO A GOOD GUY.
AND OVER THE YEARS, I HAVE FORGIVEN ALL THAT.
THIS IS A WHOLE DIFFERENT MATTER.

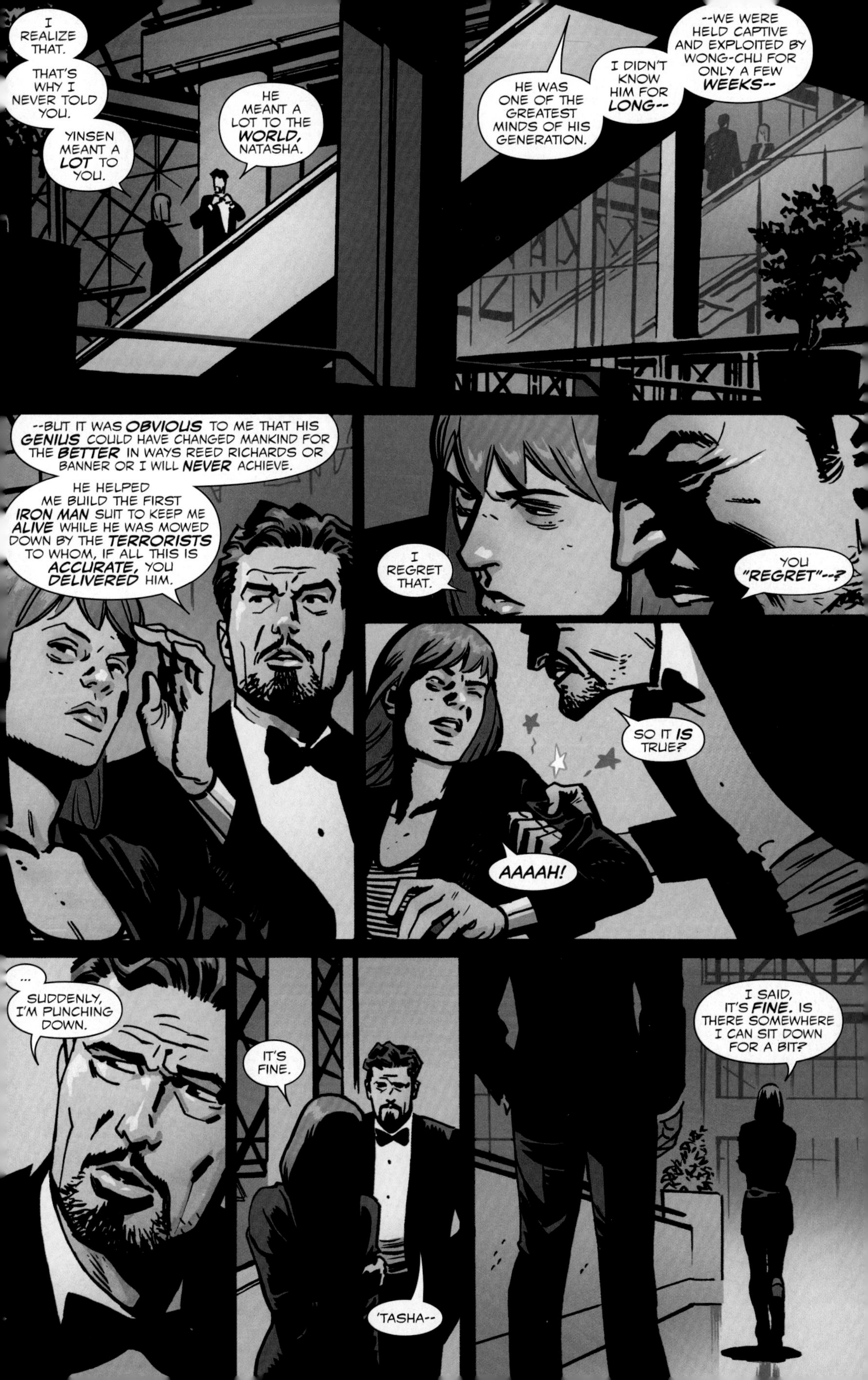
I REALIZE THAT.
THAT'S WHY I NEVER TOLD YOU.
YINSEN MEANT A LOT TO YOU.
HE MEANT A LOT TO THE WORLD, NATASHA.
HE WAS ONE OF THE GREATEST MINDS OF HIS GENERATION.
I DIDN'T KNOW HIM FOR LONG--
--WE WERE HELD CAPTIVE AND EXPLOITED BY WONG-CHU FOR ONLY A FEW WEEKS--
--BUT IT WAS OBVIOUS TO ME THAT HIS GENIUS COULD HAVE CHANGED MANKIND FOR THE BETTER IN WAYS REED RICHARDS OR BANNER OR I WILL NEVER ACHIEVE.
HE HELPED ME BUILD THE FIRST IRON MAN SUIT TO KEEP ME ALIVE WHILE HE WAS MOWED DOWN BY THE TERRORISTS TO WHOM, IF ALL THIS IS ACCURATE, YOU DELIVERED HIM.
I REGRET THAT.
YOU "REGRET"--?
SO IT IS TRUE?
AAAAH!
... SUDDENLY, I'M PUNCHING DOWN.
IT'S FINE.
'TASHA--
I SAID, IT'S FINE. IS THERE SOMEWHERE I CAN SIT DOWN FOR A BIT?

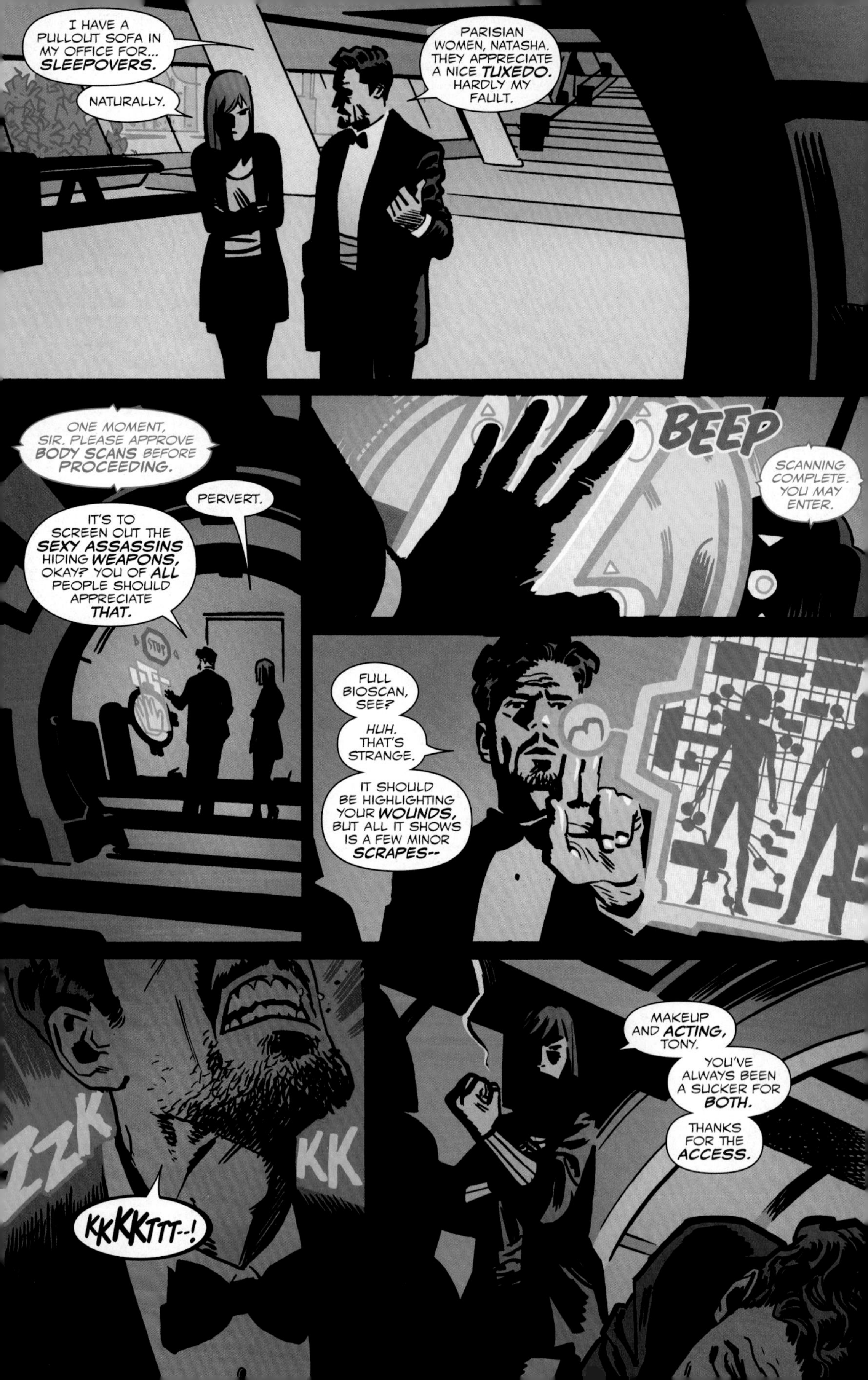

I HAVE A PULLOUT SOFA IN MY OFFICE FOR... SLEEPOVERS.
NATURALLY.
PARISIAN WOMEN, NATASHA. THEY APPRECIATE A NICE TUXEDO. HARDLY MY FAULT.
ONE MOMENT, SIR. PLEASE APPROVE BODY SCANS BEFORE PROCEEDING.
PERVERT.
IT'S TO SCREEN OUT THE SEXY ASSASSINS HIDING WEAPONS, OKAY? YOU OF ALL PEOPLE SHOULD APPRECIATE THAT.
STOP
BEEP
SCANNING COMPLETE. YOU MAY ENTER.
FULL BIOSCAN, SEE?
HUH. THAT'S STRANGE.
IT SHOULD BE HIGHLIGHTING YOUR WOUNDS, BUT ALL IT SHOWS IS A FEW MINOR SCRAPES--
ZZK
KK
KKKKTTT--!
MAKEUP AND ACTING, TONY.
YOU'VE ALWAYS BEEN A SUCKER FOR BOTH.
THANKS FOR THE ACCESS.

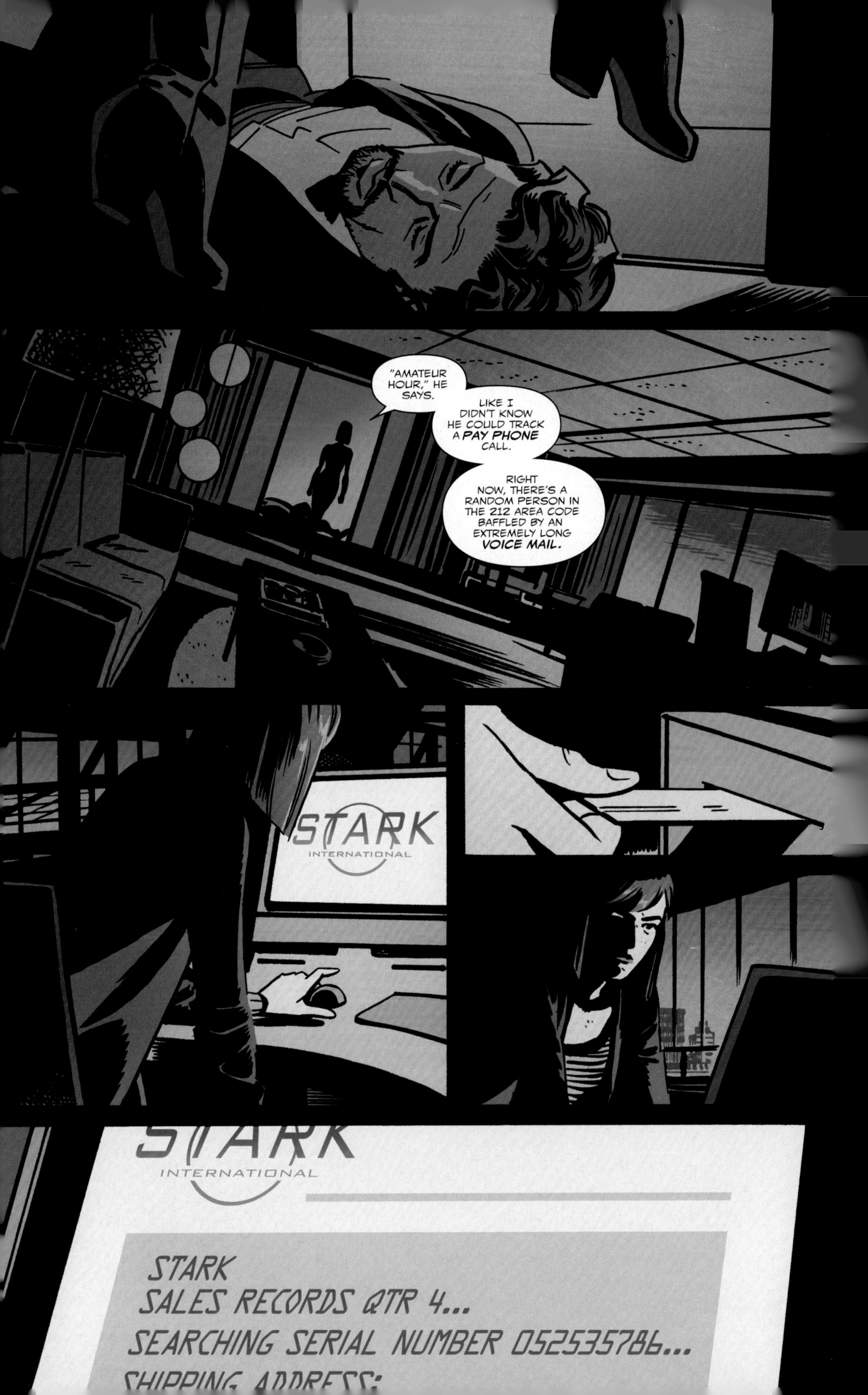
"AMATEUR HOUR," HE SAYS.
LIKE I DIDN'T KNOW HE COULD TRACK A PAY PHONE CALL.
RIGHT NOW, THERE'S A RANDOM PERSON IN THE 212 AREA CODE BAFFLED BY AN EXTREMELY LONG VOICE MAIL.
STARK INTERNATIONAL
STARK
SALES RECORDS QTR 4...
SEARCHING SERIAL NUMBER 052535786...

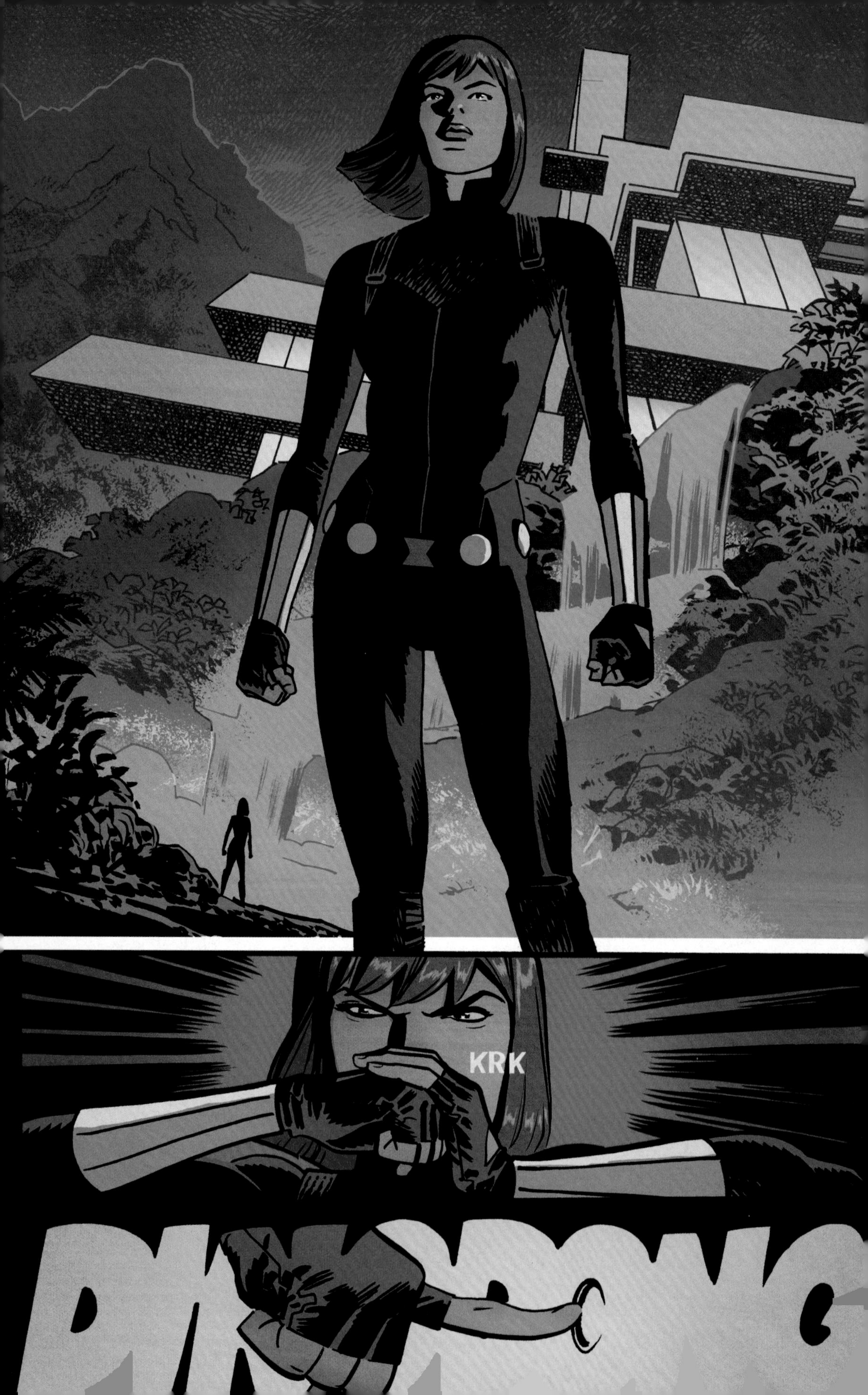
KRK

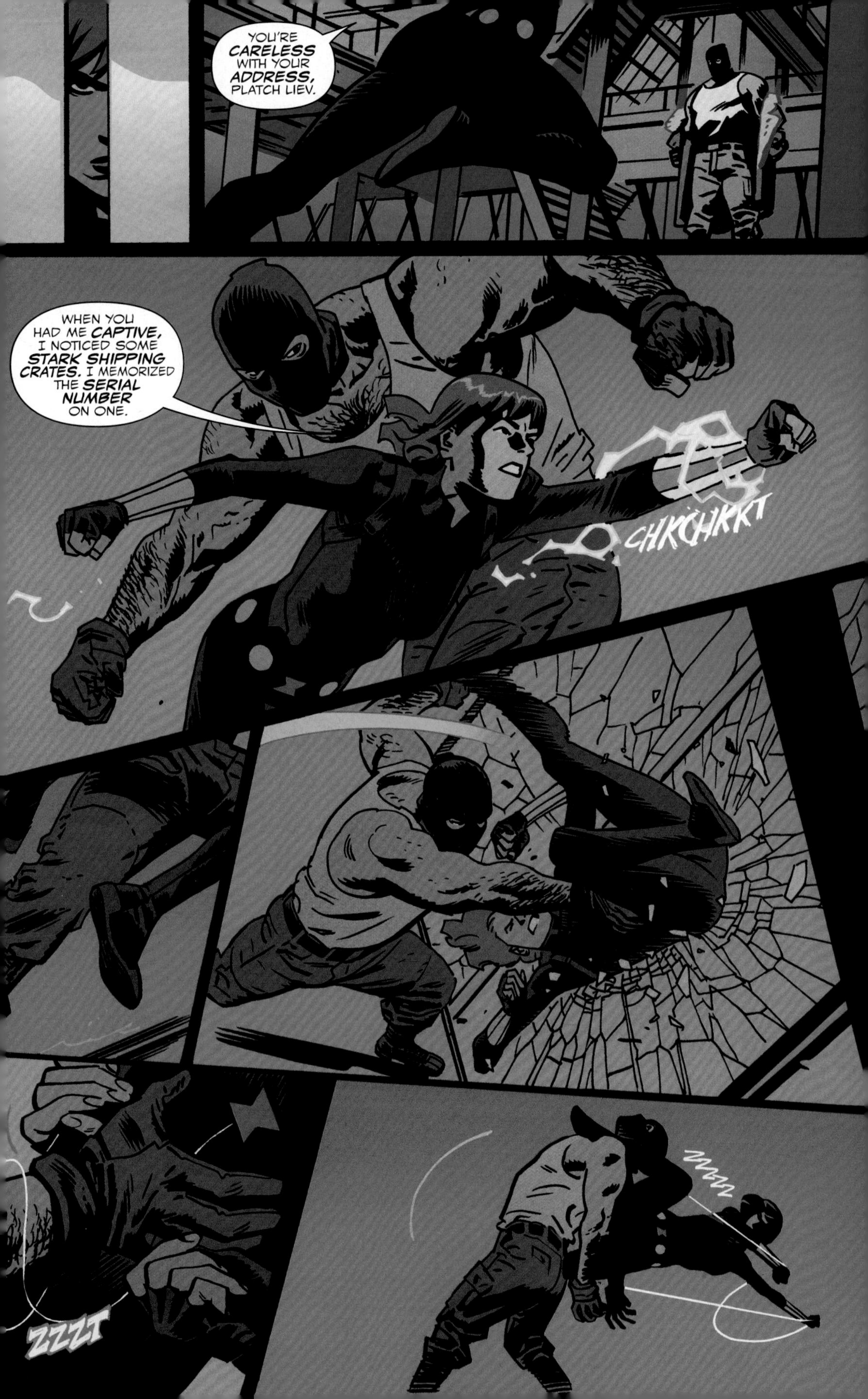
YOU'RE CARELESS WITH YOUR ADDRESS, PLATCH LIEV.
WHEN YOU HAD ME CAPTIVE, I NOTICED SOME STARK SHIPPING CRATES. I MEMORIZED THE SERIAL NUMBER ON ONE.
CHKCHKKT
ZZZZZ
ZZZT

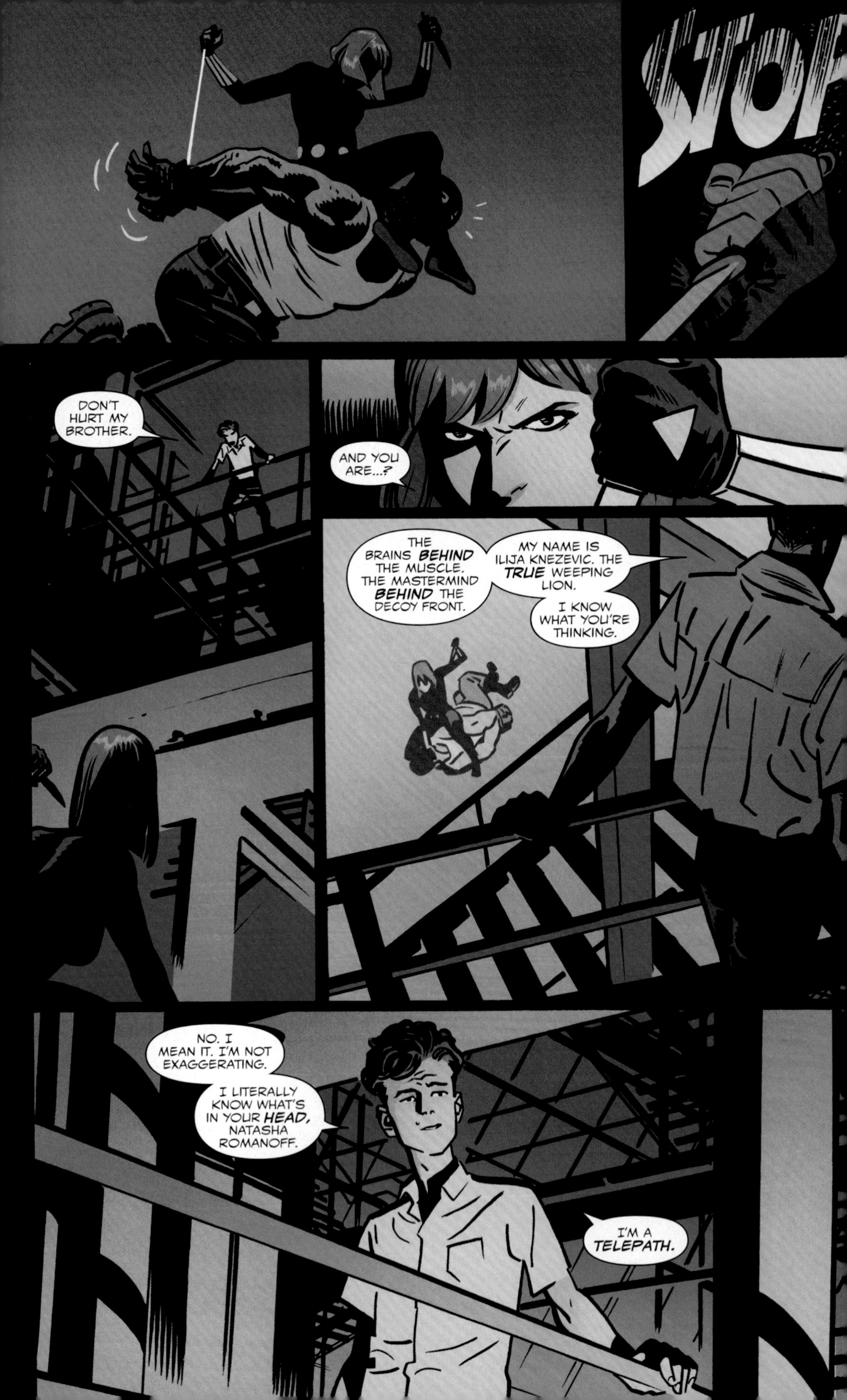
STOP
DON'T HURT MY BROTHER.
AND YOU ARE...?
THE BRAINS BEHIND THE MUSCLE. THE MASTERMIND BEHIND THE DECOY FRONT.
MY NAME IS ILIJA KNEZEVIC. THE TRUE WEEPING LION.
I KNOW WHAT YOU'RE THINKING.
NO. I MEAN IT. I'M NOT EXAGGERATING.
I LITERALLY KNOW WHAT'S IN YOUR HEAD, NATASHA ROMANOFF.
I'M A TELEPATH.

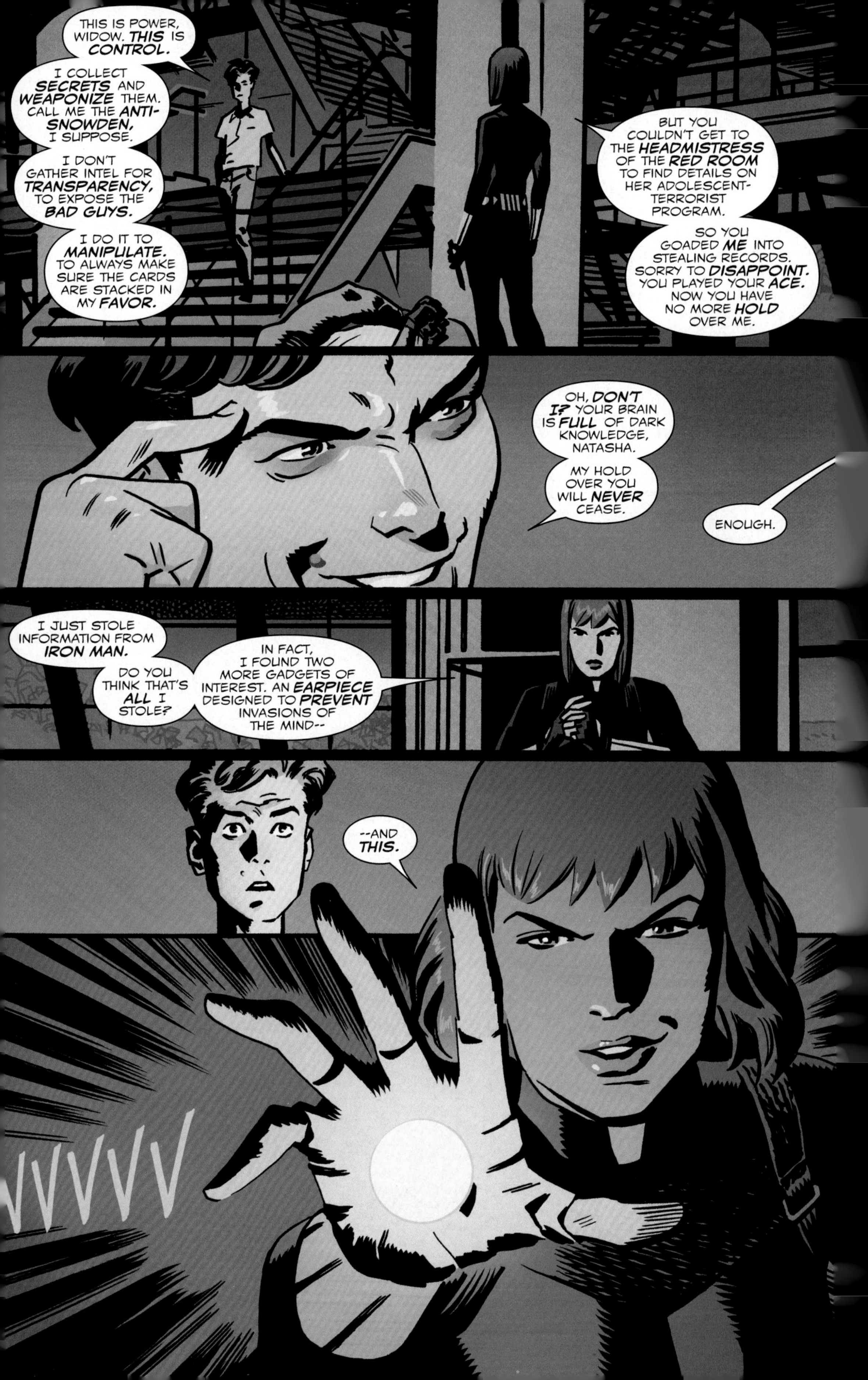
THIS IS POWER, WIDOW. THIS IS CONTROL.
I COLLECT SECRETS AND WEAPONIZE THEM. CALL ME THE ANTI-SNOWDEN, I SUPPOSE.
I DON'T GATHER INTEL FOR TRANSPARENCY, TO EXPOSE THE BAD GUYS.
I DO IT TO MANIPULATE. TO ALWAYS MAKE SURE THE CARDS ARE STACKED IN MY FAVOR.
BUT YOU COULDN'T GET TO THE HEADMISTRESS OF THE RED ROOM TO FIND DETAILS ON HER ADOLESCENT-TERRORIST PROGRAM.
SO YOU GOADED ME INTO STEALING RECORDS. SORRY TO DISAPPOINT. YOU PLAYED YOUR ACE. NOW YOU HAVE NO MORE HOLD OVER ME.
OH, DON'T I? YOUR BRAIN IS FULL OF DARK KNOWLEDGE, NATASHA.
MY HOLD OVER YOU WILL NEVER CEASE.
ENOUGH.
I JUST STOLE INFORMATION FROM IRON MAN.
DO YOU THINK THAT'S ALL I STOLE?
IN FACT, I FOUND TWO MORE GADGETS OF INTEREST. AN EARPIECE DESIGNED TO PREVENT INVASIONS OF THE MIND--
--AND THIS.
VVVVVV

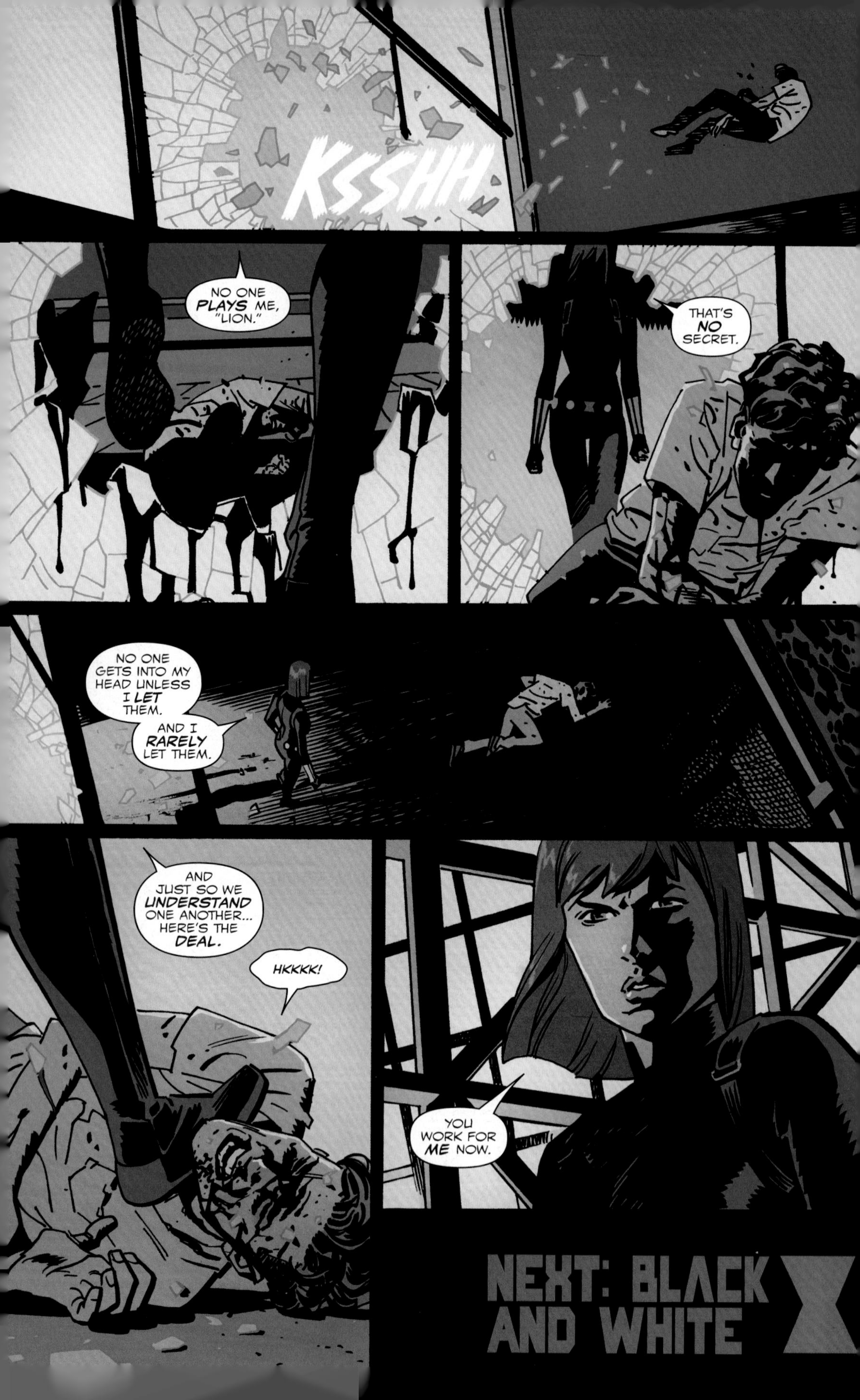
KSSHH
NO ONE PLAYS ME, "LION."
THAT'S NO SECRET.
NO ONE GETS INTO MY HEAD UNLESS I LET THEM.
AND I RARELY LET THEM.
AND JUST SO WE UNDERSTAND ONE ANOTHER... HERE'S THE DEAL.
HKKKK!
YOU WORK FOR ME NOW.
NEXT: BLACK AND WHITE

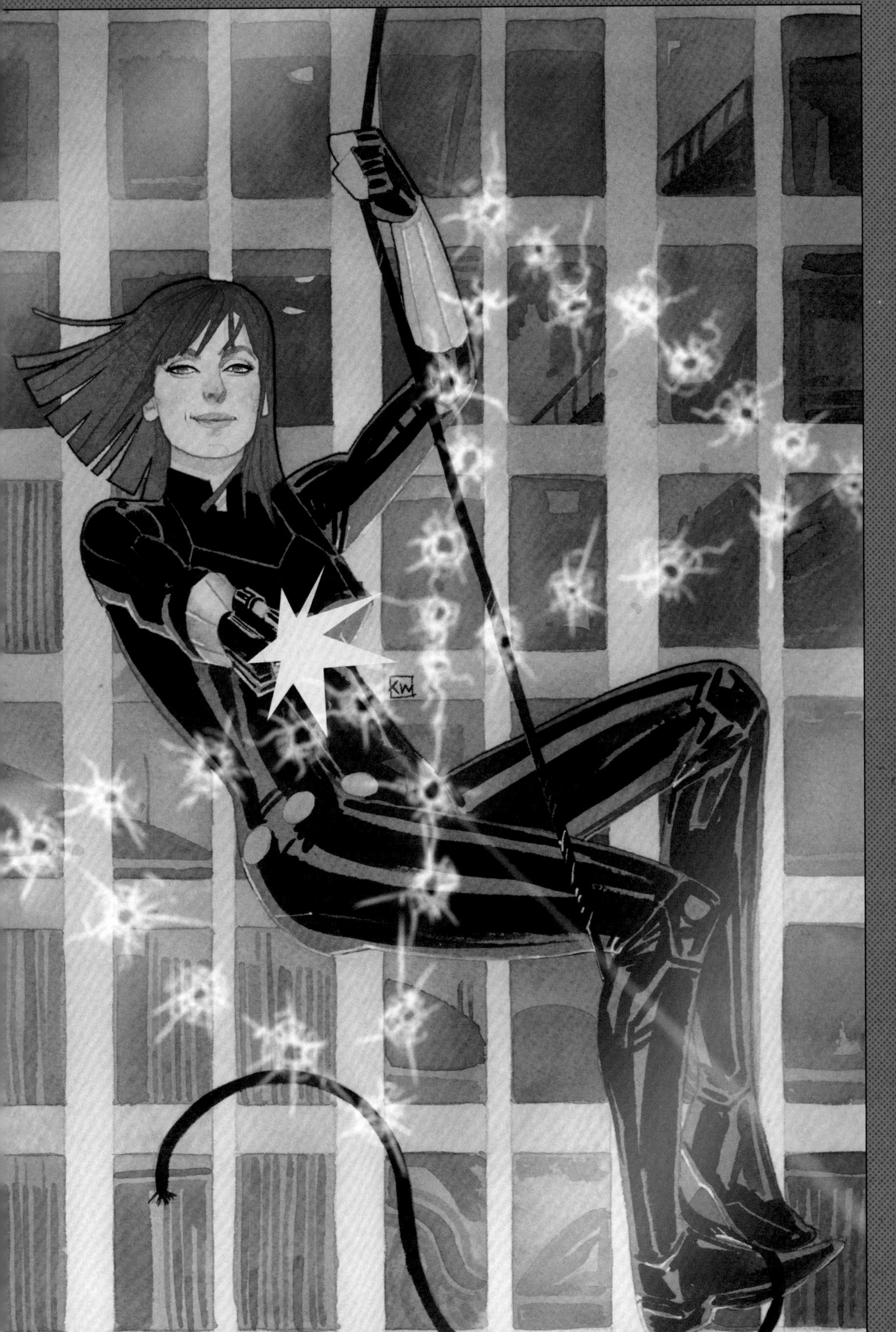

KEVIN WADA

NO. 1 WOMEN OF POWER VARIANT

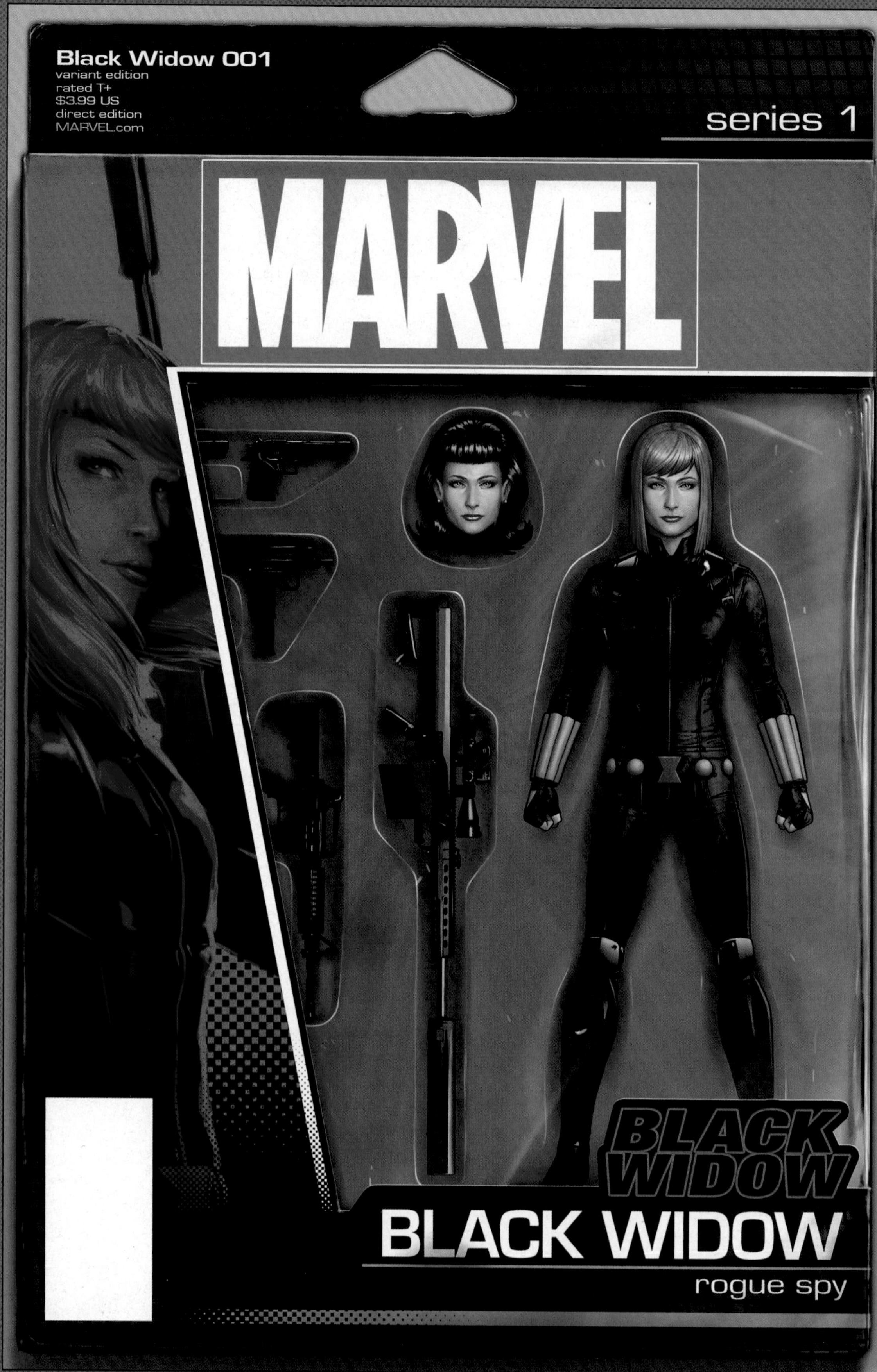

Black Widow 001
variant edition
rated T+
$3.99 US
direct edition
MARVEL.com
series 1
MARVEL
BLACK WIDOW
BLACK WIDOW
rogue spy

JOHN TYLER CHRISTOPHER

NO. 1 ACTION FIGURE VARIANT

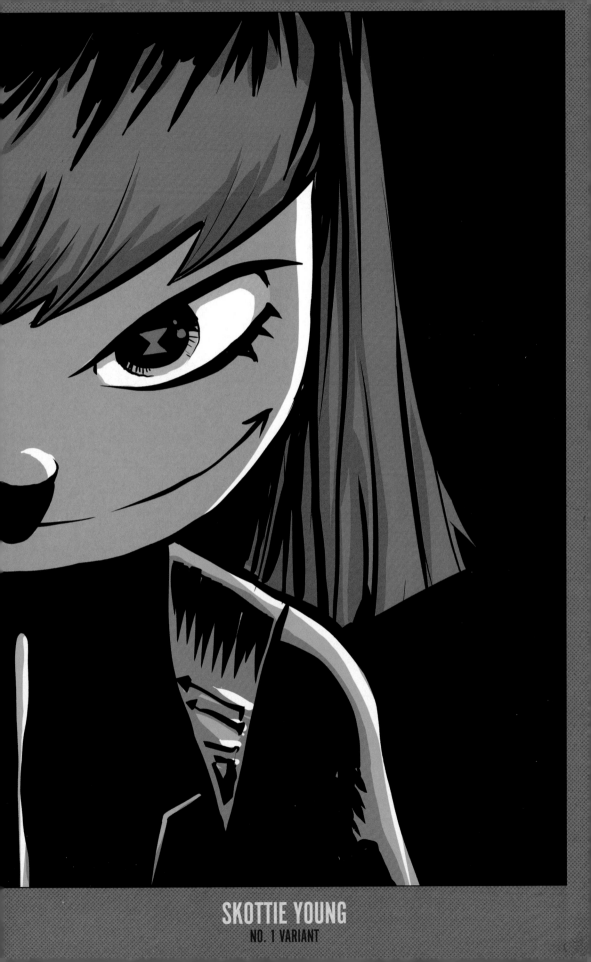

SKOTTIE YOUNG
NO. 1 VARIANT

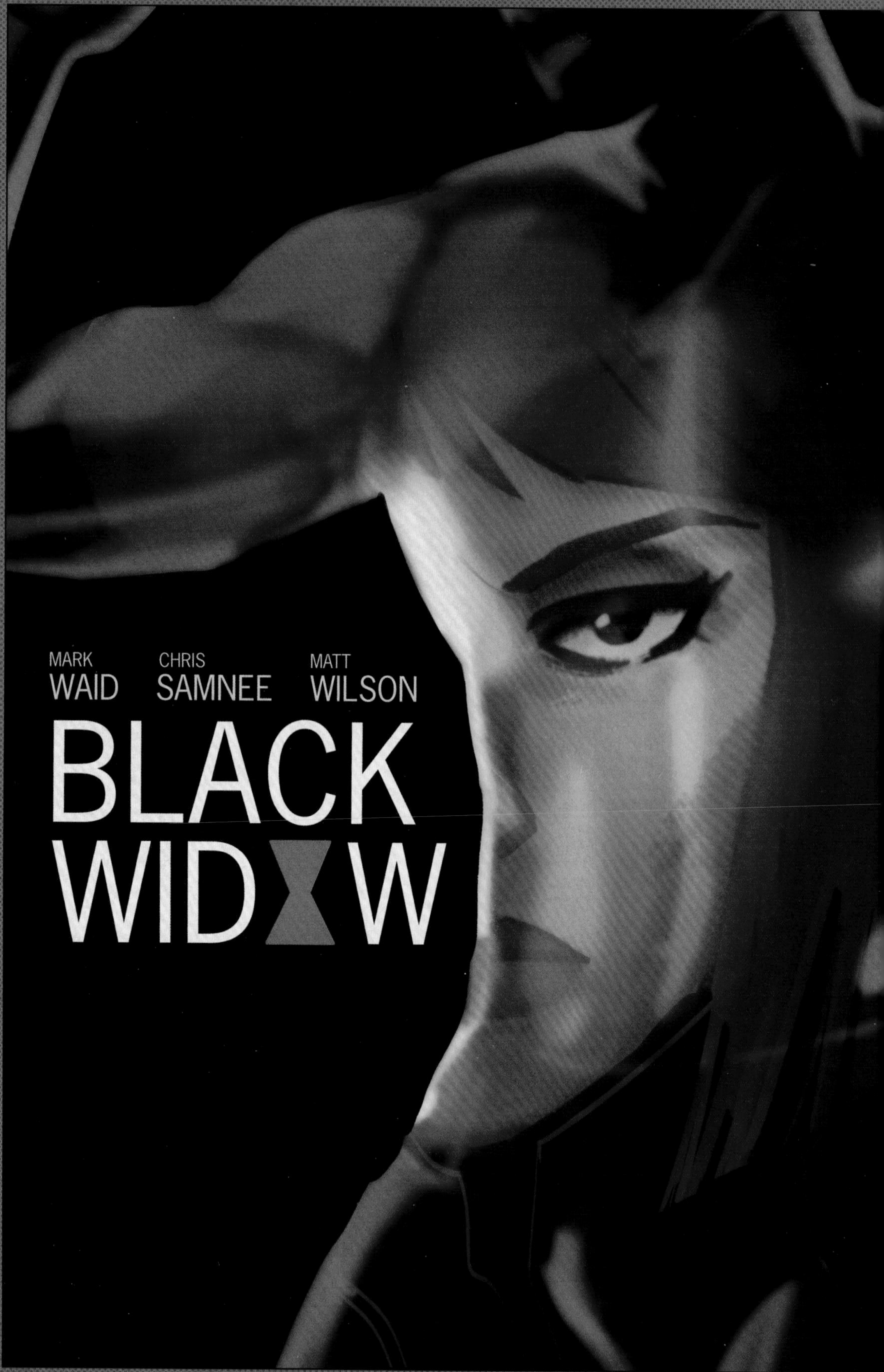
MARK
WAID
CHRIS
SAMNEE
MATT
WILSON
BLACK
WIDOW

ANNIE WU

NO. 2 VARIANT

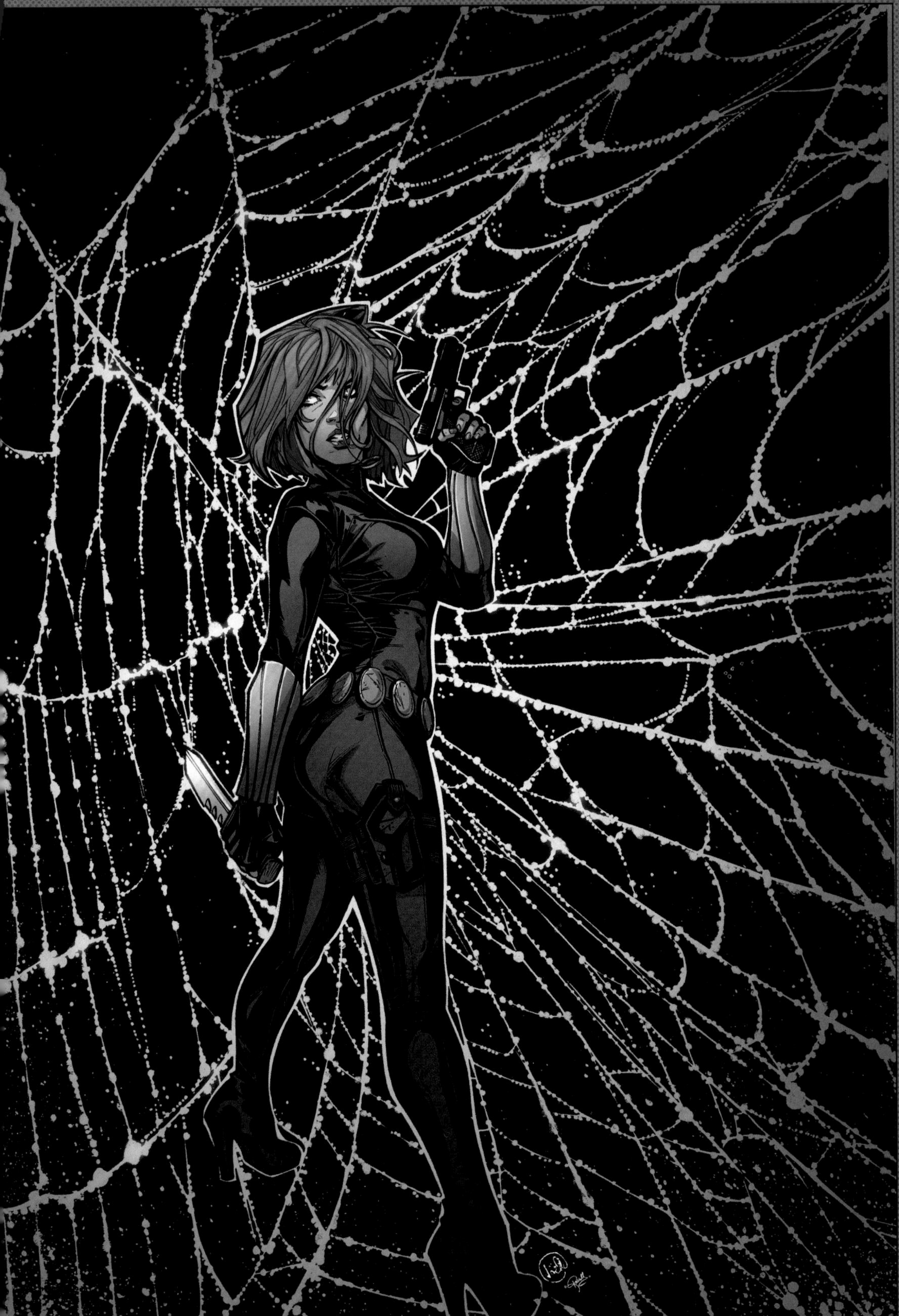

JOËLLE JONES & RACHELLE ROSENBERG
NO. 3 VARIANT

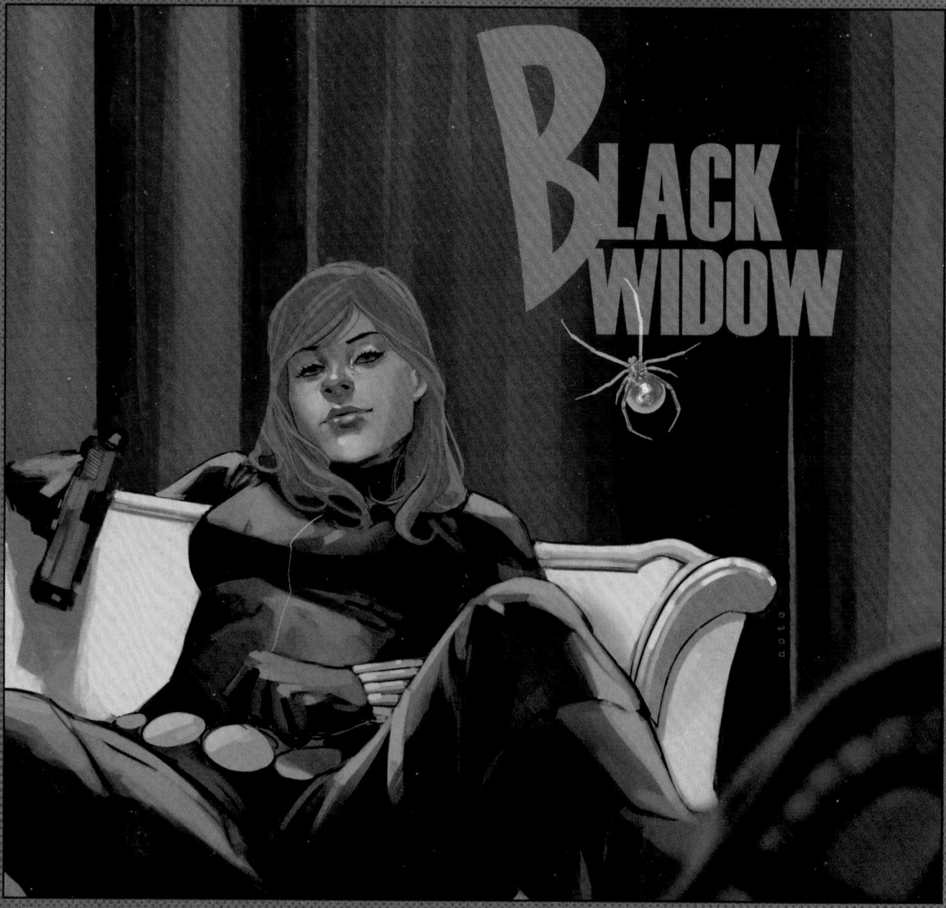
BLACK WIDOW
NOTO

PHIL NOTO NO. 1 HIP-HOP VARIANT

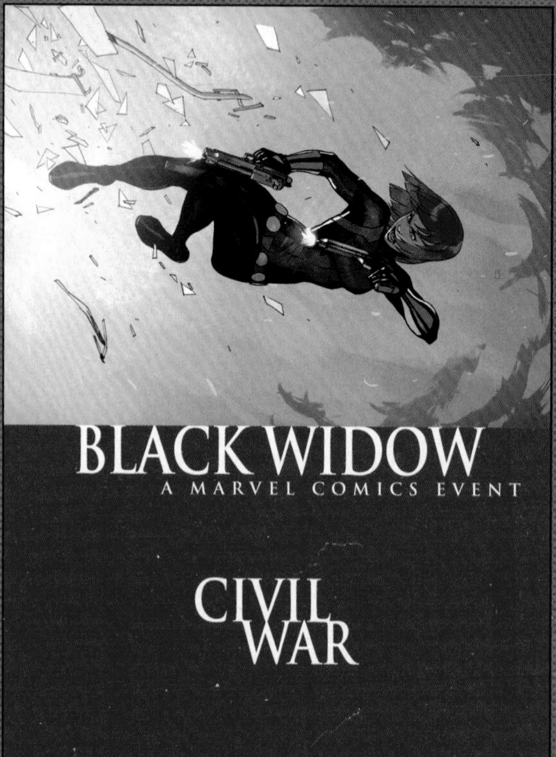
BLACK WIDOW
A MARVEL COMICS EVENT
CIVIL WAR

BENGAL NO. 2 CIVIL WAR VARIANT

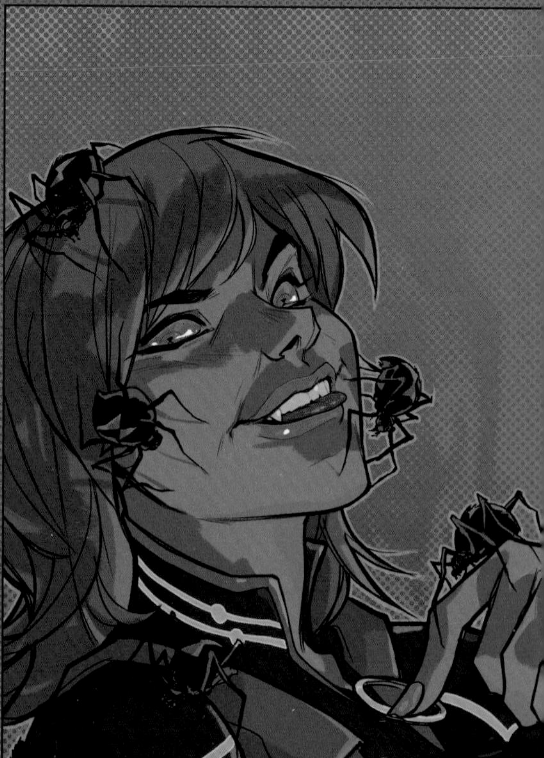
KERSCHL

KARL KERSCHL NO. 3 AGE OF APOCALYPSE VARIANT